The Holy Place

THE HOLY PLACE

Architecture, Ideology, and History in Russia

Konstantin Akinsha and Grigorij Kozlov
with Sylvia Hochfield

Yale University Press

New Haven and

London

Published with assistance from the foundation
established in memory of Philip Hamilton McMillan
of the Class of 1894, Yale College.

Designed by Nancy Ovedovitz and set in
Monotype Bulmer by Tseng Information Systems.
Printed in the United States of America.

Library of Congress Cataloging-in-Publication Data
Akinsha, Konstantin.
The holy place : architecture, ideology, and history in Russia /
Konstantin Akinsha and Grigorij Kozlov ; with Sylvia Hochfield.
p. cm.
Includes bibliographical references and index.
ISBN 978-0-300-11027-2 (cloth : alk. paper)
1. Khram Khrista Spasitelia (Moscow, Russia) — History.
2. Orthodox Eastern church buildings — Russia (Federation) —
Moscow. 3. Moscow (Russia) — Buildings, structures, etc.
I. Kozlov, Grigorii. II. Hochfield, Sylvia. III. Title.
NA5697.M627A45 2007
726.60947'31 — dc22   2007012616

A catalogue record for this book is available from the
British Library.

The paper in this book meets the guidelines for permanence and
durability of the Committee on Production Guidelines for Book
Longevity of the Council on Library Resources.

10   9   8   7   6   5   4   3   2   1

Contents

Illustrations follow pages 52 and 116

Acknowledgments

We would like to express our gratitude to individuals and institutions without whose help this book would not have been possible. We are particularly grateful to Sergei Mironenko, Director of the State Archive of the Russian Federation (GARF, Moscow); Andrei Yanovsky, Head of the Department of Written Sources of the State Historical Museum (GIM, Moscow); the late Aleksei Komech, Director of the State Institute of Art History of the Russian Academy of Science (GII, Moscow); Viktor Bezatosnyi, Head of the Department of Exhibitions of the State Historical Museum (GIM, Moscow); Andrei Serkov, Head of the Sector of Acquisition and Scholarly Description of Archival Funds of the Scholarly Research Department of Manuscripts of the Russian State Library (RGI, Moscow); Rifat Gafifulin, Curator of the Archive of the State Museum–Preserve Pavlovsk (St. Petersburg); Aleksandr Arkhangelsky, professor, Higher School of Economics (Moscow); Nikita Sokolov, editor-in-chief of the magazine *Otechestvennye zapiski* (Moscow); and Marina Golubovskaia, editor of the magazine *Otechestvennye zapiski* (Moscow).

For their responses to different parts of this project we are grateful to Olga Medvedkova, art historian (Paris); Aleksandra Shatskikh, art historian (Moscow); Aleksandr Kibovsky, historian (Moscow); and Semyon Mikhailovsky, consultant of the Guggenheim Foundation (St. Petersburg).

We are especially grateful to Artem Zadikian, photographer and historian of the city of Moscow, for his help with the selection of illustrations for this book and for generously providing photographs from his collection. We also express our gratitude to Alex Lachmann (Alex Lachmann Gallery, Cologne) and to Edward Kasinec, Chief of the Slavic and Baltic Division of the New York Public Library, for their assistance with illustrations.

Last but not least, we would like to thank Robin Strauss, our agent and friend, for her help and support in bringing this project to fruition.

Introduction

A sleek black Mercedes glides past the red brick wall of the Kremlin. The evening summer sun rippling on the surface of the Moscow River gives the scene a festive air, undampened even by the immense gray hulk of the House on the Embankment across the river. The Mercedes logo—a gigantic aluminum circle divided into three segments, similar to the small steel version on the car's hood—rotates on the roof of the building where Stalin's commissars once lived. The limo dives under the bridge, passing a few old mansions, and then glides out to the Cathedral of Christ the Savior. For a second, a gigantic golden dome is visible in the windows. The limo turns right, passes through the railing surrounding the cathedral, and slows at a ground-floor entrance. Iron gates open automatically, and a stern-faced guard examines a pass and asks the driver to open the trunk. The car then enters a garage as clean as a hospital. Guards sit in glass cubicles decorated with reproduction icons, keeping watch over ranks of expensive cars belonging to "respected" people, those who have the money and connections to park their Jaguars and BMWs in the heart of the city, in the prestigious garage of the Cathedral of Christ the Savior.

The circle is closed. A project that haunted the minds of Russia's rulers for almost two centuries is complete. Started and abandoned, moved from one site to another, the gigantic cathedral that was built by czars and demolished by commissars now dominates the Moscow skyline once again. Where the original cathedral stood, a concrete replica now rises and is reflected in the river just as the original was. Jaguars sleep in the underground garage; red icon lamps glimmer above in the spacious aisles; and a stern Old Testament god with disheveled white hair looks down from the central dome. Many Russians would like to believe that this time it will be forever.

The story of the cathedral and its destruction and reconstruction holds up an architectural mirror to Russian history, for the structures on this site were transformed into supreme ideological symbols. Alexander I yearned for a symbol of universal Christendom and a united Europe; Nicholas I wanted a manifestation in marble and gold of Russian supremacy. Stalin demanded the tallest building in the world, as an assertion of the end of history. Yeltsin was to cancel seventy-four years of Soviet history.

After the armies of Napoleon attacked Russia, Alexander I swore an oath that he would construct a cathedral dedicated to Christ the Savior when the last foreign troops had left Russian soil. But, demanding more than a monument to Russian arms, the czar wanted to express an exalted spiritual vision of a new and unified Christian Europe. Alexander Vitberg, the young amateur architect he chose to realize his vision in stone, has become a legend in Russian culture. Impractical and mystical, he paid for his utopianism with suffering and exile. Alexander Herzen, who met Vitberg in exile, turned the architect into a revolutionary icon — a heroic victim of cruel autocracy. Thanks to Herzen's account of Vitberg's life, the architect became one of the first examples of a figure that was to appear often in the history of Russian culture: the artist in opposition to power.

Nicholas I, who exiled Vitberg and scrapped his design, was interested not in uniting Europe but in dominating it with Russian military power. The "gendarme of Europe" had a passion for order and uniformity, qualities reflected in Konstantin Ton, the architect he chose to create new designs for the cathedral. But Nicholas died with his monument to Russian nationalism unfinished, his vaunted army having proved in the Crimean War that it was unprepared for modern warfare. It wasn't until the reign of Alexander III, Nicholas's grandson, that the cathedral was completed — and was immediately scorned as an outdated and vulgar manifestation of official Christianity.

As Ton's gigantic "inkwell" rose over Moscow, it became the symbol of the city at the turn of the nineteenth century. Foggy film footage preserves Nicholas II and Alexandra, the last czar and czarina, watching a military parade marching under the cathedral walls: a powerful image of the beginning of the end of Russian imperial grandeur.

After the Russian Revolution, the cathedral was the center of church resistance to the Bolshevik regime. Patriarch Tikhon pronounced his anathema of Lenin's government under its dome. Soon the followers of the disgraced patriarch were exiled from their church, which was turned over to "red" priests who praised Communism as a Christian doctrine. But their days, too, were numbered, and Russia's largest cathedral was doomed.

From the early days of the revolution, representatives of the Russian avant-garde dreamed of an architectural project that would reflect the revolutionary zeitgeist. Vladimir Tatlin's spiral tower of the Third International and Viktor Balikhin's gigantic cube memorial to Lenin both claimed to be the ultimate monument of the new world. Neither was realized.

The construction of the Palace of Soviets gave Stalin an opportunity to be the architect of the world's tallest building. He personally approved all the important decisions: the choice of the site, the destruction of Christ the Savior, and the plan for a tower surmounted by a gigantic figure of Lenin. Unlike Vitberg or Ton, Stalin's architects were executors of his vision rather than their own. But the great work was interrupted by the war, and by the time it ended, Stalin had lost his enthusiasm for building a monument to Lenin, having become the equal of his teacher. When Stalin died, the new skyscrapers he had built, the Seven Sisters, were oriented not toward a dominant Palace of Soviets but toward an empty space, a gigantic excavation in the center of Moscow.

Khrushchev was no builder of monuments to the past, and during the liberal days of the thaw, the largest swimming pool in the world filled the pit. It survived until the end of the Soviet Union, aging and crumbling along with the country.

From the beginning of perestroika, the swimming pool attracted public speculation. The destruction of Christ the Savior, a forbidden subject for so many years, came to be considered by both liberals and nationalists as an event that summed up all the crimes of the Soviet regime. Soon powerful voices were heard demanding the reconstruction of the ruined cathedral. President Yeltsin and especially Yury Luzhkov, the mayor of Moscow, were quick to see the political advantages of the idea. A new "old" cathedral built on the foundation of the Palace of Soviets would be a powerful symbol of reborn post-Communist Russia.

The travesty of reconstruction—concrete and plastic instead of marble and bronze—corresponded to the semantics of postperestroika Russia, with its jumble of red stars, hammers and sickles, and double-headed eagles. Moscow intellectuals who protested the erection of a "Las Vegas" copy were ignored. Some even decided that the cathedral they had heartily despised provided a much needed architectural focus. The new Christ the Savior is now taken for granted, having become as familiar as the Kremlin or the Seven Sisters.

Russians have a proverb: The holy place is never empty. The history of the construction, demolition, and reconstruction of the Cathedral of Christ the Savior is the story of a holy place where successive rulers of Russia wanted to realize their visions. Architects from Vitberg to Le Corbusier created hundreds of projects for the site, but all were doomed to remain paper architecture. Thinkers and ideologues worked out complex decorative schemes, and artists planned grand murals of Christ appearing to the people or of the people liberated under Communism. All were unrealized. Alexander I was compared to King Solomon erecting the temple, but the history of Christ the Savior reminds us more of another biblical construction: the Tower of Babel.

PART ONE

Vitberg's Cathedral

Chapter One

The morning of October 12, 1817, was cold and blustery, but the weather did not discourage the throngs of Muscovites who had gathered at the Sparrow Hills, southwest of the city, to take part in a solemn ceremony marking the fifth anniversary of Napoleon's flight from Moscow. At the summit of a hill overlooking the ancient capital, Emperor Alexander I would lay the cornerstone of the Cathedral of Christ the Savior, the monument designed to commemorate the Russian victory over the Antichrist and destined to become a symbol of the nation's greatness and its tragedy.

At 10 o'clock, the *Russian Herald* reported, His Majesty the Emperor, together with His August Household, arrived at the Church of the Blessed Virgin of Tikhvin in Luzhniki, not far from the Sparrow Hills. While the Autocrat of All the Russias prayed, fifty thousand troops were deployed behind the nearby Convent of the Virgin. Priests carrying icons and banners waited near the church. At 12 o'clock, the religious procession started to move and slowly crossed the bridge over the Moscow River to the Sparrow Hills.

Soon afterward, the emperor and his entourage of military and civil officials emerged from the church and ascended through lines of troops to the spot where the altar of the lower temple of the cathedral would be erected, on a natural ledge about halfway up the hills. As the blessing of the water began, a deep silence fell over the multitudes standing bareheaded under the gray sky. Only the singing of prayers was audible. After the blessing, the emperor laid the cornerstone.[1]

Despite the cold and the rain, a throng of half a million people packed the streets and crammed into bleachers erected for the occasion. They leaned from every window overlooking the ceremony and craned from roofs and balconies. "Only the brush of Raphael and the pen of King David the Psalmist could describe the scene," wrote the author of a book dedicated to the occasion. "Who of us can recollect without heartfelt emotion and profound sadness the year 1812, when Moscow, the mother of Russian cities, abandoned without help or protection, groaned under the yoke of the tyrant, the leader of the Gauls?"[2]

3

It was a moment of triumph for Alexander I, then at the peak of his fame and power. He was, said one observer, like Moses ascending Mount Sinai. It was also a moment of triumph for the architect of the future cathedral, an obscure young man who had seen the czar for the first time at another solemn religious occasion five years earlier.

A few weeks after Napoleon invaded Russia, Alexander knelt in prayer before the ancient icons in Kazan Cathedral in St. Petersburg. On this day, too, the dignitaries of the empire were present, as well as hundreds of ordinary people—petty bureaucrats, merchants, artisans, servants, and serfs—praying together, imploring God for victory.

Among the crowd, a young man with a romantic appearance followed the czar's every move. Karl Magnus Vitberg, a new graduate of the Imperial Academy of Arts, was dazzled by his first sight of the czar. "I saw Alexander in Kazan Cathedral at a time when the enemy was trampling the body of Russia, when Moscow was about to become its prize," Vitberg recalled many years later. "I saw how he appeared among the people—confused, losing his temper, as if he were embarrassed by his shortcomings. Of course this time of troubles strongly affected his soul. He who had once yielded to the powerful genius of Napoleon, who had signed the peace treaty of Tilsit, stated this time that he would not put down his arms until his death."[3]

When Vitberg spoke those words, he was a sick, forgotten man, an exile in the provincial town of Vyatka. The person listening was his fellow exile Alexander Herzen, who revered Vitberg. The former favorite of the czar told the story of the cathedral to the confirmed atheist and enemy of the monarchy, and Herzen preserved it. The friendship between these two corresponded to the words of Prince Alexander Golitsyn, the czar's spiritual mentor, who said, "There are many strange things in this cathedral." The prince was referring to the inexplicable coincidences and miracles that contemporaries believed were associated with the cathedral's construction. The greatest miracle was the victory over Napoleon.

Very few Europeans doubted that Napoleon would triumph over the Russians. An acknowledged military genius, he commanded the mightiest army ever assembled in Europe, comprising more than half a million well-trained and seasoned troops led by the most brilliant commanders of the era.

Alexander learned of the invasion during a ball at the estate of General Leonty Bennigsen, near Vilna, where throngs of nobles, civil and military dignitaries, and their families had gathered for festivities. The czar, convinced that he was doomed, hid in the nursery so that no one would see his despair. He sat among the children's toys trying to think clearly.[4]

The war began with a string of disasters for the Russians, who suffered tremendous losses as they were driven back into the heart of their country. Despite the desperate resistance at Borodino, Moscow had to be abandoned to the enemy. The fall of the ancient capital was a national catastrophe. Moscow was the Third Rome, the successor to ancient Rome and Constantinople, and the center of the Orthodox world. Not only did the city have a special role in the eternal dispute between Russia and the West, it had a special significance to the reigning dynasty. The Romanovs had ascended the throne in 1613, two hundred years before the invasion of Napoleon, after a voluntary force assembled by the people themselves saved the Kremlin from the Poles. Moscow embodied the sacred bond that linked the Romanovs to the Russian people, who had placed the city under their protection in the hope that the Romanovs would guarantee the country's sovereignty and the preservation of Orthodoxy. When Alexander Romanov abandoned the ancient capital to the enemy, he violated this sacred contract and failed as father-protector.

Alexander's hair, it was rumored, turned gray overnight after he received the news of Napoleon's entry into Moscow. Now began the most difficult period of his life, filled with anxiety, humiliation, and solitude. Courtiers, ministers, even the imperial family, panicked, demanding that the czar sign a peace treaty with France under any conditions. Alexander showed unexpected fortitude. During the critical days of September 1812, when Napoleon sent him messengers of peace from the occupied Kremlin, the czar told his adjutant Alexander Misho, "I would rather grow a beard and eat potatoes with the poorest of my peasants in Siberia than sign the disgrace of my motherland." His steadfastness saved the nation.

While Napoleon waited for the czar's answer, Moscow erupted in flames. Russian historians are still arguing about who caused the conflagration, just as contemporary observers did. Napoleon believed that the Russians had started the fire. "What kind of people are they!" he marveled. "They are Scythians. To do me a passing evil, they destroyed the creation of centuries."[5] He was fatally mistaken when he called the fire a passing evil. The

French had expected to spend the winter in comfort in their captured Moscow palaces. The fire was the beginning of the end for them.

Napoleon left the ruined city and tried to break out to Europe through regions that had not been devastated by the war, but the Russian army blocked him, forcing him to retreat by the same road he had taken to Moscow, a burned-out road of death. For the first time, the hunter became the prey, a wounded animal in hopeless flight. Retreat turned into rout. Starvation, cold, and the harrowing of muzhik guerrillas completed the defeat. In a few weeks, the half-million-strong Grand Army melted away. The unexpectedness and the scale of the catastrophe that had befallen the invincible Napoleon shocked the world, the victorious Russians most of all.

"And who, then, came to our assistance?" Pushkin asked. "The folk's resistance, winter, Barclay, Russia's God?"[6] The poet didn't even mention the role of Alexander, believing that victory had simply fallen into the czar's hands. Tolstoy would later credit the Russian people's will to resist any foreign aggressor. But the czar believed that the destruction of Napoleon was a miracle and didn't want to share his laurels with anyone except the Almighty himself. God, he said, was the only victor and liberator.[7]

The conflict awakened Alexander's religious feelings. During the war of nerves with Napoleon, when even his mother urged him to surrender, he found the Bible an unexpected source of comfort. Looking for words of consolation and support, he began reading the Holy Scriptures twice a day. It was at this time that the czar developed the mystical tendencies that would dominate the rest of his life.

The historical cataclysm merged in Alexander's consciousness with his private unease. The French invasion and the burning of Moscow forced him to ponder whether he was being punished by the Almighty for the great sin he had committed at the outset of his reign: his complicity in the murder of his father, Paul I. Alexander had known about the assassination plot but had not revealed it.

The wonder of 1812 heightened the religious feelings of the entire nation. While the monarch addressed himself to the God of the Bible, the muzhik guerrillas and the nobles who commanded them prayed to the "Russian God" described by Pushkin, the Orthodox god of the serf village. The Hussar officer Denis Davidov, who had let his thick beard grow "à la muzhik," commanded his guerrilla band wearing a peasant caftan. On his chest was an icon of Saint Nicholas, the favorite of the peasants, who was even more important in folk tradition than Christ himself.[8]

People of all classes interpreted the Napoleonic invasion as an incursion of Western pagans. The war was the *Otechestvennaia,* the Fatherland or Patriotic War. "We are Russians, what ecstasy!" Alexander Suvorov, the famous Russian military leader, had once exclaimed. After the Napoleonic War, every Russian, including serfs deprived of rights, was ready to join in this sentiment. Never before had Russians been so united and so convinced they were the chosen people.

Chapter Two

On December 17, 1812, a Russian general wrote to a high official from headquarters at Vilna. The outcome of the war was inconceivable, the general marveled. The vast enemy force had melted away in the course of weeks, and the people were crying out for a monument that would express their gratitude to God. But what form should the monument take? "One person says an obelisk; another, a pyramid; the third, a column; . . . I believe that such a monument must correspond in every way to its task and its time."[1] It had to be as extraordinary as the war itself. But Russians were not idolaters. "Obelisks, pyramids, etc., satisfy human arrogance and pride but not the noble heart of a Christian filled with gratitude. Thus my heart and my mind together call for the erection of a cathedral dedicated to the Savior in Moscow. Nothing else would satisfy everyone's expectations."[2]

The monument had to be in Moscow; it was there that the enemy had intended to deliver the mortal blow and there that providence had upset their pernicious plans. "Paying tribute to God," the writer concluded, "we will connect ourselves more strongly with our faith and our posterity. We will have a monument to Him forever before our eyes — not a monument to vanity."[3]

The author of the letter was General Pyotr Kikin. The recipient was State Secretary Alexander Shishkov. Both men belonged to the old Russian nobility, and both were members of a literary society called Lovers of Russian Speech, a group of writers, poets, and cultivated men who had been gathering in Shishkov's home for friendly literary dinners since 1807. In the society's early days, eminent writers had mingled with youngsters excited by the latest trends, but by 1812 the group had become a stronghold of resistance to Western influence. The members idealized pre-Petrine Russian culture, Kikin and Shishkov being among the most zealous defenders of the old way of life. For the first time in Russian history, the Lovers of Russian Speech embodied a distinct Slavophile point of view in opposition to the ideas of the Westernizers.[4]

Shishkov was an admiral and a poet. A defender of the purity of the Russian language, he championed the ancient Slavic tongue, loved psalms and odes in the old style, and fiercely opposed the adoption of foreign, especially French, words. It was a political, not an aesthetic, issue to him: Shishkov believed that the language formed the nation.

Russian historians have often regarded the Lovers of Russian Speech as fanatical, and even slightly comical in their worship of the past, but neither Kikin nor Shishkov corresponds to that description. They were both highly educated, gifted men. Kikin, a graduate of Moscow University, was a member of the Free Economic Society and the founder and first president of the Society to Encourage the Arts. Shishkov held various ministerial positions and for a while was president of the Russian Academy. The literature historian Yuri Lotman, who can hardly be accused of sympathy with the group, remarked acutely that "by exalting the nation as the highest value, Shishkov was in tune with the trends of the time."[5]

Shishkov and his supporters had created the conception of the Holy War for the struggle against Napoleon, based on their vision of pre-Petrine, pre-imperial Russia blessed by the Orthodox Church. It was the spirit of this Holy Russia they wanted to revive, believing that the war could not be won without it.[6] On the eve of the invasion, Alexander exiled State Secretary Mikhail Speransky, a pro-Western reformer, and appointed Shishkov in his place. The admiral was one of the very few members of the czar's inner circle who demanded that there be no peace treaty with France.

Scornfully rejecting obelisks, pyramids, and the like, Kikin proposed a return to the ancient tradition of building cathedrals to commemorate important victories. Moscow was the center of such constructions, the best known being the Cathedral of the Intercession (St. Basil's) on Red Square, erected to commemorate the storm of Kazan and Ivan the Terrible's final defeat of the Tatars in 1552. The new cathedral, too, had to be in Moscow. Captured military trophies would be displayed there, and names of the fallen would be engraved on copper plaques, "because it will console a mother to read the name of her son or a son to read the name of his father who laid down his life for the fatherland."[7] The cathedral would be both a memorial and a museum dedicated to the expulsion of Napoleon from Russia. Kikin also proposed a three-day state holiday to be celebrated annually in the cathedral. The first day would be dedicated to the faith, the second to the military, and the third to the people.[8]

Kikin wasn't disappointed in Shishkov. On Christmas Day, only eight days after Kikin wrote his letter, the czar's manifesto (composed by Shishkov) was issued, ordering the construction in Moscow of a church in the name of Christ the Savior. The salvation of Russia and the destruction of her enemies were obviously due to God's grace, the manifesto stated. To preserve the eternal memory of the Russian people's unwavering fidelity and love of the fatherland, and their gratitude to God, a church in the name of Christ the Savior would be built in the ancient capital. "Let the Almighty bless our venture! Let it be realized! Let this Cathedral stand for many centuries and let the incense of gratitude of later generations, together with love for and emulation of the deeds of their predecessors, rise to the holy Throne of God!"[9]

The czar saw the cathedral as a monument of the victory of faith over the "false philosophizing that flooded Europe," by which he meant the godlessness of the French Revolution, though he was neither a Russian chauvinist nor a hater of the West, as was Shishkov. The admiral expressed himself violently on the subject of Russian Westernizers: of those who "repeated the words aesthetics, education, enlightenment, etc.," he wrote, "I would like to stick their noses in the ashes of Moscow and tell them loudly, 'Here is what you wanted.'"[10] Alexander's nose would have been the first to suffer, in that he rejected the concept of "Russia or Europe" and supported the formula "Russia is a part of Europe."

Alexander assumed the throne with a strong desire to rule humanely and justly and thus to live down his complicity in his father's murder. Full of liberal ideas, he encouraged his inner circle, known as the Private Committee, to design projects for reform in the spirit of Western rationalism but to do it secretly. The czar feared both the landowning nobility, who opposed reform, and the peasants, who were hungry for change. No one knew his thoughts, however, because he rarely shared his feelings even with the people closest to him. "A sphinx whose mystery wasn't unraveled until his death," the poet Pyotr Vyazemsky said of him.[11]

Catherine the Great had destined her grandson to become the ruler of an empire stretching from the White Sea to the Mediterranean. She had appointed Frédéric La Harpe, a Swiss republican and an atheist, as his tutor. The wunderkind, as she called the young Alexander, was to embody the ideal of enlightened monarchy—he would be the first man of the golden age. La Harpe inculcated the future sovereign with the idea that a free personality was the foundation of a just society.

In 1796, the young Alexander confessed to his closest friend, Prince Adam Czartoryski, that he "hates despotism in any form, no matter how it manifests itself, that he loves liberty, which he believes must belong equally to all people."[12] Shortly before his death, the czar expressed a similar sentiment. "I lived and will die a republican," he told one of his generals.[13] Alexander has sometimes been painted as a cowardly, duplicitous politician who only flirted with liberalism, but these two utterances bracketing his life suggest otherwise. The story of the construction of the Cathedral of Christ the Savior also points to a very different interpretation of the czar's character.

The French emperor and the Russian czar have gone down in history as eternal rivals whose ideological opposition—revolution versus feudal reaction—has seemed as clear-cut as the political and military aspects of their struggle. In reality, the situation was more complicated. The czar saw himself as a symbol of enlightened monarchy, whereas Napoleon personified revolution. Alexander never denounced his youthful devotion to schemes of liberty and constitutional government, but he wanted them untainted by revolutionary terror. Reform had to be peaceful and initiated from the top, meaning from him. The monarch had to use the power given him by God to bestow on his people a constitution and liberties.

Most of the Russian nobility believed that the victory over Napoleon was a triumph over the West, proving the superiority of autocracy and serfdom over the bourgeois innovations introduced by revolution in Europe. Russian patriotism of the period was generally conservative and isolationist. The war, it was widely felt, ended with the expulsion of Napoleon from the motherland. "Europe is not our business," Shishkov told the czar, urging Alexander to concentrate on reconstructing his ravaged country. To Shishkov, the cathedral was a monument to isolationism.[14]

Not wishing to listen, Alexander looked for a third way, a position somewhere between French radicalism and Russian conservatism. Like Napoleon, he dreamed of European unity. Europe was to be without borders: citizens of Paris, Berlin, Vienna, Rome, and Moscow would feel at home everywhere on the Continent.[15]

Alexander had taken no part in the battles on Russian soil, but the war of 1813–15 in Europe became his war. He not only inspired the establishment of the European coalition against Napoleon but personally commanded troops. The victory of 1812 belonged to God and was a sign to the czar that he must deliver the world from the Antichrist. The liberation of Europe, on the other hand, was his own triumph, the fulfillment of his mission. He considered the French to be not enemies but victims, and the only punishment he inflicted on defeated Paris was a grandiose memorial service at the execution site of Louis XVI. An altar was erected on the spot where the guillotine had stood, and the czar relished the sight of French marshals and generals who had survived Robespierre's terror and Napoleon's campaigns as they pushed and shoved to kiss the Russian cross.[16]

Alexander's vision of a united Europe, like Napoleon's, was based on Enlightenment ideas. The vision couldn't be transformed into reality, of course, unless everyone agreed that it was a good idea. Whereas Napoleon had tried to impose European unity through conquest, Alexander proposed universal love. The year 1812 had convinced the czar that faith was the most powerful weapon in his battle against the spirit of revolution. The miraculous liberation of Russia from Napoleon provoked Alexander to create a grandiose utopian program: he would find a compromise between Enlightenment rationalism, which was for him the essence of civilization, and religious mysticism. The limits of the Russian Orthodox Church were too narrow for the czar, just as the Russian throne was too small for him.

Alexander's search for a new faith became a pilgrimage as he meditated with Moravian Brothers in Germany, prayed with Quakers in England, and met with the renowned Bavarian Catholic mystic Franz von Baader, who had written a tract urging the establishment of social policy on a Christian foundation and the adoption by Christianity of elements from other religions and mythologies.[17] Alexander became enchanted by Baroness Julie von Krudener, the evangelical prophetess of Heilbronn, who had tried and failed to ensnare Napoleon. The French emperor had thrown her sermons into the fire, but the czar—her white angel—was more willing to listen to ecstatic predictions of the Second Coming and his own leading role in that event. Whenever they shared a meal, a third place was set at the table, for Christ.[18]

In the Holy Alliance, founded at the Congress of Vienna in 1815, the czar saw the realization of his dream of an international spiritual brother-hood—a united Christian Europe. The text of the Holy Alliance decrees that religion is inseparable from politics, and that the monarchs of Europe, in the name of the Holy and Indivisible Trinity and united by ties of real and indissoluble brotherhood, will assist one another. Anton Kersnovsky, the right-wing Russian historian, dubbed the alliance the Monarchist Inter-national, but it was also a Christian International.[19] In the beginning, it was far from being a fortress of reaction. In fact, the participants, led by Alex-ander, were liberals. The czar helped establish a constitutional monarchy in France and, in 1815, granted a constitution to the Kingdom of Poland, which had become a part of the Russian empire. With this step, the auto-crat of Russia became the constitutional monarch of Poland.[20]

Chapter Three

Although a multitude of problems awaited Alexander in Russia, he found time for the cathedral project. His interest was remarkable, con-sidering his apparent indifference to everything else connected with the events of 1812. "On August 26th His Majesty not only didn't visit Boro-dino and didn't participate in the memorial service in Moscow, but even on this great day, when nearly every noble family in Russia was mourning relatives fallen in the immortal battle on the banks of the Kolcha River, His Majesty attended a ball given by Countess Orlova," wrote Alexan-der Mikhailovsko-Danilevsky, the czar's aide-de-camp.[1] (Countess Anna Orlova-Chesmenskaia was one of the mystical ladies who for a while had great influence on Alexander.)

It was as if, for the czar, the war had occurred in another dimension—as if it had been a supernatural, not a real, event. The battle of Borodino had less reality for him than his own tormented vigil over the Bible at the moment when the French army was pouring into Moscow. The cathedral, dedicated to this supernatural epic, had a central role in his private spiri-tual world. Among those who were conspicuously absent from his side at this time were Kikin and Shishkov.[2]

The first projects for a victory monument appeared before publication of the manifesto announcing the cathedral. Most were for columns, obelisks, or triumphal arches. One proposal was for a pyramid made of captured French cannons. In his letter to Shishkov, Kikin had scoffed at all such imitations by "contemporary monkeys of the ancient monkeys" and accused their authors of idolatry. He distrusted professional architects, particularly foreign ones, and thought they should be consulted only for their practical knowledge. But "taste, when feelings and heart are needed, is not their business."[3]

All the projects proposed by professional architects were classical in nature. Some were for pyramids or columns; some were for churches in the Roman or Hellenistic style. The most interesting of the commemorative designs was a triumphal column submitted by Domenico Gilardi, a russified Italian-Swiss known in Moscow as Dementy Ivanovich. His decorative program for the column, called "Russia Bestowing Peace on Europe," corresponded to the czar's wish, but the project did not reflect the required religious content.

Most of the designs were similar to the many Empire-style churches built in Russia during that period. All were based on such classical examples as St. Peter's Basilica and the Pantheon in Rome or the Greek temples in Paestum.[4] The best was a design for a cathedral in the form of the Pantheon, produced by Giacomo Quarenghi, the patriarch of St. Petersburg classicism. As a source of inspiration, the Pantheon, which was both a temple of all the gods and a tomb for august individuals, seemed appropriate for a monument commemorating the liberation of Europe, but the design was considered to lack the requisite grandeur and originality.

The most original design was submitted by the prominent St. Petersburg architect Andrei Voronikhin. Born a serf, he had become a leading figure in the development of the Russian Empire style.[5] His Kazan cathedral, where Alexander had prayed for victory, played the role of national military shrine. The only architect who took seriously the idea of the Cathedral of Christ the Savior as a national monument, he tried to blend classical forms, associated with the heroic spirit of ancient Rome, with elements typical of medieval Russian architecture: Roman columns with *kokoshnik* ornamentation (so named for its resemblance to the shape of the traditional headdress). Voronikhin crowned a ribbed dome, reminiscent of Michelangelo's dome for St. Peter's, with a typical Russian onion-shaped cupola. His most daring innovation was to enclose a single, unbroken interior space within a five-domed structure, which he managed by using decorative cupolas, designed as ancient Russian belltowers topped with hipped roofs.[6] Yevgenia Kirichenko, the historian of Russian architecture, wrote that Voronikhin's design opened the way to the future, initiating the "Russian style."[7] His was the only project that corresponded to some extent to the ideas of Kikin and Shishkov. Alone of all the entrants, he had tried to express national as well as universal values. But unfortunately his vision didn't correspond to that of the most important judge, the emperor.

A Freemason and a Westernizer, Voronikhin was sensitive to the spirit of the time, when patriotic sentiment was on the rise and a fashion for everything Russian was being established. If he had lived until Alexander formulated his project of a united Christian Europe, his design might have fared better. Voronikhin's experience and talent would have made him an ideal architect to realize both the patriotic and the humanistic conception of the Cathedral of Christ the Savior. But he died in 1814, at the age of forty-five. In that same year, a young painter named Karl Vitberg, who was Voronikhin's protégé, decided to try his luck in the competition.[8]

Karl Vitberg was deeply impressed by the czar's manifesto of December 25, 1812. "A cathedral in the name of Christ the Savior! A new idea! Until that moment, Christendom built churches dedicated to a holy day or a saint, but here was an all-embracing thought. It could only come to a sovereign filled with religious feelings, as Alexander was during that time."[9]

In the summer of 1813, Vitberg went to Moscow at the invitation of Fyodor Rostopchin, governor-general of the city, to help illustrate Rostopchin's book about the Patriotic War. For Vitberg, the victory was an event of global importance; one of his allegorical drawings was called "Alexander Liberating Europe." One day, walking in the Kremlin with Dmitry Runich, director of the Moscow General Post Office, Vitberg listened to his friend talking about the future cathedral. At that moment, he later remembered, "the idea of the cathedral united with the grace of the place recommenced in my soul."[10] Runich tried to convince him to make sketches of his ideas. Vitberg was a painter, not an architect, but he promptly vowed to change his life and dedicate it completely to the Cathedral of Christ the Savior.

For the next two years, Vitberg isolated himself from the world. Day and night, in the apartment Runich had given him in the post office attic, he studied architecture on his own. He scorned all contemporary architects as mere artisans. Vitruvius, "the philosopher of architecture," was his teacher and model. To some extent, his rejection of professionalism coincided with Kikin's bitter words about professional architects. To paraphrase Kikin, Vitberg wanted to unite sense and taste with feelings and heart.

By the time of Alexander's return from the Congress of Vienna, Vitberg had already completed his original project for the cathedral-monument. It was an enormously ambitious design, based on a complicated religious-philosophical program, which he later explained in his "Notes." The cathedral must be ecumenical, not Russian Orthodox, because its "dedication to Christ shows that it belongs to the whole of Christendom," Vitberg wrote.[11] It must be divided into three parts, expressing the Trinity of Father, Son, and Holy Ghost; the three stages in the life of Christ: Nativity, Transfiguration, and Resurrection; and the three elements of the human principium: body, mind, and soul.

Vitberg's cathedral consists of three superimposed temples. In his description, as conveyed to Herzen, the structure proceeds symbolically from the base, or crypt cut in the hill and representing the body in the grave, to a cruciform main structure representing the soul, and finally to a cylinder supporting a dome symbolic of the divine spirit.[12]

The cathedral had to be built on a hill above a river, so that the crypt could be cut into the hill. A grand terraced staircase would lead from the foot of the hill to the entrance. Flanking the staircase would be a double row of columns, cast from captured French cannons, half a mile in length. The construction would be the tallest in the world, 237 meters from the foot of the slope to the top of the cross on the dome. The cathedral itself was more than 200 meters high, 30 meters higher than St. Peter's in Rome. The belltowers were to be equipped with forty-eight bells, allowing the bell ringers a four-octave range.[13]

The crypt would be a memorial to the Russian soldiers who had died in the Napoleonic Wars, and Vitberg envisioned an enormous cemetery, lit by hundreds of flickering lamps, where the fallen heroes would be buried and the names of every one of them, from commanders to common soldiers, would be carved into the walls. The only source of natural light was to be a stained-glass window in the east wall depicting the Nativity.

The symbolism of architectural forms was combined with an equally complex symbolism of light and decoration. Vitberg, who had been a painter, refused to use murals in the cathedral, preferring sculpture and stained glass, as had the creators of the Gothic cathedrals he admired.

The dark crypt lit only by the Nativity window expressed the idea that the mortal body belonged to the earth and to death and that life entered only through the light of Christ. Darkness symbolized not only death but eternity. A low-relief frieze in black-and-white marble depicting the death of Christ and figures of the apostles served as an example of how true Christians met their end. This dark labyrinth was more like an Early Christian catacomb filled with the bodies of martyrs than a national pantheon.

Above the crypt, the second temple was in the form of a Greek cross — or of a person crucified or stretched out in prayer. In this temple, dedicated to the Transfiguration, darkness gave way to semidarkness, symbolizing the soul's eternal struggle between good and evil. Transfiguration requires spiritual strength. The frieze in this temple depicted the life of Christ and the apostles, offering examples of righteousness.

If the lower temples were for the body, the upper temple was for the spirit. This rotunda surmounted by a gigantic dome, its circular shape symbolizing eternity, was dedicated to the Resurrection. The solemn gloom of the lower temples gave way here to light streaming through stained-glass windows.

Vitberg's conception was unique. It had nothing in common with traditional classicism, even though he used classical elements. But, as Kirichenko has noted, Vitberg had a "romantic understanding of the principles of creation of architectural forms." It is difficult to agree with her, however, that Vitberg's project was almost the first realization in Russia of the idea of a national cathedral-monument. The project has nothing Russian about it; it owes nothing to Orthodox tradition, nor does it express "the social and ethical values, born in the 19th century, of national character and nationality."[14] On the contrary, Vitberg's universalist Christian cathedral corresponds to the ideal of a united Europe. Rather than the Moscow River, a more suitable site might have been the bank of the Elster, near Leipzig, where Napoleon had fallen in the Battle of Nations.

Chapter Four

In January 1816, the emperor and the architect met for the first time. When Alexander had examined Vitberg's designs and listened to his explanations, he wept with joy. "I am very pleased with your project," he told Vitberg. "You have sensed my wish and conformed with my thoughts about this cathedral. I want it to be not just a pile of stones like an ordinary building, but to be inspired by some religious idea. But I didn't expect to be satisfied. I didn't believe that anybody could be motivated by such an idea. And therefore I concealed my wish. . . . You made stones speak."[1]

In typical fashion, Alexander had assumed that no one would understand him. To his surprise, he found in Vitberg not only a collaborator but a kindred spirit. The young man stated that he had no desire to play a leading role in the construction of the cathedral. He wanted to express in architectural forms the religious and philosophical ideas that filled his mind, he explained, but he was willing to leave the practical business of building to the professionals.

The czar was even more astonished when he learned that Vitberg had studied architecture for only two years. A few minutes before his meeting with Vitberg, Alexander had remarked to Prince Golitsyn that "a man can achieve anything if he only wants to." Vitberg seemed to embody that thought. Alexander took such coincidences seriously.[2] He was personally interested in Vitberg, particularly in how he was "groomed."

Karl Magnus Vitberg was born in St. Petersburg to a Swedish noble family.[3] His father, an unsuccessful painter, immigrated to Russia, where he was reduced to teaching German to the children of noble families. He urged his son to choose a "serious" profession, encouraging him to become a mining engineer, then a sailor, and finally a doctor, all of which the young Vitberg resisted. The boy demonstrated a talent for painting and interpreted the declaration of one of his teachers — "God himself commands you to join the Academy [of Arts]" — as a divine call. His father finally relented, and Voronikhin arranged a scholarship for him. Vitberg enrolled in the department of historical painting and was awarded a gold medal and a state-sponsored trip abroad for his painting *Andromache Mourning over Hector*. The trip was repeatedly delayed, however, and the young graduate was hired by the academy as an assistant professor.

One of the people who played a key role in his grooming was Alexander Labzin, the conference secretary of the academy, who took Vitberg under his wing. Historians invariably refer to Labzin as a well-known Mason, but he was much more than an influential member of the organization. It was he who resurrected Russian Freemasonry after its suppression during Catherine's last years. On January 15, 1800, when all St. Petersburg trembled under the reign of the emperor Paul, the first secret meeting of the Dying Sphinx lodge took place in a little wooden house on Vasilievsky Island.[4]

Labzin believed he was the successor to the circle of Moscow Martinists gathered together by Nicholas Novikov in Catherine's time. These were disciples of Louis Claude de St.-Martin, a French mystic and enemy of Voltaire who was known as "the unknown philosopher."[5] The Martinists believed that the moral regeneration of humankind, not revolution or reform, would bring about a kingdom of complete harmony on earth. Pavel Miliukov, the Russian historian and politician, called the Masonry of Novikov the "Tolstoyism of the time."[6] To Labzin, the most important elements of the Martinist heritage were mysticism, practical philanthropy, and action independent of the government.

When Alexander permitted the practice of Freemasonry in Russia, in 1804, the society again became popular among intellectuals of the nobility, and numerous grandees joined the lodges. Grand Duke Constantine, Alexander's younger brother and heir, headed the list of influential Masons. Virtually all the lodges were united under the leadership of Johann Jakob Beber (known in Russia as Ivan Vasilievich Beber), one of the oldest Freemasons.

On the eve of the War of 1812, the czar granted the brotherhood special favors, thereby affording them something close to official government support. Persistent rumors circulated that Alexander himself had become a Mason.[7] But Labzin, a mystical moralist who aspired to emulate the Early Christians, continued to treat the Dying Sphinx as if it were a secret sect. Bound by the strictest discipline and forbidden any contact with other lodges, its members obeyed him completely and swore an oath to dedicate themselves and everything they valued—honor, property, and life itself— to the tasks of the order.[8] They paid serious attention to theoretical studies and religious symbols. Labzin believed that meditation led to enlightenment, as the result of which chosen "prophets" could communicate directly with God.[9]

Voronikhin brought Vitberg into the lodge, and Labzin became his spiritual tutor.[10] He wanted to create in him the new moral man in opposition to the natural but immoral man of the Enlightenment. Labzin's protection was a recommendation to the czar, who, in 1816, openly regarded him and his teachings with favor. At the czar's request, Labzin reanimated the mystical magazine *Herald of Zion,* which had been banned during the short period of rapprochement with France after the peace of Tilsit. In 1817, the *Herald* started a new department, called "Rainbow," dedicated to the problem of the reunification of all religions. The rainbow was a key Masonic symbol: its colors, associated with different religions and nationalities, blended in the united light of truth. The czar even decorated Labzin for his publishing activities.[11]

In 1822, however, the monarch and the mystic had a falling-out. The president of the Academy of Arts proposed the election of a few courtiers, including General Aleksei Arakcheev, the czar's favorite, as honorary academicians. Labzin, who was at the time vice-president of the academy, asked ironically what services these people had rendered to the arts. When he was told they were very close to the czar, Labzin, in his usual stern manner, replied, "In that case I propose to elect as an honorary Academician the coachman Ilya. He is not only close to the Sovereign, he sits in front of him." The czar considered Labzin's defiance intolerable and exiled him.[12]

That same year, Freemasonry and all other secret societies were banned in Russia. All state officials were obliged to swear that they were not members of secret lodges. By this time, the disillusioned czar saw enemies everywhere and trusted only in personal devotion.

In Vitberg, Alexander saw the heaven-sent executor of his plan. The miraculous victory over Napoleon had been followed by the discovery of an architect for the memorial. The czar interpreted the transformation of the young painter into an architect as another miracle. He not only approved Vitberg's design for the cathedral but insisted that the architect supervise its construction, although he had no desire to do so.

To contemporaries, it was the czar's reception of the unknown architect that was the real miracle. To meet the czar was the highest honor a Russian subject could be granted, and people would go to enormous lengths to attain it. The brilliant guards officer and future philosopher Alexander Chaadaev, for example, asserted that he would pay an enormous price for the possibility of a private conversation with Alexander: he would accept "promotion based on the misfortune of his comrades" and ostracism from high society. He agreed to deliver to the czar the bad news of an uprising of the Semyonovsky regiment, although military statutes demanded that an officer of higher rank be sent. One of his contemporaries commented, "In this sad case, he surrendered to the natural weakness of excessive vanity. . . . The charm of close relations, private conversation, and intimacy with the emperor glittered in his imagination."[13]

Vitberg wasn't obliged to make such a sacrifice. His friend Dmitry Runich, an important Mason, helped organize the meeting. Runich has gone down in history as an obscurantist and a reactionary as well as a careerist, but Vitberg later told Herzen that Runich was "gifted with a warm soul."[14] Runich not only convinced Vitberg to put his ideas on paper, he did everything possible to attract the attention of Alexander's inner circle. As the result of his efforts, a meeting was organized in the house of Fyodor Rostopchin, governor-general of Moscow, where Vitberg explained his project to a group of grandees. One of them, Count Lev Razumovsky, a well-known patron of the arts and a Freemason, was deeply impressed and gave Vitberg a letter of recommendation to his brother, Aleksei Razumovsky, the minister of education. Another letter was addressed to Golitsyn, who had been entrusted by the czar to gather projects submitted for the cathedral.

Like the czar, Golitsyn had been educated in accordance with Enlightenment ideals and was not conspicuously religious. Alexander, at the beginning of his reign, appointed him procurator of the Holy Synod, which made him the administrative head of the Russian Orthodox Church. According to his own admission, Golitsyn loved to visit brothels, where the young ladies he favored had no idea that he was a high church official.[15] When Golitsyn was informed of his appointment, he decided to read the New Testament for the first time, an act that changed his life. He converted to the true faith, which differed from official Orthodoxy.

Golitsyn had an important quality for a courtier: he could entertain the sovereign. One day, instead of telling the usual amusing story, the prince read passages from the Bible to the emperor, who was intrigued enough to begin reading the book, also for the first time. When the French invaded a few months later, Alexander was completely devoted to the Bible and attempting to obey its teachings. He would open the book and randomly choose a passage to use as a guide to action. "The burning of Moscow brought light to my soul," he wrote to a fellow pietist, "and the judgment of God on the icy fields filled my heart with the warmth of faith which I had not felt till then. I then recognized God as He was described in holy scripture. I owe my own redemption to [God's] redemption of Europe from destruction."[16]

After the expulsion of Napoleon from Russia, the czar acknowledged the Bible's role in the victory by establishing the Russian Bible Society, modeled on the London society. The order was signed in December 1812, almost simultaneously with the manifesto ordering the creation of the Cathedral of Christ the Savior. Golitsyn was appointed president of the new society, and the czar and two of his brothers became its patrons. Orthodox, Protestant, and Catholic priests gathered in St. Petersburg to plan translations of the Bible into the myriad languages of the Russian empire.

After the war, Golitsyn began to play a key role in establishing the ideology of the new European order in the form of a united Christian church. He became minister of education in 1816 and the next year minister of education and spiritual affairs, a new position created specially for him. Because he remained minister of posts and was therefore responsible for censoring private correspondence, he had, in effect, control of the intellectual and spiritual life of the country. He and Count Arakcheev were among the czar's closest advisers. The division of power was simple: Golitsyn was responsible for heavenly and intellectual affairs; Arakcheev, for earthly and practical ones.

Chapter Five

When Prince Golitsyn received Vitberg in his St. Petersburg office at the end of 1815, he discovered to his surprise that the young man was not just another commission hunter but an idealist who was innocent of court intrigues. Vitberg never curried favor; he seemed to expect patronage as his due. At Golitsyn's request, he explained his cathedral project to the inner circle of the prince's friends. They were the only people, aside from Shishkov's nationalists, who had supported Alexander in his refusal to surrender to Napoleon, but after the expulsion of the French, Golitsyn and his followers had fought against Shishkov's isolationism and convinced the czar that it was necessary to save Europe. Now they wanted to appropriate the Cathedral of Christ the Savior to their own purposes.

One member of this group was of particular importance: Archimandrite Filaret (Vasily Drozdov), a gifted preacher and virtually the only leading

Orthodox theologian of the time who was interested in mysticism. It was Filaret who, in his sermons of 1813-14, established the new ideology of Christian universalism.[1] He would become a metropolitan and play an important role in the construction of the cathedral.

Golitsyn's friends approved of both the project and the architect. Vitberg, who was already a high-level Mason, was accepted into the inner circle of Russian mystical pietism. The prince even invited him to attend Sunday services in his private chapel—the same nondenominational chapel in which Alexander had adopted the idea of a new inner Christianity.[2] It had been established by Golitsyn in September 1812, when Napoleon occupied Moscow and many people in St. Petersburg were preparing to flee the city. Golitsyn was convinced that the Russians would ultimately be victorious, and in this chapel he and Alexander had prayed, together with their closest spiritual companions, for the salvation of Russia and Europe. Golitsyn thought it important to show Vitberg this prototype of the Cathedral of Christ the Savior.[3]

Even during his first visit to this sanctuary of the Russian ecumenical party, Vitberg behaved not as a modest artisan but as the equal of the initiated brothers. He criticized the decoration of the chapel as commonplace. He found the blue holy gates, designed by Voronikhin, completely inappropriate and proposed to repaint them red. Golitsyn was astonished.

Voronikhin's holy gates were blue because Voronikhin, a Mason himself, knew that blue was the color of St. John's Masonry, which comprised the three lowest levels of the society. Members of these lodges were visionary evangelicals who believed that paradise on earth could be achieved through individual self-perfection. Their motto was "Let us sow the seeds of the Kingdom of Light." Red was the color of St. Andrew's Masonry, the Masonry of the highest levels. Members of these lodges were fearless fighters for the cause whose motto was "Victory or Death." If blue symbolized the philosophy of passive resistance to evil, red signified the willingness to fight for ideals.[4]

By proposing to repaint the holy gates red, Vitberg expressed the mood of the Masonic element of the ecumenical party that surrounded the czar. After the victory over Napoleon, Alexander wanted decisive changes. Much as he deplored violence, he did not rule out "reasonable violence" if practiced by an enlightened ruler dealing with unreasonable subjects. The visionaries had to be replaced by soldiers for the cause.

Golitsyn immediately commissioned Vitberg to create new holy gates, and the architect came up with a complex allegorical composition in which biblical texts played an important role. Golitsyn begged him to complete the gates before the czar's return from abroad. So before Alexander met Vitberg, he had heard praise of the young man's brilliance. Thanks to the efforts of Golitsyn and other members of the ecumenical party, Vitberg, through his project for an ecumenical cathedral, had acquired the status of discoverer of a new architecture that corresponded to the new faith. As if this weren't enough, Alexander saw in him an architect who was able to express the ideology of a united Europe. The Act of the Holy Alliance, composed by the czar himself, was a union of three monarchs—Catholic, Protestant, and Orthodox—under the patronage of the Holy Trinity. All of them accepted Christ as their sovereign. The czar could hardly fail to extend the symbolism of Vitberg's tripartite church to the Holy Alliance.

Vitberg, in the eyes of St. Petersburg officialdom, had hit the jackpot. Promotions and honors were showered on him, and in five years he rose from the lowest civil rank, titular counselor, to court counselor. The czar decorated him with the prestigious Order of St. Vladimir, third class.[5] Everyone joined in the chorus of praise. Aleksei Razumovsky, the arrogant and unapproachable minister of enlightenment, invited the young man to his home and lauded his ideas as "a new poetry of architecture." Count Ioannis Kapodistria—a state secretary, an architect of Russian foreign policy, and a proponent of the Holy Alliance—tried to convince Vitberg to publish his design, along with a detailed explanation of its symbolism. Count Mikhail Vorontsov, a hero of Borodino, begged Vitberg to build a smaller version of the cathedral on his Crimean estate.

Vitberg declined all of these flattering offers, not wanting to be deflected from his great goal. There was only one project he could not refuse during this period: Grand Duke Nicholas, the czar's brother, asked him to construct a chapel dedicated to the birth of his son in the Resurrection Cathedral of the New Jerusalem Monastery in Istra. "I asked several architects, but their projects are so ordinary. I want something new with your ideas," he said to Vitberg, according to Herzen's memoir.[6] Vitberg agreed, not only because the request came from a member of the imperial family but also because he had a special interest in the Resurrection Cathedral. Constructed in the seventeenth century, it was a gigantic replica of the Anastasis (Resurrection) Rotunda in Jerusalem built by the emperor Constantine in the fourth century to enclose the Holy Sepulchre. Constantine then enclosed both the Sepulchre and the Anastasis in a huge church, the Martyrium at Golgotha. The complex commemorated Christ's Crucifixion, burial, and Resurrection.

These three buildings were echoed in Vitberg's plan for Christ the Savior. The crypt of his cathedral suggested the Holy Sepulchre, and the middle and upper levels echoed the cross-shaped cathedral and Resurrection Rotunda.

Vitberg paid primary attention to developing an ideological program, and then, after working out its complexities, he illustrated it with architectural elements. The time was ripe for this kind of ideological architecture, since Alexander was beginning to establish policy based on the principles of the New Testament. The czar and his circle agreed with the architect, however, that the time was not right to inform the public of the cathedral's ideological plan. The building was to come as a revelation. The idea of a secret plan corresponded to the spirit of the reign. Alexander wanted to find and develop an idea in complete secrecy and then introduce it to his subjects.

Although the Gospel sources of Vitberg's project have been thoroughly researched, its Masonic foundations have been deliberately ignored. Even the architect's son, Fyodor, insisted that his father had sought to express not Masonic ideas but the principal dogmas of Christianity and the central Christian moral and psychological ideas.

For many years the conviction that the Jewish Masonic plot was the main source of Russia's ills was widespread, and the search for Masonic symbols everywhere was an obsession of nationalists and anti-Semites. The reaction among educated people was to discredit even serious investigations of Masonry and Masonic symbolism in Russian history. The only author who has addressed the Masonic roots of Vitberg's architecture was Aleksei Novitsky.[7] But there is no doubt that Vitberg was a Mason. In fact, at the remarkably young age of twenty-two, he had already been initiated into the theoretical grade, a rare honor in the Masonic hierarchy.[8] His associates were all Masons, and he was introduced to the czar by Masons. After Masonry was banned in Russia, Vitberg remained a member of the clandestine "brotherhood working in silence."[9]

On the eve of his decisive trip to St. Petersburg to meet the czar for the first time, Vitberg undertook a pilgrimage to the village of Avdotiono-

Tikhvinskoe, near Moscow, to seek the advice of Nicholas Novikov, the patriarch of the Russian Mason-Martinists. Dmitry Runich organized the visit to the man who has been called the "first real *intelligent* of Russia."[10]

Novikov virtually established the tradition of private social activity in Russia. An idealist and a mystic who believed that the world could be regenerated by individual self-improvement, he was at the same time a practical genius whose brain overflowed with schemes. He was accused of self-interest, Yuri Lotman wrote, and he did know how to make money, but he spent whatever he made on food and medicines for the destitute or on publishing books, while he himself remained poor. Lotman admired Novikov's enthusiastic and practical charity.[11] Catherine the Great, however, saw a serious danger in his activities and had him imprisoned in the Schlüsselburg fortress for four years, thereby bestowing on him a martyr's halo.

Vitberg appealed to Novikov to resolve his dispute with Labzin, who believed the young architect had become obsessed with designing the cathedral and was tempted by the possibility of making a great career. He wanted his pupil to reject everything "exterior" and quoted the Bible in support of his argument: "What kind of temple can you erect for me if I created everything?"

Vitberg's account of his conversation with Novikov can be understood fully only with the help of the secret language of Masonry. Was it possible to pay attention to the exterior, or did all attention have to be dedicated to the interior? In Masonic terminology, interior refers to Masonic service, work in the lodge. The exterior is the profane world of the uninitiated. This division of space is an important point of Masonic ideology.

Unexpectedly, Novikov supported Vitberg and reproached Labzin for his excessive severity. The patriarch of the Martinists approved the architect's main idea that "the exterior cathedral . . . must not be cold stone but a living structure, full of ideas, that isn't limited by the refinement of forms. The interior meaning must be deeply incorporated into every form."[12] The language is Masonic. Vitberg was describing a cathedral that would be filled with Masonic ideology and symbolism but would be open to all—a Masonic temple in the world of the uninitiated.[13]

Novikov understood that the discussion of internal and external temples had another aspect. Just as the establishment of the internal temple was the Masonic task, the creation of the internal church was the aim of the pietists. Alexander and Golitsyn both dreamed of replacing the external Orthodox Church, mired in soullessness and bureaucracy, with an internal ecumenical church imbued with true religious feeling. A thirst for such feeling was widespread after the terrors and victories of the Napoleonic Wars, and for a while the internal construction of the true religion became a point of intersection of the ideological aspirations of the epoch.

Labzin was one of the key figures in this process. He was a link between the mystical branch of Russian Masonry and the pietism that fascinated Alexander during this period. Labzin's faith in the internal church was fanatical. There was no room in it for Vitberg's external temple filled with intrinsic meaning. Labzin believed that the external, ritualistic side of Christianity, including church architecture, had to give place to spiritual meditation and deeper immersion in the Bible. For him, external was the enemy of internal. Novikov was much more tolerant. He immediately understood the importance of Vitberg's cathedral to the cause of Masonic and mystical enlightenment in Russia and saw that the project would attract the czar's support. Novikov was the only person who could convince Labzin not to stand in Vitberg's way. He apparently succeeded, because Labzin began to look on the cathedral project favorably.

Chapter Six

Masons believed that the brotherhood created an inner temple in their souls. The conception of the inner temple and of the tripartite character of all existence was instrumental in explaining the origin of Freemasonry. According to Masonic teachings, the fall of Adam took place in three stages: Adam's soul fell in his imagination; his mind fell while he slept; and his body fell when the serpent tempted him. He lost his likeness to God and became a mortal creature, but he retained the memory of paradise and saved in his heart the "ray of light" of complete knowledge. Adam passed it to his children, but with each generation the truth handed down by the forefathers lost some of its brightness, and hearts cooled. Chosen wise men coded the most esoteric secrets through symbols, which were transmitted from one initiate to another. The task of the order was threefold: preservation of secret knowledge, self-regeneration, and the regeneration of all humankind.

King Solomon, who was one of the chosen, decided to erect a great temple that would express the truth in stone. He entrusted its construction to another initiate, the architect Hiram Abiff. Thousands of workmen from various nations were drafted for the project and divided into three groups: apprentices, journeymen, and masters. As stone rose upon stone, the architect gradually introduced his workers to the esoteric language of symbols, corresponding to their rank.

Three journeymen who believed they had been treated unjustly by the architect plotted to force him to reveal the highest knowledge to them, but Hiram kept silent, even under torture. The three killed him with three mortal blows and hid his body. After it was found and the killers were punished, the temple was completed. During its construction the brotherhood of Freemasons—the interior temple—was established. It saved the divine knowledge in its rituals, as the building—the exterior temple—saved it in its material form.

After the destruction of Solomon's Temple, the brotherhood became the only keeper of esoteric knowledge, the living temple of truth. The brotherhood's task was to help humankind understand this truth and prepare for the transformation of soul, mind, and body through which humans would once again assume the likeness of God, like Adam before the Fall, and establish the kingdom of God on earth.[1]

In the Old Testament, and especially in Masonic lore, Solomon's Temple stood in opposition to the Tower of Babel, a symbol of humanity's pride and vain belief in reason—history's first architectural utopia. Solomon's Temple, on the contrary, brought humans nearer to God. Although the builders belonged to different tribes, they were united by esoteric knowledge and understood one another. Rather than preventing their labors, God helped them and suggested the plan of the temple.

Douglas Smith, the American historian of Masonry, wrote that Solomon's Temple "occupied an important place in Masonic cosmology as the perfect and most spectacular of structures. It served as a model for the lodges, and the legends surrounding its construction formed the basis for the initiation ritual into the Master Mason degree. The Temple's three sections are mirrored by the order's three levels: as the brother progressed to the next degree, he moved ever upward and inward toward the Temple's holy of holies."[2]

Vitberg saw himself as a new Hiram Abiff, creator of an exterior temple, like the Temple of Solomon. His cathedral project is closely based on the temple as the Masons imagined it. Its three-level structure, with entry at the lower level, parallels the Masonic brother's ascent of the staircase of esoteric knowledge until he penetrates its core.

In Vitberg's symbolic program, the lower church signifies the body; the middle church, the mind; and the upper church, the soul—a scheme that corresponds to the Masonic theory of the three-stage character of Adam's Fall and the future resurrection of humankind. The two obelisks that were to be installed in front of the cathedral corresponded to the two pillars standing in the doorway of Solomon's Temple, images of which were used to decorate every Masonic lodge. The fresco painted on the interior of the dome of the upper, "soul" temple, depicting the sky, recalled the starry blue ceiling typical of Masonic lodges.

As Vitberg described the process of creation, his selection of forms for the future cathedral resembled an occult ritual: "I imagined that God Creator was a point [*tochka*] and named it the unit, God. I took compasses and drew a circle whose center was this point. I called this periphery the plurality-creation. So I had the unit and the plurality, the Creator and the creation. How can this point be joined with the periphery? Observing the process of the drawing, I noticed that the open arms of compasses create a straight line. An infinite series of such lines creates a circle. All of them intersecting in the center create crosses, and therefore, by the cross, are united with the Creator of nature. Thus I received three shapes—a line, a cross, and a circle, which compose one mysterious figure, which completely satisfied me. And since that moment I have understood this mystery."[3]

Vitberg's lower church, the "body church," cut inside the rock and only dimly illuminated, recalled the "dark" or "black little temple," the space enclosed in a black cloth into which the blindfolded novice is led during the Masonic initiation rite. The blindfold is removed, and the novice is surrounded by darkness, as in a grave. Two coffins stand in front of him, barely visible in the gloom. In one is the dummy of a dead, decaying body. The second is empty. The novice is told: "You are in a gloomy temple lit by a weak light, which glimmers through the remains of a mortal human creature. . . . The exterior man is gloomy and perishable, but inside him is an imperishable spark owned by the Great, the Most Whole Creature, which is the source of imperishable life, who runs the Universe. Joining us with the intention to enlighten yourself, from the first step you receive one very visual lesson, that one who wishes light must first see the darkness surrounding him, and distinguishing the difference between the darkness and the light, you must address all your attention to the light."[4]

Vitberg's cathedral is a visual lesson based on Masonic and Gospel symbols, like the symbolism of light, which increases dramatically from the dim lower church to the glittering dome of the upper church.

In Vitberg's vision, a compass was the magical instrument that disclosed to him the secret of the cathedral. According to Masonic teachings, the third mortal blow was delivered to Hiram Abiff by a compass aimed at his heart, where true knowledge was sheltered. A compass open over a level, another architectural instrument, is the main Masonic emblem. The compass symbolizes the sun, while the level represents the section of the globe's surface the sun illuminates. In the space between compass and level is the world of truth. The circle drawn by Vitberg's compass replicated this Masonic symbol.[5]

The architectural profession was highly respected in the Masonic world. Masonry was established in Britain, and in Vitberg's time Masons believed that Christopher Wren was the founding father of the Great English lodge. According to one legend, Wren initiated Peter the Great into Masonry during the czar's visit to London.[6] Later it was learned that Wren had not played such an important a role but that he was a lodge member—a kind of second Hiram Abiff. Vitberg wrote that St. Paul's Cathedral was one of his models, and his own project does show certain similarities to Wren's first, unrealized plan. We don't know if Vitberg ever saw this plan, but he may have seen an engraving of the large model made by Wren that is still exhibited in London.

The history of Russian Masonry has its own Christopher Wren. His name was Vasily Bazhenov, and he was chosen by the Moscow Martinists led by Novikov to win over Catherine the Great's son and heir, the czarevich Paul. Bazhenov has a special place in the history of Russian culture. Trained in France, he was instantly sought after when he returned to Russia. It was he who persuaded Catherine to build a huge palace in the Kremlin, convincing her that destroying the ancient fortress would demonstrate the victory of Western civilization over Asiatic barbarity, the triumph of enlightenment over ignorance. The Kremlin Palace he designed was the first manifestation of architectural utopianism in Russia.

Part of the Kremlin was destroyed to make way for new construction. Bazhenov was received at court, but he made the mistake of giving Paul a few books published by Novikov and telling him about the activities of the Moscow Martinists. Immediately he was accused of political intrigue. Suspicious that Masons were trying to influence the heir to the throne, Catherine saw to it that the circle of Moscow Martinists was destroyed and had Novikov imprisoned. Bazhenov was banished, and his great plans abandoned.

Despite this experience, Novikov didn't try to discourage Vitberg from trying to win over Alexander with a plan for a gigantic cathedral based entirely on Masonic symbolism. Times had changed. Vitberg was hoping to influence not an unloved heir to the Russian throne but the ruler of Europe, who was already surrounded by high-degree Masons. The guileless Vitberg would find himself at the center of a new Masonic intrigue in which he would play the role of Hiram Abiff, his cathedral would become Solomon's Temple, and Czar Alexander would be the new Solomon.

Novikov and his followers were enthusiastic about the idea of the architect-Mason and his special mission. Most were members of Labzin's Dying Sphinx lodge. Bazhenov died before the lodge was established, but Voronikhin belonged, and in 1808 he brought in Vitberg. Among the members were men who would be his spiritual tutors and patrons, including Dmitry Runich, who became his closest friend.[7] Two famous painters, Dmitry Levitsky and Vladimir Borovikovsky, did some of their best work in connection with the lodge, providing the portraits the members exchanged as a sign of special confidence. These symbol-laden portraits were even thought to contain the souls of people who had dedicated themselves to Masonry.[8]

Vitberg also painted Masonic portraits, including one of Novikov. But Labzin believed in the power of the word, not the image, and Levitsky and other members agreed with him, so the Dying Sphinx lodge had virtually no decorations except for the Masonic symbols painted on its carpets.[9] Vitberg may have been responsible for some of these symbols: the coffin-parallelogram, the Crucifix, and the sun-circle.[10] The triform symbol for the ideal lodge—the temple, as Masons called it—was often depicted on carpets, and sometimes it was drawn on the floor with chalk and then erased for reasons of secrecy.

For Masons, Solomon's Temple was the symbol of Masonry itself as well as a material manifestation of Old Testament wisdom. Vitberg's cathedral was to be a Gospel in stone, a material manifestation of pietistic teachings. By fusing Masonic and Gospel symbolism into an organic unity, he hoped to make the cathedral a monument to Russia's—and Europe's—entry into the sphere of the new spirituality.

Vitberg was both a connoisseur of Masonic dogma and a virtuoso of mystical vigils. His life was full of portents and visions, including one in which an apparition informed him that she was a "daughter of Truth." In a recurring dream of his youth, he saw himself constructing a temple.[11] Not surprisingly, there was a miracle on the day the cornerstone was to be laid. That morning Prince Golitsyn consulted his Bible, opening the book at random, as was his practice; his eyes fell on the verse in which Hiram selects builders for the construction of Solomon's Temple. Golitsyn later recounted the miracle to Vitberg. It was at this moment that Golitsyn said, "There are many strange things in this cathedral." The Masons considered Hiram's selection of builders to be the beginning of their order. The analogy was perfectly clear to both men.

Another analogy was drawn by Aleksei Merzliakov, a professor at Moscow University, who wrote a song in which the Sparrow Hills are compared to Mount Moriah, where Solomon's Temple was erected. Alexander is, of course, Solomon; Moscow—the "city of cities," the third Rome—is also the New Jerusalem; and the Russians are the new chosen people.[12]

Chapter Seven

Very few Russians would have shared the enthusiasm of Alexander and Golitsyn for the cathedral's ideological program. The educated sector of the nobility was cosmopolitan and, after the flare-up of patriotism aroused by the war, had resumed speaking French. Most considered themselves hopelessly provincial, but the victory over Napoleon had salved their traditional inferiority complex.

Everything connected with the victory contributed to the nationalistic pride felt by all classes of society. To the public, the cathedral was a symbol not of universal Christianity or European unity but of Russian superiority to foreigners and Orthodox superiority to foreign religions. This was true even of educated people. And the masses of serfs who gathered at the Sparrow Hills to see the czar lay the cornerstone had not the slightest comprehension of Vitberg's complex program or Merzliakov's song. To them, the non-Orthodox world was divided into two parts.

In the East lived infidels, or Muslims. In the West were the *nemtsi* ("mutes"), the term applied first to all Europeans and then to Germans. Many Russian peasants did not even know, and would not have believed, that other peoples and other monarchies existed in the world.[1] To them, Napoleon represented the forces of darkness, and the cathedral was dedicated to liberation from those forces. That some "Germans" were the allies of Russia was beyond comprehension. How was it possible, then, that the architect of the cathedral was a Protestant "German"? (Vitberg was of Swedish extraction.)

It didn't concern Alexander that Vitberg wasn't Orthodox, but after the foundation ceremony he heard murmurs of discontent. The czar asked Golitsyn to tell the architect that his conversion would be appreciated but left it to Vitberg to make his own decision. Although Vitberg, who believed strongly in the unification of all Christian churches and saw his cathedral as universal, thought it would be dishonest to convert, he nevertheless fulfilled the czar's wish, not to ingratiate himself but to signal his acceptance of the new faith for which Alexander was searching. Vitberg therefore referred to his baptism as a "ceremony of unification with the Russian church." He took the name Alexander, and the czar himself agreed to become his godfather. The ceremony, at which Golitsyn represented the czar, took place on Christmas Eve 1817. On Christmas Day five years earlier, Alexander had announced his intention to construct the cathedral.[2]

The czar's attentions to Vitberg were extraordinary. The young man fell ill after the foundation ceremony, and the czar sent him his own doctor. When the two met again, Alexander permitted the architect, who was still weak, to sit in his presence. The two met often for long private discussions of every design detail, arousing jealousy among those less favored by the monarch. Even ministers and state councillors didn't have such access to the czar; Arakcheev was the only minister who could talk to him directly about affairs of state.[3] Golitsyn too had influence over the czar, and Vitberg was considered Golitsyn's man. Naturally, Arakcheev was displeased with this state of affairs and tried to replace Vitberg with his own candidate, until he decided that it would be more politic to befriend the architect than to plot against him. Suddenly the loftiest grandees were seeking the young man's favor. It was inevitable that the guileless, inexperienced Vitberg, hardly aware of what was happening to him, would become enmeshed in court intrigues.

The main problem was the selection of a site for the cathedral. Vitberg proposed to erect it in the Kremlin, but the czar did not want to destroy the ancient complex that had miraculously survived the invasion. He suggested instead a spot on the Shvivaya Hill beside the Yauza River, not far from the Kremlin, but Vitberg rejected it because it would have entailed tearing down houses that had just been rebuilt after the fire. Next the exasperated Arakcheev proposed to start construction on the site of a former gunpowder storage depot near the monastery of St. Simon. The architect was adamant, however; his heart was set on the Sparrow Hills. The discussion became heated. Vitberg pointed out that the monastery of St. Simon was also ancient and would be damaged by construction nearby. Finally Arakcheev, who believed that the cathedral was an undertaking of great national importance, gave up and supported Vitberg's proposal.

Although it is known that Arakcheev and Vitberg didn't get along well, their relationship is difficult to fathom. Vitberg's son, Fyodor, stated that his father had become a victim of Arakcheev's intrigues, but there is no evidence for such a statement. Fyodor wanted to transform his father, in the eyes of history, into an opponent of the extremely unpopular Arakcheev, who has been blamed for all the failures of Alexander's reign.[4] Whatever people thought of his politics, however, no one ever questioned Arakcheev's honesty; he was incorruptible. After the occupation of Paris, Alexander promoted him to the rank of field marshal, an honor the count rejected. The only gift Arakcheev ever accepted from the czar was his portrait, though he returned the diamonds decorating the frame. Completely devoted to the czar, but no flatterer, he was ready to fulfill his master's every wish.[5]

Arakcheev has gone down in history as the founder of the infamous military settlements where peasants were expected to be both farmers and soldiers at the same time. In fact the idea originated with Alexander, who thought the settlements would solve two intractable problems: the reorganization of the army and the reform of peasant life. Arakcheev, who never defended serfdom and was an enlightened landlord on his own estates, had misgivings about the scheme from the beginning, but he obeyed the czar's order—and was blamed for the greatest failure of the reign.[6] The settlements, where the horrors of military life were added to the misery of the serf village, were an unqualified disaster. The peasants had no desire to plow to the beat of drums; they revolted, ran away, or committed suicide. The well-intentioned Alexander, with Arakcheev's help, had created a monster.

In 1818, Arakcheev worked out an emancipation plan for the czar that had much in common with the Great Emancipation Reform of 1861, through which the state would gradually purchase the peasants and their land and subsequently emancipate the peasants. The liberation of land and the state's payment of partial compensation to the landowners were central elements of the reform of 1861. But Arakcheev's plan remained secret until the end of the reign. In 1819, however, when Vitberg revealed his construction plan to the czar, it was clear that he had adopted some elements from Arakcheev. Vitberg proposed that the cathedral construction should become a model of social reform. He wanted the government to buy eighteen thousand serfs from their landlords, along with land. Some of the serfs would work the land to supply the money for the construction; the others would become builders. After the czar studied the details, he exclaimed approvingly, "Again, something new!" The project was approved in 1820.[7]

State peasants — those owned by the crown — had not experienced the oppression so familiar to privately owned serfs, and the ruling elite believed that the liquidation of serf villages would solve the peasant question, according to the historian Sergei Mironenko. "If all the serfs became state property, the problem of 'landlords versus serfs,' which was creating an increasingly dangerous situation, would cease to exist."[8]

During this period Vitberg became close to Count Viktor Kochubei, the interior minister, who was one of the czar's "young friends" and a member of the Private Committee. Kochubei was so interested in the cathedral project that Vitberg began to treat him as if he were almost a collaborator. He agreed with Kochubei that the original dome was too small for the gigantic building and, following Kochubei's advice, enlarged it to almost twice its original size.

But it was the czar who was Vitberg's most important collaborator, paying attention to every detail of the design. For Alexander and his close circle, the cathedral construction was a major concern during the late 1810s and the beginning of the 1820s — a period when the czar was making the most vigorous attempts at reform. In 1816, the year Alexander met Vitberg, he was actively trying to resolve the peasant problem. For the first time in Russian history, serfdom was abolished in one part of the empire, Estland (Estonia). The czar traveled throughout Russia to explore the possibilities of emancipation in the Russian provinces. On May 15, 1818, only five months after the cathedral cornerstone was laid, he delivered a major speech in Warsaw before the Polish *sejm*, the first elected parliament in the history of the Russian empire. Unexpectedly, he announced that the constitution he had granted to Poland in 1815 was only the beginning and that he wanted to extend constitutional rule to all of his subject peoples, including Russians.

Addressing the Poles, Alexander pronounced the staggering words, "You must set a great example for Europe, which looks to you. Prove to your contemporaries that liberal institutions, whose holy roots are entangled with destructive doctrines that threatened the very existence of social order in our time, are not a dangerous dream but the opposite." During his stay in Warsaw, Alexander ordered Count Nicholas Novosiltsev to prepare a plan for the Russian constitution, which was completed in 1820.[9] It seemed that liberal reforms were unfolding steadily. Ecumenical activity also seemed to be flourishing.

But it was an illusion. In the five years since his victory over Napoleon, the czar had lost the aura of a monarch who could do no wrong. Everybody was disappointed in him—the liberals, because he had accomplished no significant reforms, and the conservatives, because they feared the abolition of serfdom. Until the peasant problem was resolved, it was impossible to talk seriously about a constitution. Serfs who were bought and sold could not be citizens.

Admiral Shishkov, who had played so important a role in developing the ideological program of the cathedral, had become a symbol of resistance to Alexander's liberal undertakings. To Shishkov, serfdom was a mutually beneficial union of landlords and peasants, and furthermore it was native to Russia, a view he expressed in his draft of the manifesto on the victory. Alexander had been infuriated by this eulogy to serfdom and refused to sign it. Seeing how angry the czar was, the usually stubborn Shishkov did not argue but crossed out the phrase. The czar, Shishkov later wrote in his memoirs, had developed an unfortunate prejudice against serfdom, against the nobility, and against all the old institutions, because of his education in the spirit of the French Enlightenment.[10]

Six years later, Shishkov took his revenge. During a meeting of the State

Council, he adamantly opposed a law designed to ease the peasants' lot, stating that "the spirit of the time" so frequently invoked by the supporters of change was nothing more than a "yearning for self-will and disobedience." "The spirit of the time" was Alexander's favorite expression. This open criticism was a signal for a conservative attack on the czar.[11]

Napoleon died in 1821. The czar had become accustomed to measuring himself against his great adversary, whose genius had raised Alexander's stature as a victor, even after Napoleon's fall. When he died, Alexander acted as if he were having a breakdown. Both men lost the struggle for a united Europe. Both were overcome by the growing forces of nationalism. Napoleon aroused the nationalist fervor of the Russians, the Spaniards, the Germans, and the Italians. Alexander's dream of a united Europe wasn't taken seriously by the European powers.

In the 1820s a wave of revolutions shocked Europe. "Underdeveloped" peoples were also demanding their own states. The czar was horrified by the uprisings in Greece and Italy, recognizing in them the sinister specter of the French Revolution.[12] The vision of a united Europe was not to be realized. The spirit of the time, his guiding star for so long, had been the cause of all evils. Now the pernicious spirit of the West was recognized as the cause of all troubles. Alexander's struggle with this spirit would cast a shadow over the end of his reign.

Chapter Eight

The anti-Western party at this time united Orthodox fanatics such as Archimandrite Fotius, nationalists such as Shishkov, and some of Golitsyn's former followers who had rebelled against their patron. These former Masons and "Europeans" saw that the ecumenical policy was out of favor and promptly changed course. Mikhail Magnitsky became their new ideologist. The closest collaborator and follower of Mikhail Speransky, the former state secretary, Magnitsky was a Francophile and a reformer who had been exiled after his patron's fall but soon returned to political life and decreed a counterrevolution in education. He discovered Jacobin ideological conspiracies everywhere, even in lectures on mathematics. Education, he believed, had to be founded on religion — but which religion?

Magnitsky didn't like the Protestant overtones of the new faith Alexander and Golitsyn were promoting. He had decided that the font of religious renewal flowed not from the West but from the East. It was Russia — the country that had proved its superiority on the battlefield, the country that had received Christianity from Byzantium and preserved it in its pure form — that would lead Europe in religious and ideological spheres as well. Magnitsky found strong supporters among the Orthodox clergy. The bearded priests hated the meetings of the Bible Society, where they had to sit with highbrow "Western" theologians. Fotius, the young archimandrite from Novgorod, led their revolt.

Arakcheev, seeing a chance to unseat Golitsyn, sided with Magnitsky and Fotius. By the spring of 1824, the three had succeeded in destroying Golitsyn's ideological empire. The united Ministry of Education and Spiritual Affairs was abolished, and the Bible Society lost its influence. The indispensable Admiral Shishkov, embodiment of patriarchal conservatism, was appointed minister of education and head of the censorship office (just as before the war he had replaced the reformer Speransky). It was the end of the epoch of religious tolerance in Russia, and the end of Alexander's dream of a united Europe based on a universalist Christian foundation. Now a conservative vision of the future prevailed.

Magnitsky did not reject the idea of a universal church led by the Russian czar and destined to save the world, but he saw himself, not Golitsyn, as its main ideologue. Unlike Golitsyn, who wanted to amalgamate the best features of all Christian denominations, Magnitsky wanted to return to the Early Christian church, the source whose purity had been saved by Orthodoxy and had survived only in the East. The Mongol occupation had been a great blessing, he believed, because it isolated Russia and allowed it to preserve the clear stream of Christianity while the West fell into heresy. The Buddhist, Hindu, and Muslim Orient had absorbed many elements of true Christianity and could reveal sacred mysteries. The aphorism "Ex oriente lux" (Light comes from the East), in which *lux* signified the true church, was appropriated by the Masons. Magnitsky, who had once been a Mason, now believed that secret Masonic societies were part of the Western decadence that threatened Russia, but he continued to employ the terminology and the ideas of higher Masonry.[1]

Magnitsky's clerical allies weren't interested in such complicated philosophical theories. Who needed a universal religion when Orthodoxy was available? Why search and change? The so-called uneducated party led by

Fotius simply didn't understand Magnitsky's intellectual constructions. It wasn't long before Magnitsky himself was accused of secret Masonry and patronage of Jews.

Vitberg did not take part in this ideological struggle, but because his cathedral project was at its center, he was obliged to react. He saw that Alexander was hesitating. What did the czar want? Thanks to Golitsyn's patronage, Vitberg was perceived as an exponent in architecture of the ideas of the ecumenical party, led by the all-powerful minister. But Vitberg wasn't just Golitsyn's protégé; he was an independent personality who reworked ideas received from various sources, among them Runich, who in the 1820s became Magnitsky's closest collaborator and had a strong influence on the architect.

Vitberg never acted against Golitsyn, but after 1820 his activity started to reflect the influence of Magnitsky and Runich. He ignored the recommendations of Golitsyn and Kochubei that he visit Rome to collect ideas for the cathedral and was supported in this decision by Alexander, who feared that the originality of his cathedral plan might be diluted by the experience of foreign places. Magnitsky asserted that isolation from Europe was crucial to protect the uniqueness of Russia. Vitberg himself justified his refusal to study Italian monuments, asserting that "the feeling of national pride forced me to eliminate everything foreign to achieve a more complete originality."[2]

In reality, Vitberg's project—unlike Voronikhin's—lacked specific Russian features. He worked entirely within the limits of classicism, but his sources weren't the usual ones. In the early designs for the cathedral, one can detect the influence of St. Peter's in Rome, but at the beginning of the 1820s Vitberg unexpectedly lost interest in Roman architecture, both ancient and Renaissance, and turned instead to Hellenism. The cathedral began to look more like such gigantic Hellenistic constructions as the Mausoleum of Halicarnassus. Greek influence had replaced Roman.

The Russians had received their faith and culture from Byzantium, not Rome. Vitberg always referred to the Orthodox church as the Russian-Greek church. Hellenism, to him, united for the first time the culture of the educated West (Greece) with that of the East. Wasn't the czar himself named in honor of Alexander the Great, creator of the Hellenistic empire that united Greeks and barbarians?

Nationalism had not yet triumphed in Russia, but Vitberg felt that a strong force was gathering after the 1812 war. Depressed by the failure of the

ecumenical project, the czar was toying with "Ex oriente lux." Did he want
to reanimate in the new historical situation the Greek project of his grand-
mother Catherine the Great? To create an empire with Moscow, Constantinople, and St. Petersburg as its three focal points? To unite the Russian
empire and the former territories of Byzantium? To defeat the Ottoman
Turks? Was Vitberg's Hellenism an attempt to reflect in architectural form
the czar's new priority—from West to East?[3]

It was against this background that construction of the Cathedral of
Christ the Savior began in 1820. The artistic convulsions were over for Vitberg; now he would face a less inspiring struggle with hostile forces.

Chapter Nine

In the course of a few years, the Construction Commission bought about
twenty-five thousand serfs. Because Vitberg insisted that sales be voluntary
on the part of both the serfs and their owners, meetings were held in each
village at which the peasants had to signify their willingness to participate
in a deed pleasing to God.

Villages were acquired in eleven regions of Russia, and a special administrative apparatus was established to manage them. Each village had
its own office, which was under the jurisdiction of a district office. The
peasants, who had just been liberated from landlords, were delivered into
the hands of Construction Commission officials, who were responsible not
only for supervising their labors but for teaching them how to live. They
were to be reformed as well as employed. Vitberg tried to select the officials
personally, paying special attention to their moral qualities. Profoundly
committed to social reform, he wanted to mold a brotherhood of dedicated
administrators under whose care the cathedral estates would become oases
of new life. Changing Russia all at once was impossible, but small commu-
nities might be reformed and become models for the rest of the country. It
was one of many utopian schemes that characterized the period, the most
ambitious—and the most hated—being Arakcheev's military settlements.[1]

The center of Vitberg's utopia was the construction site at the Sparrow
Hills. Workshops and storage depots were built on the site, along with
facilities for the serf laborers who came streaming in from the villages: bar-
racks, kitchens, and bathhouses, even a hospital.[2]

Vitberg was humane, unlike Arakcheev, but the results of his experiment were no less lamentable. The only authority the peasants accepted was that of the czar. It did not matter whether their overseers were kind or cruel; they wanted no one interfering in their lives. In addition, peasants did everything they could to avoid labor. Those who could afford to hired surrogates, who were sometimes completely unable to work: Mikhail Mostovsky, head of the Construction Commission office, reported that there were among the laborers "minors, the lame, the feeble, and even the armless, the blind, and the mad." In addition to all the other problems, epidemics spread among the workers; in 1824, the administration had to send them all home before the end of the season because so many were ill.[3] Making things worse, a number of the idealistic administrators Vitberg had appointed couldn't manage the peasants. One administrator hung himself in 1825 in Nikolskoe, a village near Kaluga, "because of severe depression."[4]

To his horror, Vitberg found that one of the exemplary villages he had bought, Sinzhany, near Vladimir, was the secret center of the Molokan sect, which rejected the authority of the czar and the Orthodox Church. The entire population of the village was forced to convert to Orthodoxy, and the Molokan activists were exiled.[5]

The beleaguered Vitberg had to deal not only with the passive resistance of the laborers but with the intrigues and machinations of the officials. The commission staff grew larger every day, and soon the idealists he had chosen were lost in a sea of hard-boiled bureaucrats. Bribery and theft flourished. "Vitberg was surrounded by a crowd of rogues, men who look on Russia as a field for speculation, on the service as a profitable line of business, on a public post as a lucky chance to make a fortune," Herzen wrote. "It was easy to understand that they would dig a pit under Vitberg's feet."[6]

Herzen's metaphorical hole became the foundation pit of the future cathedral. Vitberg thought it would save time if site preparation began before he completed his blueprints. While the hill beside the Moscow River was cleared for the vast excavation, he would work out the last details. But he created an ideal opportunity for thieving officials by spending all his time in his study working on his plans, which he showed no one. Nobody had any idea what was to be built. An examination of the site was made, but in the most perfunctory manner. Conditions were perfect for the numerous crooks who raked off colossal sums of money for "flattening the slope for the lower site of the cathedral." Without a plan or proper control, the slope could be flattened endlessly.[7]

Another budget item that afforded vast possibilities for theft was the purchase of materials. Hundreds of carts piled with logs, planks, and iron lumbered to the site, where their contents were unloaded in huge heaps, measured by eye, and left to rot. Tearful officials tried to convince Vitberg that hundreds of thousands of rubles worth of materials had been destroyed by bad weather. In reality, most of these materials had existed only on paper, and the money to pay for them had been stolen. The unworldy, impractical Vitberg failed to comprehend these shams.

The last straw for him was the purchase of stone. As usual, he preferred innovation to tradition. Rather than transporting stone from old quarries, he found a new one in the village of Grigorovo and proposed to move the stone on the river, which would have been much cheaper than hauling it on land. The first river shipment, which Vitberg himself managed, was successful, but when the contractors started to manage transportation, they decided to dig a canal uniting the Volga and Moscow rivers. From this point on, everything went wrong. Huge amounts of money were spent, but barges loaded with stone ran aground. All the participants in this swindle blamed one another. Some claimed that the engineers who had designed the canal were guilty; others accused the builders or inexperienced pilots.

By 1825 Vitberg had realized that corruption was not only undermining the project but endangering his position. Over his objections, the Construction Commission had signed a stone contract worth three hundred thousand rubles, which Vitberg realized would provide a rich opportunity for graft. He decided to expose the thieves and appeal to the czar to cancel the contract. His appeal was a cry of despair: dealing with evil people, he wrote, was wasting his time and ruining his health. He had no more strength to struggle against them.[8] The czar ordered Arakcheev, who was known as a scourge of embezzlers, to investigate the situation and asked Vitberg to prepare new and stricter regulations for the Construction Commission. With the czar's help, Vitberg had overcome his enemies.

At that moment came the shocking news of the czar's death. The vigorous, seemingly healthy man of forty-eight had died suddenly, far from the capital, in the little town of Taganrog. With Alexander's death, Vitberg lost his most important patron. While he mourned, he continued making plans for the future, unaware that his mission was doomed.

PART TWO

Ton's Cathedral

Chapter Ten

On September 10, 1839, at another celebration a generation later, a procession filed slowly through the Kremlin gates. In the vanguard, wearing their tattered uniforms and marching as proudly as age and infirmity allowed, were veterans of the 1812 campaign. Behind them corpulent priests in gem-studded vestments carried two venerated icons, the Virgins of Vladimir and Iver. Next came the generals who had taken part in the war, church leaders, and high officials. Nicholas I, with his family and entourage, brought up the rear. This was the sort of gesture the czar loved: yielding pride of place to the simple soldier heroes. But Nicholas, unlike his subjects, rode on a fine horse. He had learned to play the role of the father-commander.

Once again, the Moscow church bells pealed, choruses sang, and cannons boomed, as the procession made its way to the new site of the Cathedral of Christ the Savior. The Sparrow Hills site selected by Vitberg had been abandoned for a new one in the center of the ancient capital, not far from the Kremlin. After Alexander's death, Nicholas, the new "owner" of the Russian land, determined to do things his way. He wanted to start all over again, with a new site, new architect, new project. He wanted to eradicate the complex of ideas and attitudes that had been established during Alexander's reign.

Although he was deeply involved in the investigation into the Decembrist uprising, Nicholas found time, in May 1825, to establish a special Artistic Committee whose task was to answer one question: could Vitberg's project be realized?[1] Its conclusion doomed the architect. The committee decided it would be impossible to construct so colossal a building on the site he had chosen. And the cost of construction, if attempted, would be incalculable. Finally the professional architects had their chance to settle scores with the amateur Vitberg.[2] The czar had served as a military engineer in his youth. "We are engineers," he liked to say of himself. In his eyes, an engineer or a builder who didn't analyze a potential site was an adventurer or a criminal.

The project that for ten years had been lauded as the highest achievement of Russian architectural thought was now labeled impracticable.

45

Once again, a grandiose Masonic architectural design was pronounced bankrupt. For Vitberg, even worse was to come. The idealistic architect who had tried in vain to expose the thieves surrounding him was himself accused of irregularities. Nicholas sent auditors led by the adjutant general to examine the books of the Construction Commission. The results of their audit were shocking. Almost a million rubles had been embezzled and could not be traced by the auditors. It was an enormous sum, considering that the entire state budget of Russia in 1816, the year Alexander approved Vitberg's project, was 400 million rubles.[3] Construction was halted. Vitberg was found guilty by the investigators and ordered to stand trial, while his property was confiscated.[4]

Even experienced court officials were astonished when they discovered how little there was to confiscate from Vitberg, who lived in the utmost simplicity. This gave rise to rumors that he had stolen millions and sent the loot to America. But those who knew him were convinced that he was an innocent victim of his own credulity and the cunning men who surrounded him. Even the author of the official report written after the completion of the cathedral years later expressed compassion for him.[5]

Vitberg's lack of humility during the investigation and trial outraged the judges.[6] This ambitious, independent upstart personified the kind of public initiative that had been encouraged by Alexander's reforms. The new czar, threatened by the Decembrist uprising, wanted to eradicate such initiative completely. Vitberg had other enemies: liberals did not admire him or his cathedral. He represented the official mysticism of Alexander's last years, which was deplored by those who were close to the Decembrists. People of very different opinions supported the new czar's campaign against the mystics.[7]

After nearly ten years of investigative and legal procrastination, Vitberg was exiled to Vyatka, a provincial town in the foothills of the Ural Mountains. There he shared a house with the political exile Alexander Herzen, who would become one of the founders of the Russian revolutionary movement. Strange to say, Vitberg—the mystical Mason who rejected violence—exerted a strong influence on Russia's first professional revolutionary. With his tales of corruption and injustice, he taught Herzen how to hate official czarist Russia.

In return, the grateful Herzen transformed Vitberg into a martyr who would inspire generations of the Russian revolutionary intelligentsia. In his memoirs, he dedicated a long chapter to Vitberg, in which he wrote:

"The leaden hand of the Tsar not merely strangled a work of genius in its cradle, not merely destroyed the very creation of the artist, entangling him in judicial snares and the wiles of a policy inquiry, but tried to snatch from him his honourable name altogether with his last crust of bread, and brand him as a taker of bribes and a pilferer of government funds." And Herzen promised, "They shall hear in Europe of your fate, poor martyr. . . . I will answer for that."[8]

His memoirs, published in London in 1854, became the bible of youthful Russian revolutionaries. Members of the People's Will terrorist organization, Lenin, Trotsky, Stalin—all read this book when they were young. The spot on the Sparrow Hills where the teen-aged Herzen and his comrade Nicholas Ogarev had vowed to sacrifice their lives to the revolutionary struggle—the spot where the cornerstone of Vitberg's first cathedral was laid—became a place of pilgrimage, and in Soviet times a monument was erected there. The "Hannibalic oath" of Herzen and Ogarev, wrote James H. Billington, "is the real starting point of Russia's modern revolutionary tradition."[9] Thanks to these associations, the story of the pious Masonic architect migrated from the hagiography of Alexander I to the hagiography of Alexander Herzen, father of Russian revolutionary thought.

When his exile ended, Vitberg returned to St. Petersburg and continued to work on his grand project. He still took part in Masonic activities, but poverty and misfortune wore him down. A fire that destroyed most of the blueprints for the cathedral was the final blow, and in 1855 he died, a forgotten man.[10]

For a few years, Nicholas lost interest in the cathedral project. Conflicting orders issued from the imperial chancellery, one calling for a new competition for a cathedral design, open to Moscow architects only, and another ordering the construction instead of a small chapel on the Sparrow Hills. Finally, Dmitry Golitsyn, governor-general of Moscow, dared to ask the czar to announce a competition for a cathedral that would be open to foreign as well as Russian architects. Nicholas was willing to turn over the responsibility to Golitsyn and in February 1830 formally put him in charge of the competition.

The commission promised to be highly profitable, and architects in Moscow and St. Petersburg immediately set to work on designs. Everyone assumed that the competition would drag on for years, but then, unexpectedly, during a trip to Moscow in 1831, Nicholas summoned a young architect named Konstantin Ton and, ignoring the competition altogether, entrusted him with the design of the new cathedral.

Events in Europe may explain why the czar was suddenly in such a hurry. The 1830 revolution in France was followed by the Polish uprising, a more serious threat to the Russian empire, and troops were sent to "pacify" the insurgents. European sympathy for the Poles struck the Russians as the basest ingratitude. Neither conservatives nor liberals could understand how the peoples whom they had saved from Napoleon could support the Polish "traitors." Russia was swept by ardent nationalistic sentiment.

Nicholas, whose goal was a stable political system completely dependent on the autocrat's will, approved of the rapid spread of the nationalist ideology, which had the virtue of explaining and justifying the fact that Russia had become a military colossus while remaining an economic dwarf. As the historian Mikhail Geller wrote, "The economic challenge of Western Europe was answered by Russia with an ideology that proclaimed economic weakness the highest manifestation of spiritual force. The challenge of the West was understood as an ideological argument, which — as was stressed by the participants in the argument — had started a long time ago and was rooted in the opposition between Orthodoxy and Roman Catholicism, Russia and the West, Russians and Germans, i.e., foreigners."[11] The Russian nation was now credited with spiritual supremacy as the savior of the true faith and the true system of power. The ideological answer to the West was formulated in the sacred trilogy of Education Minister Sergei Uvarov: Orthodoxy, autocracy, nationality.[12] "Military Orthodoxy," the idea that all Russian wars were holy, became an integral part of the new ideology.

In this climate, Nicholas bethought himself of the Cathedral of Christ the Savior and saw how it could be turned to his own ends. The idea of building a monument dedicated to the most important military victory in the country's history had its appeal, but Alexander's symbol of Europe united would become Nicholas's symbol of Russia triumphant in opposition to the West.

The ideas formulated by Shishkov and Kikin didn't disappear without a trace, but the international neoclassical style so beloved of the old-school architects was not suitable for the new Russian project. A new man, able to create a Russian style, was required, and in Konstantin Ton the czar came across just such a man. In 1830, a competition for a new church in St.

Petersburg was deadlocked, the czar having rejected all the designs submitted as both uninteresting and too expensive to build. The impatient priest, tired of waiting for an architect who would please the monarch, found a suitable one on his own. This was Ton.

Chapter Eleven

Konstantin Ton offered a new idea: a revival of ancient Russian architectural forms. Instead of porticoes and columns, he proposed onion domes and *kokoshnik* gables. His design also had a practical advantage over all others submitted: it could be built for half the cost. The czar, who had never seen a project like Ton's, admired it so much that he ordered the blueprints sent to the Academy of Arts to teach the academicians a lesson and invited the architect himself to Tsarskoe Selo on September 24, 1831. Only a month earlier, on August 26, the anniversary of the battle of Borodino, Russian troops had finally stormed Warsaw. The sense of historical continuity was strong. At the end of October, the czar ordered Ton to start work on the Cathedral of Christ the Savior.[1]

Nicholas had found an architect who suited him — not a man of passionate imagination like Vitberg but a realistic professional. Alexander, despite his partial deafness, had appreciated good music; Nicholas preferred the sound of drums. (He was proficient with drumsticks and particularly liked military signals.)

Ton was thirty-seven years old when Nicholas favored him, and in the course of the next fifty years he flooded the country with his buildings. His architecture became synonymous with official state construction. The czar ordered that an album of sample structures designed by Ton be the only source of plans for new churches in all of Russia. A second compendium, of simple peasant constructions, followed. As the czar might have put it, Ton was the head of the architectural general staff under the father-commander. More than anyone else, he transformed the appearance of Russia, designing everything from the Great Kremlin Palace that dominated the center of Moscow to an old people's home in Izmailovo. His activity drew mixed responses, some considering him a genius who surpassed the great Italians, others dismissing him as a "commonplace practitioner lacking any gift."[2]

Ton's origins are unknown. He was said to be a Baltic German or an Englishman; he was even rumored to be descended from Moors.[3] In any case, like Vitberg, he was not an ethnic Russian. Born in St. Petersburg in 1794, the son of a simple jewelry maker, he was ennobled by Nicholas when he turned fifty. He underwent a thorough traditional training at the Academy of Arts (1803–15) in St. Petersburg and was then sent as a pensioner to Europe, where he spent nine years researching ruins and designing restorations of ancient structures, topped off by a few months in Paris studying engineering at the École Polytechnique. He began working actively as an architect as soon as he returned to St. Petersburg. Like Vitberg, he belonged to a Masonic family—both of his brothers were Masons—but it is not known if he himself ever joined the order. If he was a Mason, he was less interested in mystical thought than in the fact that Masonry was fashionable among architects.[4]

Nicholas was impressed by Ton's knowledge of classicism as well as by his training as an engineer. Although Ton knew nothing about ancient Russian architecture, he studied a few old churches and quickly grasped the essence of their forms. He was known for his rare ability to apprehend the structure of a building, as if he could see through its skin. Once, inspecting the work of a pupil who had just built a church, Ton warned the young man that the dome was about to collapse. The pupil protested that this was impossible; there were no cracks. "That doesn't mean anything," Ton answered. "Everything was badly calculated." The pupil didn't believe him, but he halted the work. The next morning it was discovered that the dome had indeed collapsed.[5]

Ton is usually called the founder of the Russo-Byzantine style, but that wasn't quite the case. Voronikhin's innovative project for Christ the Savior had incorporated elements of ancient Russian church architecture; and Ton's cathedral project is in some ways strikingly similar to the design of A. Kutepov, which was entered in the second competition. It was with Ton, however, that Russian neoclassicism finally succumbed to an era of eclectic historicism.

According to his contemporaries, Ton was not particularly well educated; his strong point was practicality, not originality. He believed the architect's responsibility was to build what the patron demanded and to build it right, meaning that the structure had to be strong and suited to its purpose. He wasn't mercenary and always tried to save the client's money.

For a few years in his youth, he had worked as an auditor of the Imperial Committee for Construction and Hydraulic Works and consequently knew well the ways of the bureaucracy; it was impossible to deceive him. He extolled the work ethic and deplored whatever he considered artistic. The painter Karl Briullov once told a young sculptor, "Don't think you will become an artist working on Ton's commission."[6]

Nicholas prided himself on being an expert on art and architecture. Not since the days of Peter the Great had Russia been ruled by a monarch who approached aesthetic questions with such confidence.[7] He personally supervised every important construction project in the country, concerning himself with even minor details. He spent days in the palace cellars inventorying the treasures belonging to the imperial house and even attributing artworks. His word, of course, was law. "No, Bruni. Don't argue. Flemish it is," he told the curator of the Hermitage about one painting. Against such judgments from the highest authority, there was no appeal.[8] Perhaps his most egregious artistic gesture was to "improve" a Dutch landscape by adding a few figures painted by his own royal hand.

Strolling one day through the Hermitage, Nicholas noticed Houdon's marble portrait of Voltaire. "Destroy the monkey," he ordered, determined to root out the revolutionary infection wherever it appeared; but officials, taking a risk, hid the offending sculpture in the cellar. The czar did succeed in "punishing" some artworks. After the defeat of the Polish uprising, Russian forces took as trophies the family portraits of the Lithuanian statesman and military commander Lev Sapega, one of the insurgent leaders. Nicholas ordered that the ancient paintings be burned. This auto-da-fé constituted a lesson for the Bolsheviks, who a century later would punish Nicholas's own creation, the Cathedral of Christ the Savior, by blowing it up.

Chapter Twelve

Nicholas himself chose a site near the Kremlin for the cathedral—a site whose symbolic significance was clear to all. The new seat of Russian national tradition would face the old. The Kremlin, occupied by the Poles in 1612 and by the French two hundred years later, had been saved by the determination and sacrifice of the people. The cathedral would celebrate not only the victory over Napoleon but also the final victory, achieved in 1831,

over those very Poles who had almost destroyed the Russian state. It would
be a monument to Russia's victory over the West.[1]

In his project for Christ the Savior, Ton quoted extensively from the
Kremlin churches, particularly the Assumption Cathedral, the exterior of
which is a cube topped by five cupolas, and the interior, a Greek cross
crowned by a dome. To stress the triumph of the Byzantine over the Latin
cross, Ton designed both the exterior and the interior of his cathedral in
the form of a Greek cross. He united two types of ancient Russian church
architecture: the cross and dome with five cupolas and the cross with
hipped roof, like the Ascension Cathedral in Kolomenskoe. But because of
its enormous size, Christ the Savior looked from the outside like a gigantic
cube. Also borrowed from the Assumption Cathedral was the segmenta-
tion of the exterior into bays, though the arched gables, or *zakomary*, came
from the Annunciation Cathedral.

Christ the Savior was to be the tallest building in Moscow and so vast
that the next tallest structure, the Kremlin Bell Tower of Ivan the Terrible,
would fit inside it.[2] It would have a complex visual relationship with the
Kremlin, not only facing the ancient fortress that Ton had recently "im-
proved"—he had rebuilt the Large Palace and the Armory in the Russian
Revival style—but harmonizing with the older buildings when it was seen
against the Kremlin background. Old and new had to be linked stylistically
as well as ideologically. To emphasize the unity of the whole complex, Ton
quoted the distinctive shape of the ribbed cupolas of St. Basil's, thus bal-
ancing his new cathedral with the old one.[3]

Together, emperor and architect created a grandiose architectural trip-
tych. In the center was the Kremlin—"the cradle of the modern Russian
empire," in the words of the Marquis de Custine. To the east was St. Basil's
cathedral, the memorial to the Russian victory over the Tatars; and to the
west stood the Cathedral of Christ the Savior, symbol of Russia's triumph
over the West.

There were obstacles to this ambitious scheme. The site chosen by the
czar for the cathedral was already occupied by a venerable building, the
ancient Alexeevsky convent, erected in honor of one of the most revered of
Russian saints. The famous metropolitan Aleksy, a statesman and church
leader of the fourteenth century, had been an adviser to Dmitry Donskoy
and an architect of the great prince's victory over the Tatars at Kulikovo.
The chosen spot had been known since ancient times as Chertolie—"the

1. The Moscow fire of September 1812, seen from the balcony of the Imperial Palace.
After a drawing by Gérard de la Barthe.

2. Andrei Voronikhin, design for the Cathedral of Christ the Savior,
the main facade, 1813.

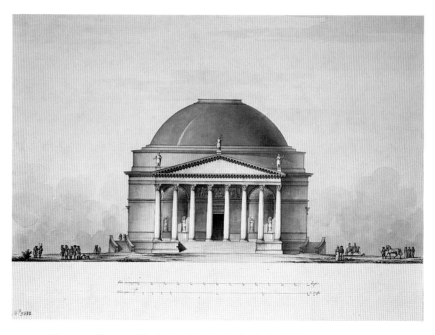

3. Giacomo Quarenghi, design for the Cathedral of Christ the Savior, 1815.

4. Alexander Vitberg, engraving after self-portrait, 1811.

(left) 5. George Dow,
portrait of Alexander I,
1825.

(below) 6. A. Afanasiev,
"Historical Depiction of
the Celebration during the
Laying of the Cornerstone
of the Cathedral of Christ
the Savior on the Sparrow
Hills on October 12, 1817."

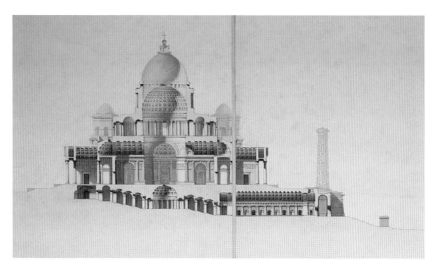

7. Alexander Vitberg's design for the Cathedral of Christ the Savior, 1817.

8. Vitberg's design for the Cathedral of Christ the Savior,
view from the Moscow River, 1825.

(above) 9. Feodor Kruger, portrait
of Nicholas I.

(right) 10. Portrait of Konstantin
Ton, based on a drawing by Pyotr
Borel'.

11. Rendering of the Cathedral of Christ the Savior, based on Ton's design, 1830s.

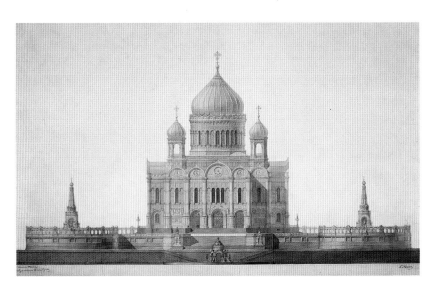

12. Ton's design for the Cathedral of Christ the Savior, main facade, 1832.

Москва.   Храмъ Христа Спасителя.
Moscou,   Cathedrale du St. Sauveur

(above) 13. The west façade of the
cathedral. Phototype published by
A. Rheinbott & Co., St. Petersburg,
late nineteenth century.

(left) 14. View of the cathedral from the
Moscow River. Postcard published by
M. Kempel', Moscow, early twentieth
century.

(left) 15. Alexander II. Photo by Sergei Levitsky, 1850s.

(below) 16. Ton's design for the cathedral, section. Phototype published by Shreer, Nabgolts and Co., Moscow, 1883.

17. Ton's scheme for the murals in the interior of the cathedral, 1854.
Drawing by I. Rezantsov.

(right) 18. Ton's design
for a ceremonial censer.
Drawing by R. Shelling.

(below) 19. Ton's design
for the main iconostasis.
Drawing by S. Dmitriev.

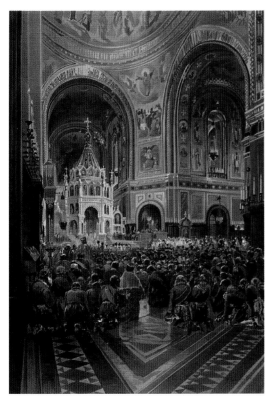

(left) 20. The coronation of Emperor Alexander III and Empress Maria Fyodorovna, 1883. Anonymous print.

(below) 21. Alexander Loganovsky's relief sculpture, the meeting of Melchizedek and Abraham, on the south facade of the cathedral. Phototype published by Shreer, Nabgolts and Co., Moscow, 1883.

(right) 22. Vasily Vereshchagin, deposition over the main altar. Phototype published by Shreer, Nabgolts and Co., Moscow, 1883.

(below) 23. Alexei Markov, *Sabaoth,* the main dome of the cathedral. Phototype published by Shreer, Nabgolts and Co., Moscow, 1883.

24. Genrikh Semiradsky, mural of the Last Supper. Phototype published by
Shreer, Nabgolts and Co., Moscow, 1883.

25. Alexander Loganovsky, Saint Sergei of Radonezh blessing Dmitry Donskoy
before the battle of Kulikovo and presenting to him the monks Peresvet and Osliabia.
Relief in the niche of the north facade of the cathedral. Phototype published by
Shreer, Nabgolts and Co., Moscow, 1883.

26. Structure of the main
dome of the cathedral.
Phototype published by
Shreer, Nabgolts and Co.,
Moscow, 1883.

27. View of the cathedral with the bathhouse in the foreground.

28. The Cathedral of Christ the Savior. Lithograph based on a
drawing by D. Strukov, 1856.

29. Panorama of the Kremlin (*foreground*) and Zamoskvorechie
from the Troinitsky Tower. Lithograph based on a drawing by
D. Indeitseva, Paris, late nineteenth century.

(above) 30. The Cathedral of
Christ the Savior at Christmas, late
nineteenth-century postcard.

(left) 31. Alexander III. Etching
based on a photo by Sergei Levitsky,
late 1880s.

devil's place." The name came from the word *chertoroi*—meaning "hole dug by the devil," which had referred originally to a stream (since filled in) that had disgorged into the Moscow River.[4] Popular superstition held that constructing the cathedral on this spot would be not only risky but blasphemous. "The feeling of mortal failure or perhaps even tragedy hung over the Cathedral of Christ like the sword of Damocles," wrote Kirichenko.[5] It took five years to convince the resolute nuns to leave their home and then to find them a new one, but the czar's will was supreme. Demolition of the convent finally started in 1837.

The people were not convinced the site was safe. It was said that the abbess had cursed the convent's destroyers and prophesied, "This place will be empty."[6] Furthermore, demolition did not proceed smoothly. According to an eyewitness, "Simple people in Moscow were saying that misfortune awaited any workman who put his hands on the Alexeevsky convent. And so? On the first day, in the presence of a huge crowd, a workman who was taking down the cross [from the dome of the convent church] fell to his death."[7] The authorities feared rioting, but the priests succeeded in calming the people.

Once the convent was demolished, however, construction proceeded rapidly. By the beginning of summer 1839, the stone foundation was near completion, and the time to lay the cornerstone was approaching. The czar decided to link the ceremony to three important anniversaries: the anniversary of the battle of Borodino, on August 26, 1812; the twenty-fifth anniversary of the occupation of Paris by Russian troops, on March 31, 1814; and the anniversary of the storming of Warsaw, on August 26, 1831.

Russians had never witnessed so elaborate a celebration. The day began with the consecration of a memorial chapel built on the battlefield at Borodino. After the service, the czar dipped his sword before the chapel, followed by an army of 120,000 men who lowered their battle standards. Three days later, the battle was restaged, with only the best regiments taking part in this colossal military game. With machinelike precision, they repeated the maneuvers of the Russian and French troops who had fought there a quarter century earlier.[8] It was a demonstration of the military might of the world's strongest army.[9]

In one important respect, however, the scenario differed from the actual conflict. Despite the valor of their troops, the Russians had lost the battle and as a consequence had been compelled to abandon Moscow. In the best case, there were no victors at Borodino, but for the restaged battle the czar in his godlike manner corrected history. One corps impersonating Russians and led by the czar himself attacked troops impersonating the French from the rear; this time around, Napoleon was defeated by Nicholas I. In his address to the troops, the czar told them that God had punished the enemy, whose bones were scattered from Moscow to Niemann. He failed to mention that after the battle of Borodino, the French had taken Moscow.[10]

The centerpiece of the celebration was the laying of the cornerstone for the new cathedral, which took place on September 10. According to a witness of the events, a certain Fedot Kuzmichev, who recorded his impressions in an imaginary letter to a Russian friend living in Paris, Moscow "boiled over with solemn rapture."[11] The ceremony began with a liturgy in the Assumption Cathedral, followed by a religious procession to the construction site. Symbolically, the new center of Russian Orthodoxy was replacing the old one. Leading the procession were fourteen decorated veterans of 1812, all demobilized sergeants, who marched silently and reverently, according to Kuzmichev. Behind them came priests and dignitaries. The troops who a few days earlier had taken part in the theatricals at Borodino greeted them with hurrahs, while the guns fired salvo after salvo. Guards battalions and bleachers holding ten thousand honored guests surrounded the enormous excavation pit. All around stretched a crowd of hundreds of thousands of common people.

Following an opening prayer, Metropolitan Filaret gave a speech in which he tried to calm the people by explaining, with the help of lofty biblical analogies, why the location of the cathedral had been changed. As in the days of Vitberg, Solomon's Temple was mentioned, but this time without Masonic implications. Filaret pointed out that King David had conceived of the temple but that King Solomon had brought it about, and not in the place initially chosen. He compared Alexander to King David and Nicholas to Solomon. The czar was not displeased by this demotion of Alexander I from Solomon to David.

Filaret's speech had another, more important purpose, which was to formulate an ideological program for the cathedral. Russia was the new Israel, Filaret told the crowd, and the Russians were God's new chosen people, whom he had saved from their enemies. The czars were the direct successors of the biblical kings. The history of Russia was the sequel to biblical history and represented the height of human development. Concluding, Filaret exclaimed emotionally: "Russians, in contemporary events we read the book of kingdoms ruled by God! Holy times are recreated in the deeds of our czars. What consolation for the faith! What hope for the fatherland!"[12]

Together with Nicholas and Konstantin Ton, Filaret was an author of the grandiose project to transform the cathedral into a symbol of Russian national superiority. Nicholas proposed it; Ton found an architectural expression for it; and Filaret developed the ideological religious program for it. The czar, of course, was at the apex of this triangle. Unlike his older brother, Nicholas was no ideologist. He possessed neither a powerful intellect nor a vivid imagination; intuition and pragmatism were his strong points. He felt rather than comprehended the importance of the "Russian idea." He used it and eventually personified it.

Nicholas's doctrine of "official nationality"—a term coined by the historian Alexander Pypin—evolved gradually. At the beginning of his reign, it was taken seriously and aroused a good deal of enthusiasm. Herzen, with his scorn for vulgar chauvinistic patriotism, and Chaadaev, who called on Russia to unite with humanity, were regarded as criminals or madmen. In the nationalist consciousness, France and rebellious Poland had merged into a single enemy—the West. This idea was to play an important role in the history of the second Cathedral of Christ the Savior.

"The most widely debated of all the 'cursed questions' during Nicholas' reign was the meaning of history," Billington wrote. "In the wake of the Napoleonic war, Russians were more than ever anxious to know their place in history."[13] Official nationality was the first Russian ideology that attempted to answer this cursed question. Russia's historical destiny was to save humankind. Allegiance to the great past would guarantee an even greater future for the country. Development depended not on reform but on conservatism, the preservation of the traditions of Orthodoxy, autocracy, and nationality.

The czar succeeded in gathering the cream of Russian culture under the banner of official nationality. Pushkin himself read to the royal family his recently composed "To the Slanderers of Russia," with its disdain for the West.[14] Glinka glorified Uvarov's triad of "Orthodoxy, autocracy, nationality" in the first Russian opera, *Life for the Czar*. The poet and diplomat Fyodor Tyutchev wrote:

It is impossible to comprehend Russia
It is impossible to measure it by the common measure
It has its own character
You can only believe in Russia.[15]

In his poem "A Russian Geography," he extended the borders of the
empire to the Nile and the Euphrates. Even Vissarion Belinsky, who later
became the leader of Russian Westernizers and liberals, was for a short time
convinced that only the czar's will could propel Russia forward and that
the czar's will was "mysteriously merged" with the will of providence: "Un-
doubtedly obedience to the czar's will is not only our advantage and our
necessity, but the highest poetry of our life, our national character." Belinsky wrote those words in 1839, at the midpoint of Nicholas's reign, when
the Russian empire was at the peak of its power. In that year, the writer and
philosopher Prince Vladimir Odoyevsky published his futuristic fantasy,
The Year 4338, in which only two major powers are left in the world: Russia
and China, the former culturally and technologically progressive, the latter
learning from its superior neighbor. America has reverted to barbarism.

The victory of 1812—or, more precisely, the mythology that enveloped
it—was the cornerstone of the new ideology. The czar's inner circle, according to the historian Viktor Bezatosny, included a number of noble generals "blessed by glory and the memory of the year 1812."[16] Society was
intoxicated with the romantic, heroic past. As Pypin noted, "Even strong
minds became accustomed to [official nationality] and adopted its theory.
The present appeared to be the solution to the historical task; the national
character was defined and the limits of aspiration marked by it."[17]

It was the Russian triumph and the successful enactment of Russia's
historical destiny that the new cathedral would express. Nicholas wanted
history made visible in the cathedral—not just the Napoleonic War but
also the history of "all the favors God has granted to the Russian kingdom,
thanks to the prayers of righteous men, in the course of ten centuries."[18]

Chapter Thirteen

Metropolitan Filaret was the only person involved in the creation of both
cathedrals. As the most respected moral authority of the Russian church for
almost half a century, he served three czars. He had composed the special

manifesto of Alexander I on the succession, and he would write the manifesto of Alexander II abolishing serfdom. But even without those deeds, Filaret occupies a significant place in Russian history as the leader of the Bible translation project. Sober and penetrating of mind, he was one of the first Russians to predict the apocalyptic shocks of the twentieth century lurking behind the outward prosperity of the nineteenth. "We are living on the outskirts of Babylon if not in the place itself," he said bitterly. At the same time, this "theological Jacobin," as his enemies called him, was profoundly conservative; he believed that photography was the devil's invention and refused to use railways.[1]

Filaret (in secular life, Vasily Drozdov) belonged by birth to the provincial priesthood, a class that in many ways still lived in the seventeenth century. Kolomna, his native town, was very much as it had been in pre-Petrine times, but the ambitious, hard-working young provincial, who was largely self-taught, had reached dizzying heights in the pro-Western capital. The tension between his origin and the position he had achieved defined many contradictions in his mind and fate. He combined a deep knowledge of Orthodox traditions with an interest in the new mystical theology. As a youth, he had developed a passion for Masonry and mysticism, visited the Dying Sphinx lodge, and discussed his sermons with Labzin, whom he admired.[2] Even after he became an archbishop, he organized Masonic gatherings in his home.[3] He is the only Mason canonized by the Russian Orthodox Church (in 1994, when his remains were reburied in the Trinity–Saint Sergius monastery). Alexander I presumably saw in him a representative of the best aspect of Russian Orthodoxy, which he wanted to incorporate into his universalist religion.

Filaret participated in the practical task of Golitsyn's ecumenical party, which was the Christian enlightenment of the Russian people. One of the few Orthodox members of the church who approved enthusiastically of the Bible Society, he became the leading force in the translation of the holy book into contemporary Russian from the incomprehensible Church Slavonic that had been the language of Orthodoxy for a thousand years.[4] He drew up guidelines for translators and personally translated the Gospel of John. The complete New Testament was published in 1820, and it looked as if every Russian would soon have access to the full sacred text. But it was not to be. Alexander's spiritual reform was already on the wane. A few months before the revolt of Fotius and his followers, Filaret received the czar's permission to leave St. Petersburg and return to Moscow. Alexander's utopian dream of a united Europe had turned into the hated "official mysticism." Filaret decided to save what he could of the project at a safe distance from the capital.[5]

In Moscow, he concentrated on the Bible translation and his role as a member of the Construction Commission for the Cathedral of Christ the Savior. The latter project went much less successfully than the former. Filaret and Vitberg got bogged down in endless arguments, provoked to some extent by jealousy, since both were favorites of Alexander and both were proud, obstinate men. But the main problem was that Vitberg was building for posterity and behaved as if he had all time in the world, whereas Filaret feared that time was against the supporters of the new spiritual order. Vitberg had no idea that Filaret was the keeper of the most important secret in the realm: he knew that Alexander had designated his younger brother Nicholas as his heir, bypassing the middle brother, Constantine. The succession manifesto, which Filaret had drawn up at Alexander's request, was hidden in the altar of the Assumption Cathedral in the Kremlin. Filaret knew that the czar might abdicate at any moment and that the epoch of reforms would end with his reign.

Vitberg and Filaret apparently had no aesthetic or ideological disagreements. In any case, Vitberg acknowledged Filaret's religious authority and as early as 1815 made changes in his project in response to the priest's criticisms.[6] But the stern, meticulous Filaret was irritated by Vitberg's artistic way of working and his constant experiments, which often gave rise to confusion. Contemporaries remembered a scandal provoked by Vitberg's insistence on using a round table for a meeting of the Construction Commission because he wanted to stress the equality of its members, from the governor-general to the humblest official. Filaret saw in this incident a manifestation of Vitberg's arrogance and a violation of discipline damaging to the cause.[7] When the storm clouds gathered over Vitberg, Filaret did not defend him. He may have begun to share Labzin's opinion that the young architect had become too concerned with worldly success. In any case, Filaret himself was in need of protection. In the spring of 1824, after Golitsyn's fall, he faced accusations of unorthodoxy, but he remained the staunchest defender of the new order against which Fotius and his followers were rebelling.

The victory was theirs. In 1825, in the yard of a St. Petersburg brick factory, the entire edition of the first volume of the Russian translation of the Bible was burned, on Shishkov's orders.[8] Russian peasants who had no right to determine their own fate were to be deprived of the right to communicate directly with their God. The abrupt end of the Bible project was a terrible blow to Filaret, but he remained determined to revive it. This was impossible during the reign of Nicholas, but under Alexander II, Filaret succeeded.[9]

Nicholas disliked and distrusted Filaret and had him kept under surveillance, but the priest was a popular and deeply respected figure, and the czar needed him to explain to the people why the cathedral site had been changed. Alexander had vowed to build on the Sparrow Hills; it was blasphemous to violate that oath. Filaret did succeed in making the change of site acceptable. In addition to offering a wealth of biblical analogies, he had the memorial plaques that had been embedded in the cornerstone of the first cathedral "purified" after their removal by taking them from the Sparrow Hills to the Assumption Cathedral in the Kremlin on the eve of the second cornerstone ceremony. From there, they could be conveyed, cleansed, to the new site.[10]

Filaret was neither a servant of the authorities nor a careerist who betrayed his youthful humanistic ideals. Although he was one of the most prominent public figures of Nicholas's reign, he was a man of the epoch of Alexander, placing moral law above earthly temptations. Although he collaborated with the state, he never hesitated to speak his mind. He condemned the transformation of Russia into a police state, and he fiercely defended the independence of the church. According to Georges Florovsky, Filaret "had his own theory of the state, the theory of the holy kingdom. It didn't correspond, however, to the official doctrine of state sovereignty."[11] He believed that the sovereign received his legitimacy from the church.

When Nicholas became keen on romantic nationalism, Filaret saw an opportunity to find common ground with the pragmatic czar. He transformed Alexander's exalted ideal of the holy kingdom into the narrower Byzantine ideal. The Cathedral of Christ the Savior became for him an ideal possibility for cooperation of church and state. During the cornerstone ceremony for the second cathedral, Filaret justified the sin of the ruler who had violated Alexander's oath and grounded the conception of the cathedral as an exclusively Russian monument squarely on the new nationalist doctrine. Nicholas must have been pleased.

But then he had to listen to a lecture. Filaret set forth the "God-ruled biblical kings" as models for the rulers of Russia. Then he addressed the czar directly: "Let the savior of the world, who saved Russia, rule your throne until the end of your days."[12] This was unacceptable to Nicholas, who couldn't imagine that any other being—God included—would rule his kingdom. His reign might be "God-saved," but it wouldn't be "God-ruled." Nicholas was determined to complete the transformation of the Orthodox Church into a state office, a process that had begun with Peter the Great. As part of that conversion, in 1836 he had appointed the cavalry general Nicholas Protasov head of the Holy Synod. Alexander had depended on Golitsyn's supple, liberal mind to reanimate the church. Nicholas employed a general to bring the church into the iron grip of the state.[13]

To Filaret, church and state were equal partners. Orthodoxy was Russia's only foundation and only hope. The problem was that the union of church and state was embodied in the czar. Thus Filaret had to keep trying to reeducate Nicholas. His next opportunity came in 1844, when he was entrusted with developing the sculptural program for the exterior of Christ the Savior. The czar himself determined that the theme of the decorations, both exterior and interior, had to be "all the favors God had granted to the Russian kingdom, thanks to the prayers of righteous men, in the course of ten centuries."[14] This meant that the decoration had to exalt the exceptional position of Russian statehood supported by Providence.

The official program of sculptural decoration Filaret proposed included images of "sacred historical events, similar or equal in importance to the events of the Patriotic war of 1812, figures of patron saints and protectors of the Russian land, some of the Fatherland's statesmen who had worked for the establishment and propagation of the Orthodox faith, and also Russian princes who had sacrificed their lives for the freedom and unity of the Russian land." The victory over Napoleon was seen through the prism of Orthodoxy and statehood in Russia.[15]

Filaret planned the sequence of the exterior decoration to match the direction of the religious processions that would make their way around the church. Such solemn processions, always moving counterclockwise, were traditional on religious holidays. Even an individual who wanted to look at the sculpture would have to submit involuntarily to the counterclockwise direction. Filaret's intent was to create a feeling of the "measured steps" of history.[16] His program had to fit into Ton's scheme, which allowed for two levels of relief figures. In the upper level were images of saints led by Christ. The lower level was reserved for historical events. Thus Filaret divided the exterior decoration according to the division of the world into heavenly and earthly spheres traditional for Orthodox consciousness.[17]

Chapter Fourteen

As decoration for the west facade, where processions assembled, Filaret proposed the theme of Russia's holy patrons and protectors. A large medallion of Christ the Savior blessing all who entered crowned the composition, flanked by smaller medallions of Saints Alexander Nevsky and Nicholas, patrons of the cathedral's creators and of all the Romanov rulers.[1] Below them, in the earthly realm, were sculptural groups demonstrating the heavenly protection of the pious Russian army. In the center, over the main entrance, angels carried a broad ribbon with the words "The power of God is with us." Angels on the left carried flags with a cross, the symbol of the regular Russian army, and those on the right held church banners, under which the militia troops had marched to Borodino. The religious character of the Napoleonic War, and of all Russia's wars, was thus stressed. In this program, Filaret followed the direct orders of Nicholas I, who had chosen the inscription carried by the angels. The entire west facade illustrated those words.

A second, related theme, the sacred meaning of Russian history, was emphasized in the two corner reliefs. On the right, David was shown handing Solomon the blueprints of the temple, and on the left Solomon was being anointed. So the cathedral was equated with Solomon's Temple, and Russian history was aligned with biblical history. Every Russian understood with pride that David was Alexander, and Solomon, Nicholas.[2]

The south facade, facing the Moscow River, was dedicated to the miracle of 1812: the triumph of a weak but faithful people over a strong but godless enemy. Crowning the arch was the Virgin of Smolensk, patroness of Russia, whose wonder-working image had been carried into battle for centuries and who was believed to have saved the nation from Western invasion many times. She was specifically connected with the events of 1812, because her icon had been carried aloft by the army during the retreat.[3] Accompanying her on the upper level were images of the saints, most of them Russian, on whose name days the major battles of the war of 1812 had taken place. The lower level was dedicated to miraculous victories of the Old Testament, including David's triumph over Goliath, and Moses' over Pharaoh. A few Russian saints were also represented, since there was not sufficient space for them in the upper level.

The east facade was the only one dedicated to the New Testament. The crowning image, over the main gates, was a pair of angels carrying the Gospel. With this image Filaret wanted to acknowledge the role of the holy book that Alexander had consulted so often in the struggle against Napoleon. The corner reliefs were dedicated to the Nativity and the Ascension, the beginning and the end of Christ's earthly existence, which were correlated with major events of the war. The czar had signed the manifesto ordering the erection of the cathedral on Christmas Day, 1812, when the French troops had been driven out of Russian territory; and Russian troops had entered Paris on Ascension Day, 1814.

At the military council meeting that considered the question of marching into Paris, Alexander had retired to consult his Bible and to pray passionately until he received a revelation: "steadfast determination of will and radiant clarity of purpose" were granted him. Opposing his generals, the czar had insisted on the risky maneuver. Napoleon, who later called the allied march to Paris a perfect chess move, could hardly have imagined how the czar had reached this crucial decision.[4]

The main image in the upper level of the east facade is the icon of the Blessed Virgin of Vladimir, on whose name day, August 26, the battle of Borodino was fought. To Russians, this battle was the moral turning point of the war; Filaret therefore placed her image precisely half way along the route of processions circling the church. Like the Russian soldiers, procession participants were following the difficult path to victory.[5] Completing the sculptural program on the east facade were important Russian saints, protectors of the land, whose lives formed a collective sacred history of Russian statehood.

The most complex ideological program was realized in the sculptural decoration of the north facade, the last on the procession route. It was dominated by three themes: the conversion of Russia to Orthodoxy; the defense of Orthodoxy against Muslims and Roman Catholics; and the liberation of the Christians of Europe from the yoke of the Antichrist.

The teachers of Christianity in the lower level, among them the Apostles and the emperor Constantine with his mother, Helena, represented conversion. Their Russian counterparts were Princess Olga (who took the name Helena when she was converted) and her grandson Prince Vladimir the Holy. The Apostles spread Christ's message to the world. Constantine made Christianity the state religion of the Roman Empire and established Constantinople as the new capital of the faith, where Olga became the first Russian ruler to be converted. Her grandson Vladimir made Christianity the state religion of Russia. The Holy Prince Daniil founded the dynasty that would begin the work of making Moscow the third capital of the Orthodox world.

Filaret's choice of subjects for the lower-level corner reliefs was influenced by Karamzin's history as well as by Nicholas's official nationality. On the right, Saint Sergei of Radonezh is shown blessing Dmitry Donskoy before the battle of Kulikovo and presenting to him the monks Peresvet and Osliabia; on the left, Saint Dionysios is depicted blessing Prince Pozharsky and Citizen Minin before the liberation of Moscow from the Poles.[6] These two reliefs were probably the best-known sculptures on the cathedral. Both events represented the protection of the faith, from Eastern Muslims and Western Catholics. In both narratives, Moscow played a central role as the symbol of Russian statehood and of allegiance to national traditions. Filaret expressed Orthodox Russia's role in the world in a way that even the most ignorant peasant could understand: the world is divided between Muslim infidels and Western "Germans," who surround faithful Orthodox Russia. Only the autocratic Russian state can repel the danger and save the faith.[7]

If Vitberg's cathedral was a symbol of unity and accord, Ton's celebrated national confrontation and the uniqueness and separateness of the Russian identity. Together with Dmitry Donskoy, the ideal monarch, and such ideal Orthodox saints as Sergei and Dionysios, the Russian land was represented by the noble Pozharsky and the commoner Minin. These two folk heroes were the only real—uncanonized—personages from Russian history who appeared among the cathedral's sculptured pantheon. They were needed for the complete expression of Uvarov's trinity: Orthodoxy, autocracy, nationality.

The sculptural program corresponded perfectly to the contemporary political situation. The West, which had invaded in 1612 and 1812, was a danger again, as was demonstrated by the Polish uprising and the revolutionary threat coming from Europe. The theme of peril from the East was no less relevant, since the Russian empire, under Nicholas, was involved in wars in the East, usually justified by the necessity to protect brother Christians—Georgians, Armenians, Balkan Slavs—from Muslim domination, which was associated in the Russian mind with the Tatar yoke.

Dominating the composition of the north facade was a depiction of the Russian army's foreign campaign against Napoleon, the salvation of Christian Europe by Orthodox Russia. Images of saints on whose days the important battles of 1813-14 took place appeared on the upper level.[8]

The religious procession that began under the west facade of the cathedral ended under the north wall, which was dedicated to the theme of the holy character of Russia's wars. A spectator walking around the cathedral was meant to experience not only the events of the war of 1812 but the history of Russia, from its conversion to the seventeenth century. Both war and history were enmeshed in a web of biblical and mystical references and analogies. The war had not yet been transformed into history; it was still a contemporary event; and the world depicted in the Scriptures was directly linked to the Russian empire's brilliant present.

Why did Filaret exclude Peter the Great from his version of Russian history? The reason was probably that while Christ the Savior was under construction, another huge church begun by Alexander was nearing completion. St. Isaac's Cathedral in St. Petersburg, dedicated to the saint on whose name day Peter was born, was a symbol of the new Russia Peter had brought into being. Kirichenko has called the Cathedral of Christ the Savior the "antipode of St. Isaac's." She writes that Christ the Savior "symbolizes another conception of Russian history, rooted in ancient Rus and Byzantium."[9] How could Nicholas, who demanded uniformity above all else, allow the existence of ideological antipodes? The answer is that he considered as sacred any manifestation of greatness in the nation's history.

Alexander I initiated the construction of the two most important cathedrals of Russia. Despite all his vacillations, he remained the czar-enlightener. A man of the eighteenth century, he envisioned the cathedrals as manifestations of the Europeanization of Russia, the victory of enlightenment over barbarism. If St. Isaac's symbolized the awakening of Russia by Peter the Great, Christ the Savior signified Russia's elevation by Alexander to the summit of European civilization.[10] The two cathedrals went up simultaneously, but after Vitberg's fall and Ton's redesign of Christ the Savior, their ideological significance changed. To Alexander, the cathedrals had signified Russia's unification with the rest of humankind; to Nicholas, they expressed the special role of the Russian nation. The doctrine of national supremacy could be based just as easily on the legacy of Peter the Great as on the Byzantine legacy rooted in biblical tradition. Its main element was the eternal role of the state chosen by God. Where the idol of the state was concerned, Nicholas was both a Slavophile and a Westernizer.[11]

Filaret had encoded a second level of meaning into his sculptural program, which had to do with the relative power of church and state. The anointing of Solomon, on the west facade, not only justified the coronation of Nicholas but also conveyed the idea that the church conferred legitimacy on the state. The relation of the two institutions is similarly stressed in the relief on the south facade depicting the return of Abraham from the slaughter of the kings. The biblical forefather is a warrior monarch, humbly placing his trophies at the feet of Melchisedek, the prototype of Old Testament and Christian priesthood, and receiving his blessing.

Filaret's choice of Russian saints is also significant, most having an association with a prince or a czar. The ideal pair, depicted on the north facade, consisted of Dmitry Donskoy and Sergei of Radonezh, heroic prince and holy monk, whose cooperation was crucial to the formation of the Moscow principality. Filaret considered Sergei one of the most important personalities in Russian history, and it was not mere chance that his image appeared twice on the walls of the cathedral.

Filaret included opposed as well as ideal pairs—a holy man of the church, for example, linked to an unrighteous czar. Everyone who saw the image of Metropolitan Philip among the Russian saints on the east facade knew that this Moscow metropolitan, who spoke out against the tyranny of Ivan the Terrible, was executed by him in 1569.[12] Filaret included these personages in his visual history of Russia for the education of his own partner, Nicholas I.

The image of the holy monarch was as necessary to this educational endeavor as the conception of the holy kingdom that Filaret supported. The holy monarch, according to Byzantine tradition, united sacral with political power. The princes Vladimir and Alexander Nevsky were therefore placed alongside such biblical kings as David and Solomon. Filaret also immortalized the martyred Grand Prince Mikhail of Tver, who was murdered by order of Khan Uzbek in 1318 after he refused to pray to idols.

To Nicholas, the Russian kingdom was divine by nature; the blessings showered upon it were proof that it was chosen by God. To Filaret, the Russian state was divine only to the extent that its rulers obeyed the will of God as expressed through the church hierarchs.

Chapter Fifteen

Filaret selected the subjects for the frescoes, thereby defining the character of the interior as well as exterior decoration. His ideological program for the frescoes reinforced the ideas expressed in the exterior sculpture. The frescoes were quite untraditional for Russian churches because they included scenes from the history of the Russian empire, which were equal in importance to the biblical scenes. Only those in the central area of the cathedral corresponded more or less to tradition, but even there new trends were apparent.[1]

For the dome Filaret chose the image of the Trinity—Father, Son, and Holy Spirit—at the moment of the world's creation. This is prehistory, the beginning of the Christian cosmos. History begins on the walls, its main event being the appearance of the Savior, whose earthly life is painted under the dome. The frescoes of the drum (*baraban*), situated between the biblical murals above and the Gospel scenes painted on the walls and pylons, depict the heavenly church. The Virgin, John the Baptist, prophets, Apostles, early saints, and finally Russian saints approach Christ from both sides, praying for humankind.

Three narratives—the Bible, the history of early Christianity, and the history of Holy Russia—intersect in the heavenly church as in a prism. All are important because, according to Filaret, they represent the realization of the divine design. The Russian holy princes Vladimir and Alexander Nevsky are included among the saints and prophets. Nobody before Filaret had dared elevate the founders of the Russian state to so high a level. The history of all humankind was transformed into a foundation for the Russian holy kingdom that crowned it.

The decoration throughout the church carried out the theme proclaimed so boldly in the cylinder of the dome. The murals in the nave depict events that followed Christ's redemptive sacrifice. These were interpreted as the history of Orthodoxy, or, more precisely, as the genesis of the Orthodox holy kingdom. According to Mostovsky, the official historian of the cathedral, every image is "closely connected with those events that were especially important for the spiritual or the civil life of our state."[2]

The cathedral is like a time machine; it transports the faithful to the space of sacred history and sacred geography, allowing pilgrims to traverse centuries and vast distances from Early Christian Rome and the Byzantine empire to Holy Russia.

The eastern and southern branches of the cross were decorated with murals depicting the pre-Russian period of Orthodoxy. There were "images of the saints of the ecumenical church who lived and acted in the East and the South from the first to the tenth century, i.e., before the enlightenment of Russia by the Orthodox faith."[3]

The west and the north wings of the cathedral were adorned with frescoes depicting the Russian millennium of Orthodoxy. The west wing was dedicated to the Russian church, and the north, to the Russian state. "In the west wing is depicted the synod of the Russian saints and holy men who enforced in our Fatherland the Orthodox faith and protected Russia from internecine wars and external enemies. In the north wing—the synod of the holy princes of Russia, relatives of the holy Alexander Nevsky, martyrs of the faith fallen for the freedom of our Fatherland."[4]

The gallery encircling the interior commemorated the victory over Napoleon, the apex of the Russian Orthodox holy kingdom, and was lined with marble plaques describing the battles of 1812–14. Walking along the gallery, visitors followed the route of the army from the river Niemann to Moscow and then back from Moscow to Paris.[5] Icons symbolically connected to the events of the Napoleonic Wars were also exhibited there.

The decorative program of the cathedral had a distinctly Orthodox-monarchist character. God created the world. The Savior was born into the world to bring humanity the gift of the true faith. The Russian holy kingdom—the highest development of Orthodoxy—was created to preserve the faith. The victory over the Antichrist Napoleon was the sign that the kingdom was chosen by God. The end of the kingdom will be the end of humankind.

The unique iconostasis, a freestanding white marble chapel twenty-seven meters high, with a hipped roof of gilded bronze, played a special role in the decorative scheme. Four rows of icons were attached to its outer walls, and inside was the altar. The structure of the iconostasis was reminiscent of ancient Russian hipped-roof churches, such as the Ascension Cathedral in Kolomenskoe. It resembled a gigantic tabernacle with a canopy over the altar and, simultaneously, a cathedral within the cathedral. It was a symbol of both the Ark of the Covenant and the czar's throne, which, according to ancient Russian tradition, was installed in a church and covered with a canopy.[6] It was quite unlike the normal Russian iconostasis in the form of a wall covered with tiers of icons.[7] This unusual structure was the mystical focal point of heavenly and earthly powers. Christ the Savior was envisioned as the Cathedral of Cathedrals, a successor to Solomon's Temple and the Church of the Holy Sepulchre in Jerusalem.[8]

In Vitberg's cathedral, worshipers had moved upward and inward, ascending as individuals to the true faith and following the path of divine comprehension from the Old Testament prophets to the Apostles, from darkness to light. Vitberg had thought of his cathedral as a living body. In Ton's cathedral, processions circled the iconostasis in a ritual of enclosing the true faith that had been given once and forever to the community of the chosen, rather than achieved by individual suffering. It was a mass movement, not an individual one. The Masonic and pietistic ideal of personal enlightenment was transformed into a Byzantine ideal of collective service.

The first and second cathedral projects were both influenced by Filaret's conception of the holy kingdom. In Alexander's reign, Filaret believed in the Christian republic of Europe. In Nicholas's reign, his ideal was the universal Orthodox empire — the new Byzantium. Only Russia's messianic role in creating the holy kingdom did not change.[9]

In 1846 Russian society learned how the cathedral had originated. That year the letter from Kikin to Shishkov was published, for the first time, in the magazine *The Muscovite*. The editor, Mikhail Pogodin, was a well-known historian and one of the leading ideologues of the epoch of Nicholas I. He believed that it was important to establish a connection between the conservative nationalism of Shishkov, which was associated with the glory of 1812, and the ideology of official nationality. The Russian messianic trend was one of Pogodin's favorite topics: "The Russian czar, without having planned it, wished it, prepared it, or designed it, quiet in his study in Tsarskoe Selo, is now closer than Charles V and Napoleon to their dream of a universal monarchy," he wrote.[10] It is doubtful that Nicholas shared this sentiment. The prophetic visions of Pogodin and Filaret were too liberal for him, not in their meaning but in their spirit.

It is not surprising that of all the creators of the second cathedral, the czar preferred the bureaucrat Konstantin Ton. The liberal intelligentsia correspondingly saw in Ton a servile votary of the official muse. To intellectuals who regarded the artist as teacher and prophet, Ton seemed a traitor to the noblest ideals. The cathedral, even before its completion, became a symbol of dead state architecture, and its creator was scornfully nicknamed "the operator." Compared to the romantic story of Vitberg's creation, the history of Ton's cathedral was a sterile bureaucratic report.

In 1839 the four central pylons and the brick walls of the cathedral began to rise, and in 1840 marble sheathing began. Of highly patriotic significance, this marble was not imported from Italy but quarried in the village of Protopopovo, near Moscow.[11] Although domestic products were more expensive and inferior in quality to foreign ones, common sense was sacrificed to the ideology of nationalism. In 1849 the central brick dome was completed, followed by the walls and the smaller domes the next year.

By 1853 the cathedral was completely sheathed in marble. An iron frame was installed between the brick walls and the marble cladding and in some places was filled with hot lead. In 1854 the iron roof and the cladding of the domes was finished. In the course of fifteen years, forty million bricks had been used in the construction.

When construction began, an Interior Ministry publication had proudly announced that the structure would "memorialize not only the glory of the reign of Alexander I, but the energetic and firm will of his wise successor."[12] In 1855, the wise Nicholas died after the shock of the crushing defeat of his seemingly invincible army in the Crimea. Rumors circulated that the monarch had poisoned himself. On his deathbed he told his heir, "I leave you the command not in good order."[13]

The unfinished Cathedral of Christ the Savior became a symbol of the unrealized hopes of the exemplary Russian czar who wanted to achieve a victory over history. The Temple of Solomon of Russian military despotism proved to be its Tower of Babel.

Chapter Sixteen

The next czar, the reformer Alexander II, was for a long time completely indifferent to his autocratic father's favorite project. Yet it was he who would do more than any other monarch to realize the cathedral, which was finished and decorated during his reign.

Financial records suggest that construction was organized somewhat irregularly during the first fifteen years of his rule.[1] Sometimes the sums allocated annually by the treasury were half the amount spent on construction even during the difficult years of the Crimean war. In 1862, when the fiftieth anniversary of the victory over Napoleon was celebrated, Alexander ordered a decrease in funding for the cathedral. Reforms that affected every aspect of Russian life were in full swing, and the czar did not want to spend lavishly on a monument to the previous era.[2] From time to time he visited the construction site, which cost nothing and invariably prompted the newspapers to report on his fidelity to tradition, thus soothing conservative sensibilities.

Alexander was doomed to maneuver among political forces. The famous statement of the imperial chancellor Alexander Gorchakov, "La Russie ne boude pas; elle se recueille" (Russia isn't brooding; she is looking inward), was adopted. It had the merit of seeming to satisfy everybody: to liberals it suggested that Russia was concentrating on catching up to the West socially and economically, while to conservatives it hinted at a respite in which to plan a military revenge for the war lost in the Crimea. Europe looked on anxiously. Russia was spending a third of its budget on defense and steadily expanding its territories in Central Asia and the Far East.

In the early years of Alexander II, the cathedral was overshadowed by other state constructions. The czar cared more about St. Isaac's in St. Petersburg, dedicated to Peter the Great and consecrated in 1858. As the Emancipation was being prepared, the czar wanted to remind his subjects of the radical spirit of Peter's reforms.

The most important commission of the first period of the reign was the Millennium Monument in Novgorod, designed by a team led by Mikhail Mikeshin and unveiled in September 1862.[3] The Cathedral of Christ the Savior might have been considered an ideal venue for the millennial events, but Alexander saw advantages in moving the festivities to Novgorod. He wanted a jubilee that would look to the future, and the cathedral was linked to the past. The onset of his reforms was intended to coincide with the millennium. According to legend, the Russian state was born when warring Slavic tribes invited the Varangians (probably Scandinavians) to rule over them, in the eighth century. The Western-based "Varangian reform" that followed was a contract between the people and their new rulers—at least that was how the czar and his advisers interpreted it.

If Moscow was the symbol of centralized, autocratic power, Novgorod represented the lost alternative: a city-state ruled by a popular assembly, or *veche*. The monument's shape referred both to the bell that tolled for the opening of the veche and to the crown of Monomakh, symbol of the czar's power. Linking these two seemingly contradictory ideas was deliberate, for the czar hoped to suggest a tie between the Russian autocratic idea and the Western parliamentary idea. This attempt to take only the best from opposing systems was typical of Alexander II.

At the apex of the monument, an angel blesses a kneeling woman who symbolizes Russia. Below are six scenes central to Russian history, each featuring a reforming czar. Olga Maiorova, who has studied the monument, stresses that it is dominated by the themes of origin and renewal. The history of Russia is interpreted as a "chain of brilliant reforms realized by the supreme power." The main idea is the "rebirth of the era of reason and liberty" under Alexander II.[4]

According to the historian Richard Wortman, the millennial celebration was designed to demonstrate the czar's adherence to the model of popular monarchy borrowed from the West. At this time Russia was enamored with the success of the "democratic empire" of Napoleon III.[5] As a result, the anniversary of the victory over Napoleon I was somewhat muted: it was no longer clear what Russians should be proud of, because France seemed triumphant in 1855. In this climate, the ideology of Russia's cosmic triumph over the Antichrist, on which the Cathedral of Christ the Savior was based, was irrelevant. The structure was now associated with the decrepit old monarchy. The new monarchy needed symbols like the Millennium Monument.

All this changed drastically in the second part of Alexander's reign. In 1863, the Poles rebelled and were again repressed, which brought the czar into a diplomatic conflict with the West that threatened to turn into a military one. He crossed himself every time he signed a note to the French or the British government. His personal life was also in turmoil. The sudden death of the twenty-two-year-old czarevich Nicholas in 1865 was a terrible blow. Alexander saw God's punishment in the loss of his handsome, intelligent heir. The next year, he became the lover of Princess Yekaterina Dolgoruky, a young maid of honor. "Now I count you as my wife in the presence of God and will never leave you," he promised her. He kept his word, dividing himself between his two families and fathering four children with Dolgoruky.[6]

On April 4, 1866, the czar survived the first attempt to assassinate him, when a former student named Dmitry Karakozov tried to shoot him as he was stepping into his coach after a walk in the Summer Garden. Alexander was shocked to learn that the would-be assassin was not an avenging Polish patriot but the son of an ancient Russian noble family from the Saratov region. Even more shocking, Karakozov acted because he thought reforms had not gone far enough. The czar was mistaken in his belief that the abolition of serfdom had secured him the absolute love of his subjects. The only consolation was that Karakozov's shot was spoiled because a simple peasant named Osip Komissarov jostled his arm. Like Ivan Susanin, the savior of the first Romanov czar, Komissarov came from the Kostroma district, a coincidence that Alexander and his courtiers saw as a miracle. Thus was born the myth of the folk-savior having protected the czar not only from foreign enemies but from Russian revolutionaries.[7]

Ten days later, the Senate ruled that April 4 would become a holiday commemorating the czar's salvation, to be celebrated with religious processions and the tolling of bells. Although Alexander approved of this decree, Filaret made clear his disapproval, asking caustically whether it was expedient to remind the people every year that an uprising against the czar was possible.[8] He did agree, however, to conduct a thanksgiving service on April 17, Alexander's birthday, and chose the unfinished Cathedral of Christ the Savior as the setting. It was there that the hymn "God Resurrected" mingled with the anthem "God Save the Czar," performed by a military orchestra. Filaret explained the symbolic meaning of the event in his sermon. The cathedral, he said, was a memorial to the first salvation of Russia in 1812. Providence had led the people to pray there, for the first time, for the second salvation of Russia, in 1866.[9] With this sermon, he gave a new reading to the ideological program of Christ the Savior, interpreting it as a monument to the miracle of autocratic Russia's salvation. This miracle was abstract and unconnected to real events, not even the events of 1812.

That same year, the magazine serialization of *War and Peace* began. To the intelligentsia, Tolstoy's masterpiece was a much more important monument to the victory of 1812 than the Cathedral of Christ the Savior. At a moment when public culture was developing, Tolstoy's version of the victory, which gave the most heroic role to the people, was more convincing than the official account.

Although the czar continued to believe in progress and civilization, he drifted into the currents of nationalism. Reforms continued, but sporadically and lethargically. A culture war had developed, with liberal and conservative factions within the government struggling to influence the czar's soul. Everybody seemed to be expecting him to produce a miracle, while he was waiting for God and destiny to save the dynasty and Russia. It was at this time that Alexander II began to show an interest in Christ the Savior. The cathedral represented, first, an obligation to his father's memory, but it also assumed a mystical significance for him, as it had for the first Alexander. In December 1866, he inquired when the building would be finished and how much money would be required for the task. The State Council ordered the Construction Commission to draw up a plan and a budget, which it delivered in 1869. The completion of the cathedral would require 5,870,000 rubles and would take twenty-five years unless annual expenditures were significantly increased, in which case construction could be completed in seven years. The czar chose the latter option. Spending on the cathedral, which had been drastically reduced in the reformist 1860s, was doubled in the stagnant 1870s. The goal was to finish the work for the czar's twenty-fifth anniversary, in 1880.

Economic constraints were not allowed to slow construction. Even when a terrible famine struck in 1874, more than half a million rubles was spent on building, and in 1877, when war with Turkey brought the country to the brink of bankruptcy, the record sum of 750,000 rubles was allocated. There is a persistent legend that ordinary people financed the cathedral; the truth is that private individuals donated only 42,260 rubles for the construction of Vitberg's cathedral and only 20,247 rubles and 50 kopeks for Ton's.[10] The myth originated because Nicholas I wanted every donation published in the newspaper *Moskovskie vedomosti*. The public was touched by such announcements as "Soldier Grigory Sedelnikov from Vyatka wishes to donate one ruble for the construction of the Cathedral of Christ the Savior." Publishing such an announcement cost the state one ruble.

The total cost of constructing the cathedral was more than fifteen million rubles over fifty years.[11] In comparison, Alaska was sold to the United States in 1867 for eleven million rubles, or $7.2 million.

Chapter Seventeen

When Nicholas I ordered Ton to create a cathedral in the "Russian style," he was referring to the architecture, not the decoration. In Ton's first plan, of 1832, both the exterior sculptures and the interior paintings were classical in style. The fashion for ancient Russian painting had not yet developed, and there was no tradition of native sculpture. The Orthodox priesthood, in fact, rejected sculpture entirely, considering it akin to idolatry. In 1846 Nicholas ordered Russian sculptors trained in Italy to create high reliefs for the facade of the cathedral.[1] His favorite was a skillful naturalistic sculptor named Alexander Loganovsky, whose work the czar followed closely.

The historian Ivan Zabelin provided the best description of these sculptures: "Bishops in robes and miters with crosses in their hands are seated in the corners above the arches. They are squeezed in, sitting with their legs dangling, in indecent poses. Poor things, they have no room to turn up their toes. What is this? Russian sculpture? It has no simplicity, no greatness, no decency."[2]

Loganovsky died in 1855, the same year as his august patron, but he succeeded in completing thirty-three of the forty-eight sculptural groups and fourteen of the twenty medallions. After his death, a group of sculptors completed the work. Among them was Baron Peter Klodt, the famous animalier who created the prancing horses for the Anichkov Bridge in St. Petersburg.

The only aesthetic decisions Alexander II made regarding the cathedral involved its interior decoration, and then only in the later part of his reign. Initially, he did not interfere in the painterly project his father had approved in 1854.[3]

Ton's early sketches of the cathedral interior, executed in 1832, show that originally he limited the amount of space for paintings, which he envisaged in the classical style.[4] Nicholas did not want foreign painters working in the cathedral, but he held Russian artists cheap. By the mid-1840s, however, the Russian school had developed and received international recognition. The czar was not concerned that most of its stars were not of Russian origin and had been trained in Italy. It was enough that they were Russian subjects.

In the 1840s Ton and his assistants produced new designs of the interior. Nicholas wanted the most important decoration assigned to Karl Briullov, who had become famous in Europe because of his monumental canvas *The Last Day of Pompeii*. Although the priests did not like Briullov's academic style, enriched with baroque effects and flavored with fashionable romanticism, the czar visited his studio often to examine his sketches.[5]

Another important artist called on to work in the cathedral was Alexander Ivanov. Unlike Briullov, this brilliant artist-philosopher was unaccustomed to the czar's favor. Valuing his creative freedom above all else, he initially treated the cathedral decoration as a burden that would distract him from his magnum opus, a huge painting of Christ appearing to the people, but his Slavophile friends convinced him that through his work in the cathedral he would become the leader of a new national school of art that would encourage a spiritual revival.[6] He consented, to his ultimate frustration and humiliation.[7]

The highest manifestation of the ancient spirit was icon painting, and even before Ivanov received an official commission, he began preliminary work on a huge icon of the Resurrection. In his plan, his painting of Christ appearing to the people would face the iconostasis decorated with his Resurrection. He therefore began researching the ancient iconographic variants of the composition. This was not the superficial stylization characteristic of Ton but a true representation and understanding of the Byzantine-Russian tradition.[8] Ivanov's sketches show what quality he could have achieved in the cathedral.[9] In the end, however, it was Briullov who was commissioned to paint the Resurrection; he eventually produced a technically perfect but empty composition. Ivanov's ideas were rejected, and he refused further participation.

It wasn't until 1854, when the roof was finished, that the problem of the interior decoration became crucial. Briullov was dead by this time, so Nicholas had to reconsider his aesthetic priorities. Preparations were under way for the war with Turkey, and jingoistic frenzy was at its peak. During an inspection of the cathedral on September 3, 1853, the czar announced that he wanted the interior decorated with murals executed in the "ancient oriental, not in the new Western manner," so that it would be transformed completely into a "national monument."[10] These orders reflected new political priorities. The aim of the war was control over Constantinople, the ancient Byzantine capital. One of the issues was whether the Catholic or the Orthodox Church would control the Christian churches in Palestine.

In 1854 a new program was introduced to decorate the interior of the cathedral in the ancient Russian style. Saints were to be depicted in the style of icon painting. All compositions were to correspond to the Orthodox canon. There were to be tiers of images covering the entire space of the vaults and walls.[11] At about the same time, the czar ordered the construction of an iconostasis modeled on the Church of the Holy Sepulchre in Jerusalem.

After Nicholas's death, in 1855, Alexander II continued his father's undertaking. In 1858, after the consecration of St. Isaac's in St. Petersburg, the painters Fyodor Bruni, Aleksei Markov, and Pyotr Basin, who had worked on its decoration, were commissioned to paint murals for Christ the Savior.[12] At the same time, the new czar approved sketches of icons for the iconostasis that were executed in the style of those in Zion Cathedral in Tiflis, which had been painted by Prince Grigory Gagarin, who had tried to revive Byzantine and ancient Russian painting.[13] His murals in Tiflis, completed in 1850, were admired by the empress Maria Alexandrovna, Alexander's wife.[14]

In 1856 Gagarin established a class in Orthodox icon painting at the Academy of Arts, taught by Timofei Neff, a salon portrait painter who later executed icons for the iconostasis of Christ the Savior in the Gagarin style. Some of the academy's leading figures were trying to revive—or, more accurately, to discover—the "ancient" style, but the results were not impressive.[15] Only Bruni, rector of the department of painting, succeeded in creating a deep if dismal mystical mood in his *Descent into Hell* and other paintings for the cathedral. The aging academics, trying hard to suppress their academic skills, complained about the absence of money and yearned for the golden days of Nicholas.

Everything changed when, later in his reign, Alexander II became seriously interested in the cathedral. The plan approved by Nicholas in 1854 was abandoned. On April 28, 1867, Alexander ordered that the galleries should be decorated with "subjects referring to the great events of the Patriotic War and the epoch of the current reign." The new plan was to create something like the Millennium Monument in the painterly program. Filaret was entrusted with the choice of subjects, but in November he died.[16] The work was continued by Bishop Leonid of Yaroslavl, Filaret's former parish priest, and, to a lesser extent, by Metropolitan Inokenty. Both protested the inclusion of secular subjects in the painterly program, to no avail.

Despite their protests, another version of the program was composed, which included, along with religious subjects, the Napoleonic War and the "historical events that took place in our Fatherland" before and after the war, such as the Mongol invasion in the thirteenth century, the conquest of Central Asia, and the reforms of Alexander II. The overall theme of the proposed secular murals was the military expansion of the empire and its reformation, treated as a continuous development of Russian statehood.[17]

As a result of a visit to the cathedral on July 14, 1873, Alexander II chose a compromise version of the competing decorative schemes. "The names of troop units and, if possible, the names of heroes fallen in battle, as was done in the church in Sevastopol" were to be incised in the gallery walls. Instead of battle scenes, there would be images of the saints on whose days the battles took place.[18] The remaining space would be decorated with religious subjects, which were chosen by Leonid and, after his death, by the parish priest Amvrosy (Kliucharev). Major revisions to the earlier plan were dropped, although changes were made. The cathedral did not become a grandiose ideological repetition of the Millennium Monument.

In 1875 the emperor officially rejected the program of murals in the ancient style by approving a new program. It wasn't only the difficulties connected with the revival of ancient Russian painting that killed the old program. The czar himself had pro-Western taste and wanted a plan that would differ from his father's. The renewed fashion for Russian antiquity, admired by the empress and the crown prince, did not correspond to the European spirit of Alexander's reforms.[19]

In the beginning, the empress accompanied the emperor during his visits to the cathedral and took part in discussions about its decoration.[20] When Alexander began his affair with Princess Dolgoruky, the estranged empress withdrew, visiting Moscow only rarely, but their son Grand Duke Vladimir Alexandrovich, as vice president and later president of the Academy of Arts, was involved in the construction and decoration, and it was he who reported to the czar during the 1870s. Since the crown prince was also interested in the cathedral, we can say that the entire royal family was involved. But, as Ton wrote, the cathedral was built "according to the personal taste of His Highness."[21]

Alexander could not change the decorative program completely, but he could influence the style of the paintings. In this situation, young academic rebels found their way to the cathedral. In 1863 a few students who rejected academic painting for realism had left the academy to establish a commune, or *artel*. In 1870 this movement gave birth to the famous Partnership of Traveling Exhibitions, whose members, known as Wanderers, created a new epoch in the history of Russian art, the epoch of critical realism. The painter Ivan Kramskoi was their leader. (During Soviet times Kramskoi was glorified as the founding father of Russian democratic realistic painting and was treated as a predecessor of Socialist Realism.) This artistic rebel was invited by his old teacher, Aleksei Markov, to participate in the decoration of the main dome of the cathedral.

Markov was a secondary artist but a good man, who got on with both his superiors and his pupils. Ton commissioned him to decorate the main dome, for which he was to be paid one hundred thousand rubles as a reward for his loyalty to the academy. It was only because Markov needed qualified assistants to handle this immense job that Kramskoi and his friends had the chance to work in the cathedral. Later many of them accused Markov of exploiting young artists and suspected Ton of taking kickbacks from Markov and other academicians who received profitable commissions. The young artists joked, "Add more gold tone!" in a play on the architect's name.[22] Did the honest old campaigner succumb to the temptation of easy money? It is not at all certain. After Ton's death, Prince Dolgorukov wrote to the czar that the architect had left his family "in an unfortunate state of affairs, with debts and without money."[23]

The painters working in the cathedral made no attempt to resolve complicated ideological or creative problems. The best of them were ambivalent about their commissions. They did not want to tie themselves to dull official work, but it was hard to resist the temptation of taking part in such an important project, being noticed, and being well paid. When Kramskoi decided to participate, he explained his reasons to his wife: "I believe that this work is so important to my career that I am ready to endure any yoke just to fulfill the task, because when the work is finished . . . it is possible that I will be noticed. . . . I feel as if I am playing a big card game, staking all on one card."[24]

Kramskoi's card was a good one. Not involving himself in the troublesome search for the ancient style, he created, with his collaborators, the grandiose composition *The Triune God,* skillfully executed in the style of Briullov with the addition of a certain degree of naturalism. For the cause, the militant realist easily turned himself into an academic painter. Forgetting for the moment about ideological art, Kramskoi and his friends tried to prove to the government and to their artistic competitors that they were skilled, professional painters, and they succeeded. From the technical point of view, the painting of the dome was of high quality. The young rebels proved to be competent professional artists who had to be taken seriously by their aesthetic opponents.

Kramskoi's decision to participate hadn't been mere opportunism; it was the "reasonable egotism" advocated by Nicholas Chernishevsky, author of *What Is to Be Done?* and the ruling influence over the "generation of nihilists" of the 1860s. His attitude contrasted sharply with Ivanov's idealism and the academic-bureaucratic approach of Briullov and Bruni. Ironically, the future success of realist painting was due in part to the participation of the Wanderers in the creation of reactionary academic murals in Christ the Savior.

Ilya Repin, the leading painter of the Wanderers, refused to take part in the decoration, but group members Vladimir Makovsky, Illarion Prianishnikov, and others did not refuse their piece of the official pie and received their share of mockery.[25] Not all were as successful as Kramskoi. The Wanderers were genre painters who lacked experience with monumental painting and consequently made mistakes in perspective and size. These favorites of the liberal public had to endure the ridicule of the academics who chided them with remarks like this: "It seems that you put boots on your Holy Virgin." Because of faults in perspective, her feet looked too big.[26] In turn, the realists openly made fun of the boring compositions and dull colors of Vasily Vereshchagin (not to be confused with his namesake, the famous painter of battle pieces), a pillar of the conservative art establishment who in the end produced more paintings in the cathedral than any other artist.

During the 1870s Ton was gradually withdrawing from the works. His deputy, Alexander Rezanov, assumed the main role, and his correspondence with the architect Semyon Dmitryev, who was in charge in Moscow, reflects the problems of the last stage of construction.[27]

The major role in developing the final decorative program was played by Lev Dal, an architect and the son of Vladimir Dal, the famous folklorist and the author of the *Explanatory Dictionary of the Living Great Russian Language*. Their project was a complicated compromise, which was typical for all state undertakings during this reign. It represented something between the original classicist project of 1832 and the ancient-style project of 1854.

From the latter, the new program inherited the system of lining up murals in tiers. In addition to this, Lev Dal, a serious researcher of Byzantine and Russian art, worked out a plan to decorate the walls with painted ornaments stylized in imitation of the antique. The spirit was described by Alexander Benois as "Bolognese fancy-dress ball," academic painting with naturalistic elements and a willingness to borrow anything from anybody. It was decided to save some features of the Byzantine-Russian icon-painting tradition only in the images of saints that were to be painted on the pillars and the spaces between the windows.

The painterly decoration of the cathedral was shared by realists and academic painters, represented by two generations of artists with vastly different attitudes and beliefs. Not surprisingly, the final effect was cacophonous; the interior of Christ the Savior was a triumph of pastiche. The only person who tried to preserve stylistic unity was Alexander II, who made the decision to get rid of the venerable academics' experiments in the ancient style despite the expense. The czar's disappointment with Bruni's paintings literally killed the former favorite of Nicholas I; the royal criticism brought on a stroke.[28] Basin didn't survive the destruction of his murals, either. Young artists repainted the gloomy compositions of both masters, replacing them with gay, almost secular decorativeness.[29] It was this decorative style that became general in the cathedral. The monumentality typical of the old academicians was lost. The young generation did not have their skills.

Finally, the murals leave the impression that all the participating artists were simply doing hackwork. It is difficult to detect in them any sense of the time, although the five years of their making were for Russian society a period of intense moral and creative searching. It was a time of revolutionary and government terror, chauvinist Pan-Slav frenzy, and the Russian-Turkish war.

Representatives of the opposing camps of Wanderers and academics, Ivan Surikov and Genrikh Semiradsky, respectively, painted the most interesting murals in the cathedral. Both had accepted the commissions for financial, not creative, reasons.[30] Surikov, a young Siberian who later became Russia's best historical painter, developed his skills in the cathedral. He painted four murals of ecumenical councils in which one can see his gift as a colorist, but they do not reflect the quality of the work he began immediately after the completion of the murals, his masterpiece *The Morning of the Execution of the Strelets*.[31]

The complete opposite of Surikov, Semiradsky was a talented but cold academic painter, famous for his spectacular pictures with classical subjects. A Polish Catholic, he decorated the side chapel dedicated to Saint Alexander Nevsky, which included the most anti-Western painting in the cathedral, *The Envoys of the Pope Meeting Alexander Nevsky*. Semiradsky's participation in the "Russian national monument" was notable considering how painful Russian-Polish relations were. Such a collaboration would not have been possible during Nicholas's reign. Nor would it have been possible to use Italian and Belgian marbles, which Alexander permitted.

Semiradsky involuntarily betrayed the confidence of the czar by making Alexander Nevsky look less sympathetic than the Catholic cardinals who, according to legend, wanted to convert the Russians. One newspaper claimed that the saintly prince looked like a petty tyrant rolling in luxury.[32] But this exercise of interpretive liberty was rare; there was place in the murals only for stilted personages, not real characters. The Construction Commission prohibited Surikov from using Greek models for his murals, demanding not original but typical images. They ordered the hair and beards of some of the figures to be shortened. In addition to the petty complaints of the commission's artist members, the painters had to put up with endless quibbles from the priests on the commission who demanded strict adherence to dogma.

As a result, even the best murals in the cathedral were sentimental and artificial. By inviting artists from different aesthetic camps, Alexander II may have intended to create a miniature model of Russian society united by service to the highest values. But the only thing uniting the artists was their adherence to academic prescriptions.[33] The aesthetic principles that divided realists and academics were not reflected in the interior decoration. Instead of sublime religious drama in the spirit of Alexander Ivanov, the decoration was reminiscent of opera stage design in the academic style. "The interior painting was rouged, powdered, and pomaded. All depicted are opera singers, tenors, baritones with the grimaces of opera singers or simple opera extras," wrote the historian Ivan Zabelin. He continued with a jeer at Kramskoi: "Sabaoth is good—an opera baritone, about 50 years old, powdered."[34]

Despite their shortcomings, however, exact copies of the sacred historical images chosen to be depicted in the cathedral, stamped on the back with the signature of a religious official, were collected all over Russia. These homemade copies played the role of iconographic models for artists. No one cared about their style.[35]

The inconsistency of the paintings—Western in style, Russian-Byzantine in content—was true of the cathedral as a whole. It was a world of Asiatic luxury, in which every element, from the splendid mosaic floor to the gilded bronze gallery railings, was made of the most costly materials. No expense was spared. Everything that could be gilded was gilded—chandeliers and icon frames as well as railings. More than nine hundred thousand pounds of gold were used for the domes alone.[36] The grand chandelier, a gigantic three-tier behemoth made of bronze and weighing more than three and a half tons, gleamed gold, as did the bronze tabernacle-shaped roof of the chapel-iconostasis. Even wall ornaments were covered with twenty-four karat gold.

Precious metals, gems, and rich enamels were used to decorate liturgical vessels, furniture, and priestly garments. More than 660 pounds of gold went for crosses, censers, and vessels.[37] Commissions were given to the best jewelry makers: Khlebnikov, Postnikov, and others. They used as a model the heavy, ornate style of the Moscow kingdom of the end of the sixteenth and seventeenth century—a style that came to be known as "à la Russe." It later became internationally famous thanks to Fabergé.

If the painted decoration was the brainchild of Alexander II, the applied art objects reflected the taste of Crown Prince Alexander Alexandrovich (the future czar Alexander III), who was responsible for most of the commissions.[38] The Russian style was part of the political program of the Russian party, which pinned its hopes on the crown prince.

Stylistic cacophony was the hallmark of the entire cathedral, interior and exterior. But this mixture of different styles unexpectedly gave birth to an impressive image—that of Russia poised between East and West.

Chapter Eighteen

With the completion of the cathedral in 1880, the question arose of how to use the consecration for propaganda purposes. The political situation had changed since the construction of the Millennium Monument. The victory over Turkey in 1878 had revived pride in the country's military might, and the liberation of Orthodox Slavs from the Ottoman Muslim yoke had given rise to a messianic Pan-Slavic ideology, based on the old idea that Russia was a chosen country. This time, Russia's mission was the unification of the Slavs. The main achievement of Alexander's reign was seen as the return of Russia to great-power status under the banner of Pan-Slavism.

According to Billington, "Pan-Slavism began in the second half of Alexander's reign to replace in many minds official nationality as the ideology of tsarist Russia."[1] In this climate, when there was hope for the establishment of a neo-Byzantine empire with its capital in Constantinople, the "Russian-Byzantine" Cathedral of Christ the Savior proved to be very useful.

The cathedral was to be one of the focal points for the twenty-fifth anniversary celebration of Alexander's accession to the throne. The consecration was planned for August 26, the day of Alexander's coronation in 1855 and of the battle of Borodino.[2] But the celebrations never took place. On May 22 Empress Maria Alexandrovna died, and Princess Dolgoruky, who for fourteen years had been living with Alexander and their children in the Winter Palace, demanded that her Sasha keep his word and marry her. To the horror of the imperial family and the court, the two were secretly married at Tsarskoe Selo on July 6, 1880, and at the end of August they left for a honeymoon in the Crimea.[3] The Moscow celebrations were postponed to 1881.

While the cathedral stood empty, awaiting consecration, Alexander added another celebration to the list of festivities — the fifteenth anniversary of his escape from Karakozov's bullet in 1866. The czar had survived five assassination attempts, and the cathedral was to become a monument to his miraculous salvation.[4]

The imperial family and the court saw a greater threat to the throne than terrorists. Immediately after their secret wedding, the czar conferred on his morganatic wife the title of Princess Yurievsky — a contrived title combining the name of her ancestor, Prince Yuri Dolgoruky, with his, Roman Yurievich Zaharin-Koshkin. The czar was rumored to be contemplating even greater honors for his new wife. The preparations were secret, but it was believed that the anniversary celebrations would include her coronation.[5] The Cathedral of Christ the Savior would become a symbol of the renewed monarchy and the resumption of reforms. The court rejected the princess, but the reformist ministers led by Loris-Melikov supported her. And then, six months before the jubilee, the czar was killed by a terrorist. Princess Yurievsky's coronation never took place. The consecration of the cathedral was once again postponed.

On the morning of his assassination, Alexander II approved a plan drawn up by Interior Minister Loris-Melikov to summon an elective consultative assembly, an important step toward the establishment of a parliament. The czar postponed formal approval of the plan until the next meeting of the cabinet of ministers. But it was his successor, Alexander III, who presided over that meeting and made it clear that his father's wishes would not be fulfilled. The so-called constitution was a dead issue.

Standing at the new czar's side was his former tutor and most trusted adviser, the jurist Konstantin Pobedonostsev. This former liberal lawyer, one of the architects of the Judicial Reform Act of 1864, had become procurator of the Holy Synod and the fiercest defender of the autocratic principle. At the new czar's first cabinet meeting, Pobedonostsev delivered a fiery speech blaming the murder of Alexander II on liberal policies.

Pobedonostsev convinced the new czar to sign a manifesto asserting his faith in autocracy, "which we are called upon to maintain and to protect, for the welfare of the people, from all attempts directed against it." A year later, he squashed a plan set forth by the new interior minister, Count Nicholas Ignatiev, a Pan-Slavist, to summon a zemsky sobor, or "council of the land," based on the national assemblies of ancient Russia. Such assemblies were intended to support autocracy, not to interfere in politics.[6]

As crown prince during his father's reign, Alexander III had opposed the reforms and had seen in the zemsky sobor an alternative to a Western-style parliament. He was sympathetic to many Slavophile teachings and went about wearing high boots and a coat that suggested a muzhik's tunic. When he became czar, he accepted Ignatiev's proposal, and discussions began about convening the assembly in 1883, the 270th anniversary of the election by a zemsky sobor of Mikhail, the first Romanov czar, in 1613. Ignatiev proposed that the gathering take place in Christ the Savior, a few days after the czar's coronation in the Kremlin. The three thousand delegates, most of them peasants, would listen to the czar's speech and then communicate it directly to others.[7] But the cathedral was not to be the place where democracy in the ancient Russian style would be revived. Pobedonostsev told the czar sternly that he didn't need public opinion: "It makes no difference what kind of popular gathering it is—it is revolution and the downfall of Russia."[8] The project was rejected, and Ignatiev discharged.

Historians have not been kind to Pobedonostsev. He was "like a frost that hinders further decay, but he would never get anything to grow," according to the conservative Konstantin Leontiev. The finance minister, Count Sergei Witte, considered Pobedonostsev an extremely well-educated and cultivated individual but a "nihilist by nature." Completely devoid of "living creativity," he approached everything with a dry critical attitude.[9] Yet this cold skeptic was a man of strong feelings. Describing the most important questions of the faith, he used images and liturgical forms rather than logic. In a letter to the Slavophile writer Ivan Aksakov, Pobedonostsev wrote that monarchy in Russia was simply a matter of faith. "There are subjects that can only be directly apprehended and felt but can't be subjected to stern logical analysis."[10]

Pobedonostsev gave a new interpretation to the Cathedral of Christ the Savior—and it was he who had the last word. This dry man of reason believed that the instinctive religious faith of the common people was Russia's main treasure and its salvation in the battle against Western rationalism.[11] Tradition—the "stability of patriarchal everyday life"—and the "inherent wisdom of the people" had to be protected because they would save the monarchy.[12]

Napoleon had once commented that the Russian emperor would become invincible on the day he grew a beard—when he became a real Russian muzhik, like his people. Alexander III was the first Russian emperor who followed this advice. Big, burly, and bearded, he looked to the people exactly as a real czar should look. Pobedonostsev's royal pupil perfectly embodied the image of monarchy that could be "directly apprehended and felt."

The ideal czar needed an ideal symbolic environment in which to communicate with his subjects. In his famous manifesto of April 29, 1881, in which Pobedonostsev wrote about the "Russian land," referring to the seventeenth-century Moscow state, he explained that it wasn't the silent obedience of his subjects that gave the czar his right to rule but "the warm prayers of the pious people" said for him in the Orthodox Church.[13]

All his life Alexander III continued to play the role of a seventeenth-century czar, tirelessly constructing cathedrals in the seventeenth-century style—places of symbolic communication of the people with their czar. The model of the ideal people's cathedral where the ritual of the protective monarchy took place was the Cathedral of Christ the Savior.

For two years, the cathedral had awaited the coronation of the new czar, but Alexander was in no hurry for the ceremony to take place. He was too busy establishing order in the country, firing liberal ministers, and oppressing revolutionaries. From his father, he had inherited the idea that the coronation festivities should include the consecration of the cathedral, which would bestow unprecedented honor on the building. The schedule of coronation festivities, which included the cathedral consecration, was approved on April 16, 1883.[14] The czar had approved the religious part of the ceremony a month earlier.[15]

Pobedonostsev composed the ceremony, using as models the consecration ceremony of St. Isaac's as well as the project for the consecration of Christ the Savior prepared for the Construction Commission by Vicar Amvrosy (Kliucharev) of Moscow and edited by Metropolitan Ioanniky.[16] Although the ceremony was to take place on Ascension Day, May 26, the traditional prayer that was read on Christmas Day was chosen, because it was on Christmas Day that Napoleon had been expelled from Russia and that Alexander I had pledged to erect the cathedral.[17] A prayer dedicated to the miraculous expulsion of Napoleon was thereby transformed into a prayer dedicated to the miraculous salvation of the monarchy.

The Assumption Cathedral, where the coronation ceremony was held, was large enough only for courtiers and priests, so the first common prayer of the czar and his subjects took place in Christ the Savior. Another innovation was the series of religious processions that were held all over Moscow, as impressive in scale as military maneuvers.

On May 26, Their Imperial Highnesses entered the cathedral arm in arm, accompanied by cheers, bells tolling, and choirs singing.[18] More than seven thousand people, which included the imperial suite, ministers, the diplomatic corps, high-ranking officials, and delegations from all over the empire, as well as correspondents from all the major newspapers, filled the vast cathedral. Surviving veterans of 1812 stood in a separate group.

When the altars had been consecrated, all present, including the emperor and the empress, sank to their knees in prayer, each person lighting a candle. Then began the most solemn part of the ceremony, as the religious procession left through the western doors and started to move around the perimeter of the cathedral, under the gaze of the biblical and Russian heroes carved on the walls. The czar led the procession, walking slowly on a red carpet. Behind him came the czarina and a bevy of courtiers. Flanking them on one side were tall, portly priests holding banners, and on the other, guards carrying aloft their regimental colors. The sweet smell of incense mingled with the acrid odor of gunpowder that lingered in the air. "High, white, and gold-domed, the cathedral rose majestically above the masses of people surrounding it," wrote a contemporary.[19]

The consecration not only wedded the new czar to Russian history but was seen as a sacrament unifying ruler and people. Two years after the assassination of Alexander II, the house of Romanov wanted to show the world that the People's Will, one of whose members had carried out the assassination, was no more than a powerless gang of renegades that, despite its name, acted against the will of the people. The cathedral served as a symbol of the victory of Alexander III over the revolutionaries in the struggle for the people's love and loyalty—a victory that was equated with the triumph over Napoleon.

Chapter Nineteen

No monument in the history of Russia has been more harshly criticized than the Cathedral of Christ the Savior. Critics included both conservatives and liberals. According to Alexander Ivanov, Moscow grumbled that the cathedral was a "gigantic cupboard where nothing corresponds to the devout rules for church symbolism." Alexander Herzen wrote that "all new churches constructed by Nicholas and Ton were full of hypocrisy, anachronism, and looked like five-headed cruet stands with onion domes instead of stoppers." People of the next century shared the opinion of contemporaries. Igor Grabar, author of the first multivolume history of Russian art, regretted that "instead of Vitberg's giddy romantic dream, an ugly, bulky, and cumbersome thing, dreadful in its disproportion and repulsive in its awful stylistic eclecticism, rose over Moscow." Prince Trubetskoi, the well-known religious philosopher, expressed a similar sentiment: "The Cathedral of Christ the Savior is a monument to expensive nonsense—it is a gigantic samovar around which all of patriarchal Moscow gathers."[1]

Ordinary people loved it, however. Long before it was completed, the cathedral had become one of Moscow's landmarks; everyone visiting the capital, down to the poorest peasant, had to see the construction site. Prints and postcards bearing the cathedral's image were distributed to the far corners of the empire and had their honored place in the "red corners" of peasant huts, where the icons were hung. Servants and artisans glued views of the cathedral to the inner lids of their storage chests, along with portraits of the royal family.

When the scaffolding was removed, in 1858, the cathedral dominated the skyline. Moscow was still a relatively small city of low buildings, and the cathedral was visible from every point. The view from its galleries was also spectacular; one could survey the entire ancient capital, from its gold-domed churches to its picturesque hills.

The building's gigantic size and rich ornamentation—the very features that repelled connoisseurs—awed and delighted ordinary people. It was precisely the pastiche of Russian and foreign elements, the mix of familiar with exotic and strange, that appealed to them. Immediately after the consecration, the masses poured into the building, which they had watched in wonder for such a long time as its walls rose higher and higher. "Many visitors . . . behaved in the cathedral as if they were at home. They sat on the benches, on the steps of the bishop's ambo . . . ate eggs, cracked nuts, and nibbled sunflower seeds while waiting for services. Mothers fed their children, others walked back and forth and, not trusting their eyes, touched every object, kissed icons, wanting to understand how they were painted stuck their fingers into them, and scratched ornaments. When told, 'Don't touch,' they were insolent, and it was often necessary to use the power of the police to make such visitors leave. To admit only respectable and well-bred visitors meant giving the crowd a chance to push in."[2]

Displeased by this domestication of the cathedral by crowds of unruly commoners, Prince Vladimir Dolgorukov, governor-general of Moscow, ordered the gates closed during hours when there were no services. The open-door policy had lasted for only two weeks, since officials could not

manage the mobs of up to fifteen thousand people at a time. But Pobedonostsev ruled that the "pious and patriotic wish" to see the cathedral
and understand its meaning had to be satisfied.[3] The number of attendants
was increased, and the doors were opened again from early morning until
midnight.[4] He was delighted that people treated the cathedral as a place of
prayer given to them by God and the czar and was ready to fight with the
"strangers" — officials — who ordered the people to behave themselves as if
they were their masters.

Pobedonostsev understood the role of the cathedral as a mass spectacle.
It was probably the most successful mass-culture project of prerevolutionary Russia. Entering the richly decorated interior, common people found
themselves in an atmosphere of luxury, patented piety, and legendary history. The cathedral was a gigantic encyclopedia of the Russian Orthodox
world that was accessible to every illiterate peasant. One could wander inside it for hours, awed by the greatness of that world or enjoying the details
of the holy stories. The history of Russia was as legendary and lofty as the
story of the Bible. At the same time, the cathedral was soon as comfortably
overgrown with rumors and fables as was traditional Orthodoxy, with its
superstitions and folk beliefs.

The murals created a broad historical panorama in which sacred history, the history of ancient Russia, and the events of the Napoleonic War
were equalized by their visual similarity. On one wall Dmitry Donskoy was
depicted preparing for battle with the Tatars, and behind the next column Russian troops were entering Paris. One could witness an Ecumenical Synod in Constantinople and, ten steps away, the Passion of Christ in
Jerusalem. The archaeological accuracy with which, on demand of Bishop
Leonid, both academics and Wanderers painted such details as Metropolitan Pyotr's miter were especially useful for the purpose. Leonid commanded, "An artist must remember that at the moment of the Assumption
the Virgin was 48 years old."[5]

The cathedral proved to be quite at home in the world of Pancake Week
festivities, Palm Sunday religious processions, Sunday and folk panto-
mimes. Unlike St. Isaac's, it wasn't oppressive. On the contrary, it filled
visitors with wonder and pride in being Russian. People approached it not
from a clean, swept St. Petersburg avenue but from a dusty, unpaved Russian road. Prince Dolgorukov complained that the thick layer of highway
dust that coated the sculptures and penetrated the interior was destroying

the costly ornaments and furnishings.[6] The square around the cathedral was not paved until a few years after the consecration, the Moscow city council having pleaded a shortage of funds. Although the Kremlin was only a few steps away, the area around the cathedral was considered dangerous and had been dubbed the Valley of Wolves. There were ramshackle hovels and wretched little taverns, the haunts of disreputable people. The riverbank remained unpaved. Respectable citizens were afraid to walk in the vicinity at night.[7]

City officials demolished some of these offensive buildings, but the area remained colorful nonetheless. Fishermen gathered on a raft that was permanently anchored in the middle of the river, directly opposite the cathedral. These free spirits, their pockets full of worms, recognized no authorities. As was frequently observed, they did more drinking than catching fish. A bathhouse was nearby, and in all seasons naked men ran from the steam rooms to dive into the river.[8]

The cathedral was at the center of a bitter debate about whether Russian society or the Russian state deserved credit for the victory over Napoleon. This dispute arose during the preparations for the jubilee celebrations of 1912 and became more acrimonious as the event approached. Traditionally the victory of 1812 was celebrated with both a religious procession and a military parade. This had been the case since the first foundation ceremony of 1817. By the 1840s, it had also become traditional for the Sunday closest to October 12, the day the French troops left Moscow, to be celebrated with a religious procession. After the service in the Assumption Cathedral, the Moscow priests walked around the Kremlin carrying wonder-working icons. After the consecration of Christ the Savior, a separate procession starting there was added to the ceremony.

By the end of the nineteenth century, the system of state-church holidays was established. Assumption Cathedral was the center of festivities dedicated to the salvation of Moscow, whereas Christ the Savior was the site of celebrations honoring the salvation of Russia and Europe.[9] The liberal intelligentsia tried to oppose this system centered on Christ the Savior by imposing its own secular system, centered on the construction of a museum devoted to the war of 1812. This faction wanted the museum built close to the cathedral as a visual manifestation of the opposition between true people's patriotism and its official version.[10] For them, it wasn't God, the monarchy, or even the army that had been most responsible for the victory; it was the people. The museum was to house not military or religious relics but diaries and memoirs of the Napoleonic period, newspapers and folk prints dedicated to the war, and memorial objects belonging to the participants.[11] These plans were opposed by supporters of the state line, and a special committee for the establishment of the museum became a stage for heated discussions.[12] Nikolai Pozdeev, staff architect of Christ the Savior and a leader of the state party, tried hard to save the military-Orthodox character of the upcoming celebration. He wanted to reinforce the role of the cathedral as the main monument of the war of 1812 and worked to secure the transfer of military relics—banners, keys to the cities taken by the Russian armies, and the like—to Christ the Savior, where they could be placed in the sacristy or in a special chapel built nearby.

In the meantime, a battle for the right to be considered the heirs of the victors of 1812 started in the Russian press. In the Duma elections of 1912, the government supported priestly candidates, and articles with titles like "In Memory of the Heroic Priests of 1812" appeared in the papers. The Moscow church newspaper *Tserkovnie vedomosti* (Church gazette) published in installments a text by Mikhail Sobolev, titled "The Cathedral of Christ the Savior in Moscow as a Monument to the Great Favor of God and the Heroic Deeds of Ancestors Demonstrated in the Difficult Time of 1812." Liberal newspapers, on the other hand, wrote that "priests betrayed the people in 1812." It was noted that Tolstoy had not mentioned any priests in *War and Peace*. Liberals protested the official version of the "people's war" and supported the idea of the museum.[13]

The erection of the monument to Alexander III on the square in front of Christ the Savior put an end to these discussions. The decision to establish the museum was postponed and then, with the start of World War I, forgotten. The monument was planned immediately after the death of the "czar-peacemaker." Its cost, unlike the cathedral's, was paid by donations from the people. Ivan Tsvetaev, a professor at Moscow University and father of the poet Marina Tsvetaeva, suggested its placement near the cathedral, but the decision to install it during the jubilee celebration of the war of 1812 belonged to Nicholas II and his circle. The well-known sculptor Mikhail Opekushin was chosen to depict the czar at the moment of his coronation in 1883, during which celebration the cathedral was consecrated, thereby stressing the monarchist element in the mythology of the cathedral.

Alexander III was depicted seated on the throne, crowned and holding the scepter and orb of monarchy. The intention had been to portray him as he had been during the coronation ceremony, aware of the greatness of the moment, but the sculptor was generally considered to have failed. The ceremony, however, was spectacular. Grand Duke Gavriil Konstanti-novich described the arrival of the sovereign to the square, which was lined with troops. After the service, the royal family proceeded to the shrouded monument, where the sovereign unsheathed his saber and commanded the troops to present arms. The photographers who had been stationed on the cathedral steps swarmed around the base of the monument, irritat-ing everybody, to get the best shots and were chased away by Grand Duke Sergei Mikhailovich.[14]

None of those present could know how little time was left to the royal family, the monument to Alexander III, and the cathedral itself. Within a few years, the only thing remaining of that day would be the photographs and film footage shot by the brash photographers who had been brushed aside by the grand duke.

PART THREE

The Last Days of the Cathedral

Chapter Twenty

On March 11, 1918, an unusually solemn service took place in the Cathedral of Christ the Savior. Since the previous August, church dignitaries from all over the former empire had been gathered in the cathedral for a synod. Their original aim had been to reform the ancient institution, which had been released from state control by the provisional government. But with the Bolsheviks' seizure of power, the church had entered a time of severe trouble.

Metropolitan Anthony of Kharkov summed up the situation in a sermon. The Orthodox Church, he lamented, had fallen into even worse slavery than it had suffered under Muslims, Western heretics, or even Tatars. Churches had been plundered and their clergy killed. Religious instruction had been banned and seminaries closed. Military units had been deprived of their priests. The metropolitan accused his compatriots who had been led too easily into sedition: "A large number of the Russian people betrayed their beliefs, openly rejected the holy faith, indulged in the most foul vices. They rob, kill, blaspheme, betray their motherland to enemies and sell their souls to the devil."[1]

Anthony called the devil by name: the Bolshevik government had led the Russian people into temptation. They had been deceived by leaders who were "non-Russians" or convicted criminals. A reactionary and a well-known anti-Semite, the metropolitan was referring to Jews, who many church leaders believed composed the core of the Bolshevik movement and were responsible for all the country's troubles.

After the sermon, the archpriests carried icons of Christ and the Virgin into the center of the cathedral. The newly elected patriarch of Moscow and All Russia, Pimen, followed by the metropolitans, archbishops, and bishops, mounted the rostrum, and a solemn service began. Protodeacon Konstantin Rozov entered the pulpit and in his famous bass voice chanted the anathema against heretics and all who "blaspheme our Holy Faith and revolt against the Holy Church."[2] His condemnation resounded throughout the vaults of the vast cathedral, lit by thousands of candles. After the echoes died away, the patriarch and church leaders, dressed in their glittering robes, prayed together for the destruction of the Bolsheviks.

That same day, the Bolshevik government arrived in Moscow, the new capital of revolutionary Russia.

The Russian Orthodox Church was not ready for the catastrophe. Like Russian society in general, it was divided, and by the end of the nineteenth century, its divisions were glaringly apparent. A substantial part of the priesthood remained, as it had always been, "the foundation of the monarchy" — reactionary, anti-Semitic, and distrustful of any hint of reform. But a large minority of priests and church leaders were calling for changes: the replacement of incomprehensible Church Slavonic with modern Russian; the democratization of the Byzantine-style hierarchical structure; even the eventual independence of church from state. But until the February Revolution the reformers had no hope of prevailing.

The czar's abdication took church leaders by surprise. The new democratic government proclaimed freedom of conscience and broke the bond between church and state. Lessons in the catechism ceased to be part of the school curriculum.[3] Despite these dangerous steps, the church recognized the provisional government. A prayer for the "Motherland saved by God" replaced the ritual prayer for the emperor, his court, and his army.[4] Almost all circles in the church supported the restoration of the patriarchy, which had been abolished by Peter the Great in the seventeenth century. Conservatives considered it a move away from state control, while liberal elements saw it as the first step toward institutional reform.

The provisional government treated the synod as an event of the highest political importance. Despite the war and the growing standoff with the Petrograd Soviet, both Prime Minister Alexander Kerensky and Duma President Mikhail Rodzianko traveled to Moscow to participate in its opening session. In his speech Rodzianko expressed the Duma's hope that the synod would be able to "conciliate and unite all Russian people."[5]

In September the delegates discussed the forthcoming elections to the Constituent Assembly that would give the Russian republic a new government. They hoped that the voice of the Orthodox delegates would be strong enough to influence the political future of the country. "Let us call to the high Constituent Assembly those people who love their church and can stand for her. Let there be gathered at the Assembly not names ending with 'feld' and 'blum,' not pseudonyms, but the names of real Russian people. Let our synod defend the boon of the Orthodox multitudes of Russia," proclaimed Archpriest Alexander Khrapovitsky (who was to die in the gulag and be canonized in 2000, along with Nicholas II).[6]

All such hopes were swept away by the events of October.

On October 28, as the delegates prayed for the Conciliation of the Motherland, they could hear the battle raging outside.[7] Metropolitan Tikhon of Moscow called for a religious procession to appeal for peace, but events developed too rapidly. During the next few days it was possible to reach the cathedral only under cover of darkness. The troops of the revolutionary council were fighting for control of nearby streets, and military cadets defending the provisional government installed their machine guns in the cathedral bell towers. Bodies lay around the building, visible to the delegates.

The synod sent a delegation to plead with the Red commander not to destroy the ancient Kremlin. He promised them to stop the shelling, but the bombardment continued nonetheless, smashing a large hole through the dome of the Ascension Cathedral and damaging the Cathedral of the Archangel Michael and the Bell Tower of Ivan the Great. The patriarch's sacristy and the Small Nicholas Palace were looted. The tops of some of the watchtowers were destroyed, and the icons installed over the gates were used as targets.[8]

Even the Bolsheviks were shocked by the savagery of the battle in the heart of Russia. Commissar of Enlightenment Anatoly Lunacharsky was so upset by the bombardment of the Kremlin, which he could do nothing to prevent, that he resigned (temporarily) from the Council of People's Commissars.[9]

The writer Ilya Ehrenburg, who had just returned to the country from his Paris emigration, was also shocked.

They were fighting in Moscow. Cannons spat
Hellish stench at the white churches,
And the Patriarch wept,
Pressing himself against the wounded heart of the Holy Virgin.
The Kremlin walls, spared of cruel hands
During the days of Napoleon,
Bent under the shelling—
They had nothing more to protect.[10]

On November 3, when the battle was over, a thanksgiving service was organized in the cathedral. Two days later the synod elected Tikhon, the metropolitan of Moscow, as patriarch of Russia. The new leader of the church predicted that martyrdom awaited him: "The news of my election as patriarch is for me a scroll on which is written, 'Weep, lament, and grieve.'"[11]

To many Russians, the restoration of the patriarchy was the only good news in the country, which was rapidly sliding into chaos. Moscow was running short of food and fuel. "The Don Cossacks have 'entrenched' themselves and are not rushing to help us. They give us neither coal nor bread and are not letting anybody in," one Moscow citizen noted in his diary. Political developments were incomprehensible. "Ukraine and Finland have declared republics and treat our disaster with scorn. The Caucasus has established something 'independent' too. Great Russia is falling apart and crumbling away. Autonomy is established in Bessarabia. Only the church is attempting to hold its ground. On Sunday Tikhon was elected patriarch of Moscow."[12]

From the moment of his election, the patriarch actively opposed the Bolshevik government. He looked on helplessly as the revolutionaries killed in battle were ceremonially interred in Red Square, near the Kremlin wall (thus beginning its transformation into the most prestigious cemetery in Soviet Russia). The secular funeral accompanied by revolutionary songs was completely foreign to Orthodox tradition. Two days later an Orthodox memorial service for all those killed during the events of October was held in the Cathedral of Christ the Savior, but the church's call to the citizens of Moscow to unite in grief for the dead on both sides fell on deaf ears.[13] Russia was divided by an abyss of social hatred.

On January 19, the patriarch addressed an epistle to the Council of People's Commissars. "Come to your senses, madmen! Stop these cruel, bloody massacres. Otherwise face the fires of hell and the damnation of your progeny."[14] The government responded with brutal repression. An icon of the Savior installed on the wall of the Moscow Duma was replaced by the Marxist slogan "Religion is the opium of the people." In the Moscow markets food was wrapped in pages torn out of Bibles confiscated from the Synodal Printing Office.[15]

A serious standoff between church and state took place during the first celebration of May Day, in 1918. The holiday devoted to the solidarity of the international proletariat coincided that year with Lent. The Bolsheviks did everything they could to convince the conservative population of Moscow to celebrate the Red holiday, but believers immediately named it "Judas Easter" and tried to prevent participation in the May Day demonstration. The popular Moscow priest Ioan Kedrov implored his flock: "Brothers and sisters, if we have even a little bit of faith in Christ, our Savior and God, we cannot attend this pagan holiday."[16]

More unspeakable events were on the way. On July 6, *Izvestia,* the official organ of the Central Executive Committee, reported that the committee had approved the execution of Citizen Nicholas Romanov. The newspaper also reported, falsely, that the ex-czar's wife and children had been evacuated to a safe location.[17] Patriarch Tikhon immediately held a memorial service for the murdered czar in the chapel of his residence and asked priests all over Russia to pray for the victim. Two days after the newspaper announcement, Tikhon stated in his sermon: "Obeying the teaching of the word of God, we are obliged to condemn this deed, because if we do not do so, we, and not only the executioners, will be responsible for the blood of the murdered ones."[18]

Chapter Twenty-one

It had become clear to everyone that Tikhon was the only authority in the country who could challenge the dictatorship. Because the government had occupied the Kremlin and placed its churches off-limits, the Cathedral of Christ the Savior had become the patriarch's seat and, therefore, the center of resistance. Archpriest Alexander Khotovitsky, describing his vision of the cathedral's new role to the besieged synod, declared that it was time for the cathedral to justify its historical existence. It had to be a place of continuing contact between the patriarch and the people, where thousands could gather "under its immense vaults to see their Father making the Bloodless Sacrifice for the Russian people, teaching the flock and blessing it. Let the Russian people know where to find their holiest Patriarch."[1]

But the government had no intention of leaving the church alone. On February 2, 1918, came the dreaded decree from the Council of People's Commissars that separated church and state. In effect, it meant that thousands of priests, who until October had been government employees and received monthly stipends, found themselves deprived of any means of

support. The numerous churches and monasteries, including all their pos-
sessions, became state property.

The cathedral was also suffering. Like the Russian empire itself, it glittered on the outside but was crumbling inside. The gigantic building had
never been renovated. The interior decorations had been damaged by cold
and damp because the heating system had never been completed. A thick
layer of soot, deposited by thousands of candles, obscured the paintings
on the upper walls. When the number of candles was reduced because the
congregation could no longer afford them, semidarkness reigned in the immense, dank spaces.[2]

Despite the difficulties, however, Khotovitsky did not abandon his
vision of the cathedral's historical role. With the blessing of the patriarch,
he established the Brotherhood of the Cathedral of Christ the Savior to
collect money for maintaining the building and paying its clergy the sal-
aries due them.[3] Another of the brotherhood's goals was to arouse "zeal
for the Orthodox Church and a feeling of love for the Motherland" in the
Russian people.[4] In 1918 such ideas were dangerous. The revolution was
still in its internationalist stage, and Marx's words "A proletarian has no
motherland" were inscribed on its banners. The state could not tolerate a
counterrevolutionary organization like the Brotherhood of the Cathedral of
Christ the Savior for long.

Khotovitsky proved to be an able manager. During its short life, the
brotherhood succeeded not only in installing a temporary electric lighting
system and constructing a Golgotha in the cathedral but in establishing
a popular chorus and a library. Work began on the restoration of the sacristy. Despite limited means, the brotherhood became involved in reprinting Mikhail Mostovsky's *Historical Description of the Cathedral of Christ
the Savior in Moscow,* originally published in 1883. Khotovitsky and his
colleagues did not, however, limit their publishing activities to reprinting
historical literature. The church underground was also distributing thousands of mimeographed copies of the patriarch's epistle to the Council of
People's Commissars. Like later samizdat, it was copied by innumerable
hands and made its way to the farthest reaches of the country.

By the end of 1918, the cathedral clergy had become so concerned about
the patriarch's safety that believers guarded his quarters day and night,
fearing that he might be arrested at any moment. Fantastic plans were made
to ring all the church bells in Moscow and organize huge religious proces-

sions if he were imprisoned. Some thought he should avoid the fate of the czar by escaping abroad, but the patriarch bluntly rejected the proposal, saying that only enemies of the church would benefit if he fled.[5]

On November 11, the government made its first move against him. Tikhon's quarters were searched, and he was put under house arrest.[6] He was not released until December 24, so that he could attend the Christmas Eve Mass in the cathedral. But disturbing rumors about his fate were circulating among the people, and the Bolsheviks wanted to exhibit him alive and well. But the time of compromise was coming to an end. The state was not going to retreat before the last remaining reactionary force in Russia was destroyed.

In 1919 the campaign of opening holy relics started all around the country. According to Orthodox doctrine, the flesh of saints was incorruptible. Their remains, treasured in monasteries and churches, were revered by believers and had become objects of pilgrimage. The state thought it could prove the falsehood of church teachings by demonstrating the true content of the gilded shrines held sacred by generations of Russian people. Guarded by soldiers with fixed bayonets, the commissions entrusted with the examination of relics burst into monasteries and churches. In some places, the forced exhumations provoked clashes with believers; in others, holy relics were stolen and hidden on the eve of the appearance of the commissions.[7] Newspapers published detailed reports about the earthly remains of the saints, whose bones were photographed and filmed.[8] This was the triumph of materialist science over superstition.

In May 1920 the Bolsheviks decided to examine the remains of Saint Sergius, one of the most revered Russian saints, which were interred in the Trinity–Saint Sergius Monastery, not far from Moscow.[9] This undertaking turned into a serious military operation. Unable to remain silent any longer, the humiliated patriarch wrote a letter to Lenin demanding that this blasphemy be stopped. The only answer he received was an order prohibiting him from conducting services in any Moscow church without special permission from Mikhail Kalinin, head of the Central Executive Committee, which made it virtually impossible for him to appear in the cathedral.[10] That same year the activities of the brotherhood came to an end. Khotovitsky was arrested for violating the decree of separation between church and state by establishing a children's Sunday school.[11] The government was tightening the noose.

In 1921 drought brought severe famine to the Volga region, leaving hundreds of thousands of peasants on the verge of starvation. A Church Committee for Famine Relief was established, and the patriarch resolved to sacrifice some church treasures to save human lives. But the government wasn't satisfied with that. Military units armed with machine guns attacked churches, stripping them of all their gold and silver objects. Chalices and crucifixes were confiscated, icon covers torn away. Government propaganda asserted that the patriarch and the church were rolling in luxury and refusing to share their wealth to save the starving masses. The people were not convinced, however. All over Russia, the confiscation of church valuables provoked uproar and armed clashes. Numerous revolts were brutally suppressed, and mass arrests of priests followed.

The wave of confiscations did not spare the Cathedral of Christ the Savior. Hoping to avoid the sacrifice of sacred objects, the congregation collected fifty-four pounds of silver and offered it to the state instead, but officials seized both the silver and the objects. In May, fifty-four priests from different parishes were arrested and tried for "concealment of church treasures."[12] The patriarch was called as a "witness."

Vyacheslav Menzhinsky, head of the State Political Department (the secret police) and Yevgeny Tuchkov, secretary of the Anti-Religious Commission of the Communist Party Central Committee, interrogated the patriarch and pressed him to issue a statement against the Russian church abroad, which actively supported armed resistance to the Bolsheviks. He refused. The patriarch's policy was to avoid direct involvement in politics. He had refused to bless the White armies, realizing that such a step would be suicidal for the church.[13] Nevertheless, the Soviet press portrayed him as a supporter of counterrevolution. The poet Vladimir Mayakovsky composed a verse that corresponded perfectly to the official interpretation of Tikhon's political role:

Patriarch Tikhon is calling
People to revolt against Soviet power.
Tikhon is reaching abroad,
And calling back the White Guards

.   .   .   .

Don't be naughty, father-patriarch,
We will not surrender our freedom to anyone.[14]

On May 19, 1922, the patriarch was placed under house arrest in the Donskoy monastery, where he was isolated and subjected to endless interrogations, an indication that his trial was being prepared. The government intended to accuse him of counterrevolutionary activities, resistance to the division of church and state, and other charges.

In November, 105 priests and laymen were arrested and tried for "an attempt to retain in their hands church valuables and to overturn Soviet power, using the famine as the cause."[15] Among those arrested were Khotovitsky and the lay members of the brotherhood. According to the official charge, this "criminal group" was gathering secretly to carry out their "felonious intentions."[16] The trial gave a boost to a young prosecutor named Andrei Vishinsky, who would become internationally known during the show trials of the 1930s. Vishinsky demanded the death penalty for thirteen of the accused, including Khotovitsky. Tikhon's plea for a pardon of the fifty-four priests was ignored, and eleven were executed.

The imprisoned patriarch was tormented by reports of these attacks, but he had other worries as well. Not all his enemies were dressed in the uniform of the secret police. Some wore the sacerdotal robes of the church. They were the *obnovlentsi*—derived from the word for "renovate" or "renew"—and their aim was to reform the church. These groups wanted to establish connections with the Bolshevik government and were willing to pay the high price the commissars demanded for their support. The priests of the so-called Revolutionary Church who opposed the anti-Bolshevist politics of the synod and the patriarch found themselves transformed into puppets of the new regime.[17] Trotsky, who took an active part in the formation of the government's antireligious policy, considered the Revolutionary Church a temporary ally he could use to split the Orthodox Church. After that, the obnovlentsi would no longer be needed and could be destroyed.

Chapter Twenty-two

Early in May 1922, at the beginning of the trial of the fifty-four clerics, the priest Sergei Kalinovsky, a leader of the Living Church reformist group, sent a letter to the All-Russian Central Executive Committee proposing that the government protect priests and laity "who recognize the justice of the Russian socialist revolution" and calling for the establishment of a state church.[1] The aims of the obnovlentsi, however, were not limited to winning government support and taking control of the common clergy. One of their targets was the patriarch himself. On May 9, 1922, a delegation of obnovlentsi leaders, including Archpriest Alexander Vvedensky, traveled from Petrograd to Moscow. For a few days, they trod the corridors of power and apparently reached an understanding with Bolshevik officials. On the night of May 12, the church reformers appeared in Tikhon's quarters, accompanied by two GPU (secret police) officers. They held the patriarch responsible for the death of the eleven executed priests and charged that his policy had led to a civil war between the church and Soviet power. They requested that he retire and turn over his office and seal to representatives of the Living Church. The furious Tikhon replied that he could be defrocked only by the synod.[2]

A few days later, the obnovlentsi paid Tikhon a second visit. Under pressure, and realizing that he couldn't lead the church from prison, he appointed Agafangel, the metropolitan of Yaroslavl, as temporary head of the church and ordered him to come to Moscow to prepare a second synod. The reformers were entrusted with turning over the synod documentation to Agafangel, though they ignored this order. Instead they created a new body, the Main Church Directorate, and usurped power themselves. They explained this coup with a lie; the patriarch, they claimed, had appointed them to rule the church.[3]

One of the participants in the putsch, Archpriest Vvedensky, deserves a closer look. The most active representative of the reform movement, and the most flamboyant, he had become popular in intellectual circles in 1911, when he published an article on why Russian intellectuals were not believers, based on an opinion poll he had organized while still a student at St. Petersburg University.[4] Unlike the usual run of Orthodox priests, Vvedensky was a true intellectual of the church. An admirer of contemporary French philosophy and an ardent follower of Henri Bergson, a connoisseur of modernist painting and a gifted musician, he was a Renaissance man and might have become an important church leader under different circumstances. But his arrogance and his Faustian bargain with the regime, which he seems to have entered into with pure idealism, led him into the trap that snared many brilliant Russian intellectuals.

During the government's war with the patriarch, Vvedensky not only tried to convince the rebellious bishops to obey the Bolsheviks; he also wrote articles accusing the imprisoned patriarch of antistate activities.[5] Hungry for popularity as well as governmental approval, he wanted desperately to be the leader of the Living Church and to be recognized by the West as Russia's spiritual primate.

Vvedensky succeeded in establishing himself as a Soviet celebrity, owing to his public debates with Lunacharsky on such topics as the existence of God. His striking appearance fascinated his contemporaries. He was as "energetic as a genie released from a bottle, a tall, dynamic man with an expressive face and a large aquiline nose. His face had something devilish. In any case, the expression 'devilishly beautiful' was applicable to him."[6] Some of his friends were convinced that although he found his profession interesting and profitable, he did not believe in God. He was known as an orator and had many female admirers, whose love letters he would fish out of his pockets and tear up in public.[7]

In 1923 Tikhon's supporters were ejected from the Cathedral of Christ the Savior because the Living Church wanted to take over the building. Vvedensky, who had already started to refer to himself as a metropolitan, thought that control over Russia's primary religious structure would add to his credibility. The government obliged him by getting rid of the pro-Tikhon clergy, but even this intervention couldn't help the self-proclaimed metropolitan attract a flock. Most of the faithful continued to view Tikhon as their spiritual leader.

A supporter of the imprisoned patriarch remembered watching the "pseudo-metropolitan" arriving at the cathedral in a sleek black taxi. "His appearance was eye-catching because of his extravagance: the little square moustache, fashionable during the 1920s; the Mephisthophelean beard (during the 1930s the 'metropolitan' shaved it off); the characteristic aquiline nose, bristling black hair, constantly half-open mouth, throaty voice, jerky movements. The ecstatic admirers known as 'sisters in white kerchiefs' met him on the steps."[8] But the church was almost empty. A few dozen people were scattered about, their adoring eyes fixed on their idol in his extravagant robe embroidered with icons, similar to one Tikhon had worn.[9]

The Greek writer Nikos Kazantzakis visited the cathedral during the period when it was occupied by Vvedensky and was deeply affected by the scene. "The boundless temple which had been the boast of czarist Russia was empty, unlighted, and unheated, the multicolored processions of gilt-haloed saints freezing in the desolate winter darkness. The little old lady who kept watch at the offertory table over an empty plate containing not a single kopeck was not sufficient to warm this whole sacred, shivering flock with her breath, which issued like smoke from her mouth and nostrils." Wandering about in the semidarkness, Kazantzakis heard the sweet sound of men and women singing psalms in the gallery above. He climbed the spiral staircase and found himself in a gilt chapel, with lighted candles, "kneeling people, and the sanctuary filled with deacons, priests, and prelates dressed in gold, dressed in silk." The past seemed alive here. "The men were for the most part old, with side whiskers; they seemed like former noblemen, or like doormen in noble houses. The women had their hair cowled with snow-white wimples. Christ glittered on the iconostasis, well fed and rubicund, his breast covered with decorations — human hands, eyes, and hearts of silver and gold."[10]

In 1923 the cathedral was the setting for an important propaganda event, the Second All-Russian Synod of the Russian Orthodox Church. Vvedensky formulated the main task of the second synod in his book *Church and Revolution*, which was essentially a relentless attack on Tikhon and his followers.[11] The synod's purpose was "the final liquidation of 'tikhonovism.'" Adopting the crude language used by government propaganda organs, Vvedensky wrote that it was finally time to "destroy all this reactionary scum" and to create "normal" relations between church and state.[12]

The second synod was planned as a total repudiation of the synod of 1917–19. Organized by the Living Church, the Union of the Ancient Apostles Church, the Renaissance, and other reformist groups, the assembly included sixty-six moderate supporters of Tikhon. The participants succeeded in achieving representation of seventy-two of the seventy-four dioceses of the Russian Orthodox Church, but Tuchkov, secretary of the Anti-Religious Commission, was disappointed. The government's war against the church had provoked the outrage of clergy, politicians, the press, and the public in many countries, from Poland to America, and Tuchkov hoped to use the second synod to turn Western opinion in a more favorable direction.[13] If the synod was properly organized, he told Vvedensky, the entire West would be attracted to Moscow. Although Vvedensky assured him the West would come, only one representative of a foreign church showed up to participate, and even the Moscow-based envoys of the patriarchs of Constantinople and Alexandria decided to ignore the openly political event.

Just five years earlier the cathedral had echoed to the dread syllables of the anathema pronounced on the godless Bolsheviks. This time the words were different. The synod sent "greetings to the supreme organ of workers' and peasants' power and to V. I. Lenin, the leader of the world." The Communists were lauded for realizing the ideals of the New Testament. "The great October revolt realizes the great principles of equality and labor expressed in Christian teaching. All over the world, the powerful exploit the weak. Only in Soviet Russia has the struggle against this social dishonesty begun," wrote the synod participants in their address.[14]

Vvedensky, using all the power of eloquence, proclaimed that the teachings of Communism and the teachings of Christ were identical. "Marxists, communists, Soviet power do not follow Christ. Marxists, communists, Soviet power work for the realization of Christ's precepts. Can you say that they are antichrists?" Furthermore, Vvedensky thundered, the revolutionaries who had suffered martyrdom in czarist times would help to create the kingdom of heaven on earth. Mentioning Dostoevsky and Marx, Vvedensky compared the Russian Revolution to the Second Coming.[15] This idea dominated synod discussions, along with the glorification of Soviet power in general and Lenin in particular.

The synod's final resolution directed church members not to equate Soviet power with the power of the Antichrist. On the contrary, Soviet power was the only power in the world dedicated to realizing the kingdom of heaven on earth through state operations.[16] The bearded Orthodox priests made a substantial addition to Christian teaching by denouncing capitalism as the eighth deadly sin. Yet even this "cordial support" for the Bolshevik cause was not sufficient for the government or the GPU. It was necessary to destroy the "scum." The synod obediently moved to strip Tikhon of his power, depriving him not only of his office but even of his priesthood.[17] But when Tikhon was informed of their decision, he rejected it as noncanonical.[18]

In the West, the synod did not have the effect Tuchkov had hoped for. Western opinion was summarized in the words of one foreign newspaper, reprinted in *Izvestia:* "It is not necessary to be a churchgoer or even a believer. It is enough to be a human being who has not lost all human dignity to accuse these descendants of Judas Iscariot."[19]

Suddenly, on June 26, 1923, a laconic statement about the liberation of the imprisoned patriarch was published in Soviet newspapers. The government had lost the battle against the powerless old man who had demonstrated such unexpected resistance. The plan to replace Tikhon and his followers with the Living Church had proved a mistake. It was the beginning of the end for the obnovlentsi. They continued to use the cathedral, though services became infrequent. The chill, the twilight, the dampness that oozed from the walls, all discouraged people from entering. On one occasion, it was decided to burn "unnecessary" old books and office papers, but the warmth generated reached barely more than a meter away from the stove. Vvedensky preferred to hold services in the gallery, where it was slightly warmer and dryer.[20] In 1928, he too was ordered to leave the building. The state no longer needed the Living Church.

Lilacs still bloomed in the park around the cathedral, and courting couples still sat on the steps in the evening to enjoy the sight of the city lights reflected in the river. But the building was dead, "deprived of God."[21] Its spiritual death would soon be followed by physical destruction.

PART FOUR

The Tower of Babel

Chapter Twenty-three

In 1919, as a tribute to the revolution, the Visual Arts Department of the People's Commissariat of Enlightenment commissioned Vladimir Tatlin to design a monument to the Third International. The location was not specified, because the future capital of the dictatorship of the proletariat had yet to be determined. This commission reflected the importance Lenin gave to the Comintern (the Communist International), which had been founded in Moscow in March 1919.[1] The delegates who gathered in the Kremlin to hear Lenin speak about the glorious new era were certain that the worldwide triumph of Communism was inevitable, if not in a few months then in a few years at most.

Tatlin believed that the new culture required an entirely new kind of monument. As the art critic Nikolai Punin, who was close to avant-garde circles, explained: "He believes that it is necessary to put an end to [monuments in the form of] human figures. Contemporary monuments must, first of all, correspond to the common urge toward synthesis of the different types of art we observe today. . . . The very plan, the very project of a monument, not in details but in general, must satisfy the architect, the sculptor, and the painter."[2]

Tatlin's conception was a gigantic steel tower four hundred meters high — the tallest structure in the world — in the form of two conical spirals soaring upward around a tilted girderlike spine painted red. Suspended within this steel skeleton would be three enormous geometric structures of glass — a cube, a pyramid, and a cylinder — to house the administrative and legislative bodies of the Comintern, the new world government. These three structures would rotate at different speeds. The cube, at the base of the tower, would house the legislature and require a year to complete its revolution. Above was the pyramid, housing the Comintern's executive offices, which would rotate once a month; and above the pyramid was a cylinder, for mass communications, which would rotate once a day.[3]

Realizing the vital role propaganda would play in the new society, Tatlin paid special attention to the information center that was to crown the

tower. It would feature not only a radio transmitter and telephone and telegraph stations but powerful light projectors that would cast slogans onto
the cloudy skies. A gigantic cinema screen would transmit news flashes
over long distances, and a fleet of automobiles and motorbikes decorated
with a tower logo would distribute proclamations, appeals, and leaflets to
the whole city. Propaganda would be inescapable.[4]

Advanced critics, who had shuddered at the unsightly plaster busts of
revolutionary heroes that were becoming ubiquitous throughout Russia,
considered Tatlin's tower an alternative to garden-variety agitprop. Many
understood well that the design was a conceptual artwork, a symbol rather
than a plan for a real structure. The actor Konstantin Miklashevsky called
it a "greenhouse for growing pineapples." The avant-garde artist Ivan Puni
labeled it a manifestation of "ideological absurdity," while the critic Nikolai
Radlov described it as a "horrible beast, ridiculous and naive, with a radio-
telephone horn on its head and the Legislative Assembly of the Third International in its belly."[5]

In Berlin, Belgrade, and New York, Tatlin's tower was interpreted by
admirers as a symbol of both the October Revolution and the Russian
avant-garde. The idealistic, unrealizable project satisfied a widespread
yearning for a new cathedral of Bolshevism. The Czech avant-garde artist
Karel Teige, who was sympathetic to Tatlin's aims and admired his innovative approach to architecture, wrote that Tatlin had tried to combine the
utilitarian and the spiritual. During the Renaissance the triangle had been
the symbol for such unity, but for Tatlin it was the spiral. "Remember the
words of Trotsky: 'The powerful steel spiral . . . opening itself to the future,
can be an image of the ideological content of the revolution.'"[6] But Teige
thought Tatlin had gone too far and objected to the irrational character
of his design. Why should a palace with auditoriums and offices be in the
shape of a tower? Why did all these spaces rotate? "A tower is an efficient
shape for a radio station, an observatory, a lookout, a lighthouse, but not
for public halls. We can imagine a skyscraper—but a tower?"[7]

The gigantic scale and hierarchic tripartite structure of Tatlin's tower
recalled Vitberg's cathedral. Although neither man had any architectural
training, their visionary projects were nonetheless destined to become
unique expressions of the zeitgeist. Tatlin was even more of an idealist than
Vitberg. He dreamed of revolving glass structures and light projected into
the sky of 1919 Petrograd, a city where people heated their apartments by

burning their libraries, their pianos, and their furniture in portable iron stoves, ironically called *burzhuiki* (bourgeois). With fanatical zeal he constructed a monument to the future in a city where a horse that fell dead on the street was stripped of its flesh in minutes by starving people.

Tatlin was still working on his project in 1922, when political events unexpectedly intervened to change the nature of the commission. On December 30 of that year, the First Congress of Soviets of the Union of Soviet Socialist Republics, meeting in Moscow, adopted a decree that established the socialist commonwealth of nations. In the jubilant atmosphere that filled the hall after the pronouncement of the new Soviet Union, Sergei Kirov, one of the founders of the Trans-Caucasian Republic, delivered a visionary speech that corresponded to the mood of the event.

"I believe that the moment will soon arrive when there will no longer be enough seats for delegates from all the republics of the union," Kirov said. That was why he urged the Central Executive Committee to construct a fitting monument within which the representatives of labor could meet. That monument should be erected in the capital of the Soviet Union, on one of the best and finest squares, where the workers and peasants would find everything necessary to "broaden their horizon." At the same time, the building had to be "a symbol of the growing might and triumph of communism, not only among ourselves, but also over there, in the West."[8]

"Comrades!" Kirov concluded, "perhaps then the European proletariat—for the most part still asleep, still skeptical of the triumph of the Revolution, still doubtful of the correctness of the tactics of the Communist Party—when it beholds this enchanted palace of workers and peasants, will realize that we are here to stay. . . . Perhaps then they will understand that at last the moment has come to shake the damnable capitalist world, so that everything that has oppressed us through the centuries is hurled into the abyss of history."[9]

Kirov's speech reflected the new spirit of the Bolshevik movement. The revolutionary idealism of 1919 had dissipated. The adoption of the New Economic Policy (NEP) in 1921 and the abandonment of War Communism had resulted in a normalization of everyday life. Private stores selling caviar, champagne, and other luxuries had sprung up. Life was much easier, but for many militant communists, this "temporary retreat," as the party leadership described the NEP, was a betrayal of the ideals of the revolu-

tion. For many radicals, 1921 marked the beginning of a period of "fatigue,"
in the words of the literary critic Pyotr Kogan.[10] The world revolution that
had seemed inevitable a few years earlier had been a dream. Attempts to
establish soviet republics in Hungary and various regions of Germany had
failed. Disappointed by the lack of revolutionary zeal among the Western
proletariat, the Bolshevik leadership was turning toward the undeveloped
countries of the East. A note of bitter disillusionment resounded in Kirov's
speech when he urged the audience to "let our friends and our foes see us
as 'semi-Asiatic.' For all that they superciliously say of us, we can adorn this
sinful earth with edifices that our enemies have never dreamed of."[11]

The palace Kirov imagined, unlike Tatlin's tower, was constructed not
for some abstract "world Sovnarkom" (Council of People's Commissars)
but for the government of the newly established Soviet Union. Kirov had
no doubt where the palace should be erected, "on one of the best and finest
squares" in the capital. From now on, it would be up to the world to follow
the example of the new country. The Bolsheviks had no intention of waiting for anyone to join the revolution. Kirov's speech sounded more like an
exercise in revolutionary rhetoric than a realistic proposal.

A year later, in 1923, the Moscow city council announced a competition
for designs for a building that would house both government offices and a
cultural center. It would be erected in the very center of Moscow, on the
site of Okhotny Ryad, the historic meatpacking district, and it would be
immense, a reflection of the leaders' wish to surpass the capitalist world
in everything, including the size and grandeur of its buildings. The new
palace would house an auditorium big enough to hold eight thousand
people, with a podium for the three-hundred-member presidium, as well
as a smaller auditorium for twenty-five hundred. There would also be a
meeting hall for the Moscow city council, designed to hold twenty-five
hundred; a meeting hall for the Communist Party Committee of Moscow;
two concert halls, for one thousand and five hundred people, respectively;
a dining hall for fifteen hundred; and the Museum of Social Knowledge.
The palace would be magnificent, in keeping with the ideas it symbolized,
but its opulence must be expressed in simple, contemporary forms rather
than in any specific historical style.[12]

The country's leading constructivist architects, including the Vesnin
brothers and Ilya Golosov, submitted designs, but to the intense disappointment of the avant-garde architectural community the first prize was

awarded to Nikolai Trotsky, whose pompous project reminded people of an "overblown cross between Ledoux and Palladio."[13]

With the exception of the Vesnin brothers, whose project incorporated a skyscraper, none of the contestants included a tower as an element in their designs. In any case, the project was never realized. The colossal palace of labor was forgotten, along with many other dreams of the revolution. But the ghost of the gigantic tower continued to lead a spectral existence: the need to create an architectural symbol of the revolution had entered the mass consciousness, and soon a new occasion arose. On January 21, 1924, Lenin died.

Chapter Twenty-four

The dead leader had to be commemorated. Within weeks of Lenin's funeral, before the shock of his death wore off, discussion began about a monument befitting a person of his stature. In an article published in *Izvestia*, Leonid Krasin, Lenin's close friend and comrade in arms, called for a commemoration in the form of architecture, "the most democratic, the most popular of all the arts."[1] This would be no ordinary monument, Krasin proclaimed, but a "place that will surpass in importance both Mecca and Jerusalem."[2]

His article inspired a flood of letters to the newspaper. A Comrade Orlov, an official in the Foreign Affairs Commissariat, who believed that the monument should exalt ideas rather than personalities, proposed that a colossal tower, like the Eiffel Tower or perhaps even higher, be erected above Lenin's grave. At the base would be giant flywheels whirling to recreate the sounds of factories, and on the top a rotating globe as well as a radio-telegraph transmitter connecting it with the entire world.[3] Another correspondent, who believed it was necessary to commemorate personalities rather than ideas, proposed a colossal figure of Lenin pointing toward the West that would rise high over the Kremlin. At night it would be bathed in red light. Ten years later these two ideas—the tower and the colossal figure of Lenin—would be combined.[4]

One of the most ambitious designs came from the young architect Viktor Balikhin, a member of the avant-garde Association of New Architects (ASNOVA). His vision of Lenin's monument, which he described in

a letter to *Pravda* of March 15, 1924, united aspects of Tatlin's project with
Kirov's proposal. Balikhin's monument to Lenin would be no less than
"the headquarters of the World Revolution, the headquarters of the Third
Communist International, the center of the World Union of Soviet Socialist
Republics." All national and international revolutionary congresses as well
as conferences and mass meetings would take place within its precincts.
Furthermore, Balikhin was convinced that the proletarians of the world
would unite to construct it. "Generations of Red architects from all over
the world will be inspired by this monument; it will act as a giant magnet,
drawing the pattern of all the buildings, roads, squares, and cities within its
force field and pulling them towards it, like a pole."[5]

Balikhin's monument was in the shape of a gigantic cube. Interestingly,
he wasn't the only representative of the avant-garde who believed the cube
to be the most appropriate form for Lenin's memorial. The artist Kazimir
Malevich wrote that Lenin's crypt must be "like a cube, like the symbol of
eternity, because He is inside it for eternity."[6]

Like Tatlin, Balikhin envisioned light projection as an important element
of the memorial complex so that Lenin's teachings, slogans, and reports of
the revolution's worldwide successes could be shown on giant screens and
read by thousands. "Projectors will illuminate neighboring villages and
hamlets, parks and squares, compelling everyone to address his thoughts
to Lenin even at night."[7] Balikhin knew exactly where his monument-cube
should be installed. In a letter to *Pravda,* he stated that the "best place for
it in Moscow is the place where the Cathedral of Christ the Savior stands.
The cathedral has no value as a historical or artistic monument. . . . There
is no fundamental reason to leave intact the cathedral, which could become
an insuperable obstacle to the realization of the greatest idea."[8] His scheme
was too extreme for *Pravda,* however, and the editor returned his letter
with a note informing him that the newspaper would look ridiculous if it
published his grandiose plan, which would entail demolishing entire city
blocks as well as the immense cathedral.[9] Balikhin was undiscouraged. In
1924 his design was exhibited in the Kremlin during the Fifth Congress
of the Communist International. But then, for the next eight years, it was
forgotten by everyone except the architect and his ASNOVA colleagues.

Although the ghosts of a tower and of a Lenin memorial may have
haunted the imagination of both professional architects and ordinary

(above) 32. Moscow River embankment, 1889. Photo by Ivan Barshchevsky.

(left) 33. Christmas card, late nineteenth century.

34. Parade in front of the cathedral during the unveiling of the
monument to Alexander III on May 30, 1912.

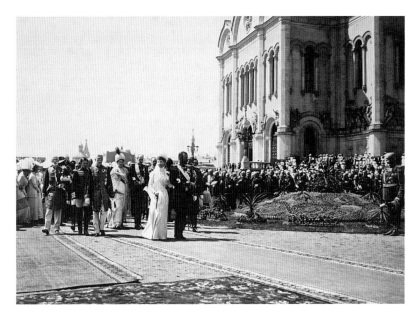

35. Emperor Nicholas II and Empress Alexandra with their suite in front of the
cathedral on the centenary of the battle of Borodino, September 1912.

36. Religious procession on the centenary of the battle of
Borodino, September 1912.

(above) 37. Vladimir Tatlin, sketch for the Monument to the Third International, from Nikolai Punin's *Pamiatnik III Internatsionalu,* published in Moscow, 1920.

(right) 38. Photo of the demolition of the monument to Alexander III on the cover of *Novy LEF* (New Left), 1927, designed by Alexander Rodchenko.

39. Alexei Samsonov, new detachment of Red commanders, *Prozhektor*, June 1929.

40. Demolition of the cathedral on December 5, 1933. Still from documentary footage by Vladislav Mikosha.

(above) 41. The cathedral
after the demolition on
December 5, 1933. Still from
documentary footage by
Vladislav Mikosha.

(right) 42. Pyotr Riabov,
Moscow of the Future,
woodcut, 1930s.

43. The reliefs by Alexander Loganovsky after their removal from the facade.

44. The Commission for Registration of Valuables of the Cathedral of Christ the Savior. Still from documentary footage by Vladislav Mikosha.

45. Commission for the Construction of the Palace of Soviets, 1930.
Lazar Kaganovich is in the foreground.

СТРОИТЕЛЬСТВО
МОСКВЫ

1933 5-6

(left) 46. Photomontage
featuring Boris Iofan's
first design for the
Palace of Soviets. Cover
of *Stroitel'stvo Moskvy*
(Moscow Construction),
1933.

(below) 47. Iofan's design
(section) for the Palace of
Soviets. From *Stroitel'stvo
Moskvy*, 1933.

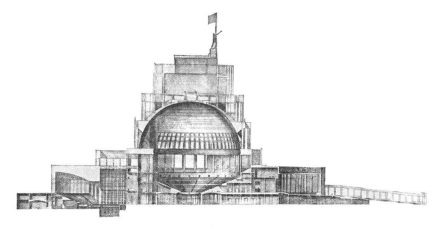

СРАВНИТЕЛЬНАЯ СХЕМА ВСЕХ МИРОВЫХ ПАМЯТНИКОВ АРХИТЕКТУРЫ И ВЕ

1. Кельнский собор—160 м.
2. Пирамида Хеопса—137 м.
3. Штрассбургский собор—142 м.
4. Церковь Стефана в Вене—139 м.
5. Церковь Мартина в Ландсхуте—137 м.
6. Собор Петра в Риме—143 м.
7. Антверпенский собор—130 м.
8. Церковь Михаила в Гамбурге—143 м.
9. Амьенский собор—126 м.
10. Фрейбургский собор—126 м.
11. Хефренская пирамида—126 м.
12. Руанский Собор (Колокольня)—151 м.
13. Собор в Шартре—122 м.
14. Собор в Метце—118 м.
15. Шпиц Петропавловской крепости
в Ленинграде—109 м.

48–49. Schematic drawing comparing the greatest monuments in the world with Iofan's Palace of Soviets. From *Stroitel'stvo Moskvy*, 1933.

...ЧАЙШИХ ЗДАНИЙ МИРА И ПРОЕКТА ДВОРЦА СОВЕТОВ АРХ. Б. ИОФАН

19. Церковь Павла в Лондоне—109 м.
20. Миланский собор—108 м.
21. Ульмский собор (незакончен) ныне—161 м.
22. Ратуша в Брюсселе—90 м.
23. Башня Азинелли в Болонье—98 м.
24. Собор в Малине—107 м.
25. Орлеанский собор—105 х.
26. Дворец инвалидов в Париже—104 м.
29. Исаакиевский собор в Ленинграде—97 м.
31. Франкфуртский собор—84 м.
33. Колокольня Ивана Великого в Москве—97 м.
34. Реймский собор—81 м.
35. Базельский собор—64 м.
36. Пантеон в Париже—79 м.
37. Башня Кутб—Минар в Дели—73 м.
38. Церковь Театинеров в Мюнхене—73 м.
39. Руанский собор—75 м.

40. Вестминстерское Аббатство в Лондоне—69 м.
44. Собор Нотрдам в Париже—66 м.
45. Монумент в Лондоне—61 м.
47. Фарфоровая башня в Нанкине (разрушена)—64 м.
49. Айя София в Константинополе—78 м.
51. Башня в Пизе—55 м.
57. Акведук в Ниме—47 м.
60. Башня Антония в Риме—44 м.
65. Здание телефонной станции в Нью-Йорке—215 м.
86. Эмпайр Стэт Билдинг в Нью-Йорке (318) 407 м.
87. Вульворт Стэт Билдинг в Нью-Йорке—(233) 255 м.
89. Транспортейшен Стэт Билдинг в Нью-Йорке—(165) 203 м.
89. Зингер Стэт Билдинг в Нью-Йорке—(186) 209 м.
90. Крайслер Стэт Билдинг в Нью-Йорке—(262) 330 м.
91. Эйфелева башня—300 м.
92. Принятый в основу проекта Дворца Советов проект арх. Б. Иофан—220 м.

50. Solomon Teligater's plan for the reconstruction of Moscow, dominated by the Palace of Soviets. Flyleaf of the book *General'nyi plan rekonstruktsii goroda Moskvy* (General plan of reconstruction of the city of Moscow), 1936.

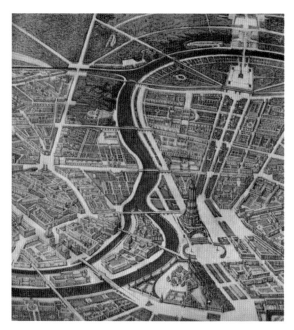

51. Lenin and Stalin superimposed on a map of the future Moscow. The Palace of Soviets is to the left of Stalin's head. Teligater, cover, *General'nyi plan rekonstruktsii goroda Moskvy*, 1936.

(above) 52. Model of the Palace
of Soviets exhibited in the
Soviet Pavilion at the New York
World's Fair in 1939. In the
background is Yuri Pimenov's
panoramic *Parade of Athletes.*

(left) 53. The Soviet pavilions at
the World's Fair in Paris (1937)
and New York (1939) compared
in height to the Palace of
Soviets. Photomontage by N. A.
Peshkova and I. N. Ralitsky,
from *USSR in Construction,*
1939.

54. El Lissitzky, the Palace of Soviets with the Kremlin in the background. Photomontage from *USSR in Construction*, 1937.

55. Muscovites enjoying the heated swimming pool in winter, 1980s.

(above) 56. A contemporary copy of Alexander Loganovsky's sculptural
group being raised into position. Saint Sergei of Radonezh blesses
Dmitry Donskoy before the battle of Kulikovo.

(below) 57. The face of God, part of the Trinity painted at the apex
of the dome. Photo by Artem Zadikian.

(above) 58. The funeral of former president Boris Yeltsin, April 25, 2007, in the cathedral reconstructed during his presidency. Photo by Aleksei Kaluzhsky.

(below) 59. The Cathedral of Christ the Savior.
Photo by Konstantin Kokoshkin, 2005.

Soviet citizens, the Cathedral of Christ the Savior was a reality. Abandoned by the obnovlentsi at the end of the 1920s, the colossus loomed over the city, locked and empty — "deprived of god," in Kataev's words.[10] But it was still the largest building in Moscow and an inescapable reminder of the not-so-distant past.

In 1923, during his brief exile in Berlin, Viktor Shklovsky, the avant-garde theoretician, recollected the horror of the first postrevolutionary years: "Ravens flew over the Cathedral of Christ the Savior in a spiral net as if they were trying to encircle Moscow. The ravens flew in hordes, and I felt like an infantryman smashed by a cavalry attack. A few ravens — still, they were many — circled the dome of the cathedral like flies. It looked dirty. Ravens screamed and made a commotion and cawed and shrieked in the air over the city that was half hidden in dirty snow."[11] Shklovsky remembered the cathedral in summer as well. A member of the outlawed Socialist Revolutionary party, he took refuge in the thick bushes that surrounded it when he was hunted by the Cheka.[12]

To Shklovsky, the cathedral was a symbol of doom. A little later, in Russian literature of the mid-twenties, it became a sign of stability. Mikhail Bulgakov, in his satirical futuristic tale *The Fatal Eggs* (1924), which describes scientific experiments leading to the creation of an early Soviet version of Jurassic Park, uses the cathedral to frame surrealistic events. At the beginning of the tale, the cathedral is visible through the windows of Professor Persikov, the hero. "Reflections of varicolored lights flashed through the plate-glass windows of the room, and far and high above, next to the dark, heavy cap of the Cathedral of Christ, hung the misty, pale crescent of the moon."[13] At the end of the narrative, when the nightmare is over, the cathedral reappears as the symbol of returning normalcy: "And in the spring of 1929, Moscow once more was dancing, glittering, and flashing with lights. Again the rolling of mechanical carriages rustled on the pavements, and the crescent of the moon hung, as though suspended on a fine thread, over the helmet of the Cathedral of Christ."[14]

In his memoir, *Novel without Lies*, published in 1926, the poet Anatoly Mariengof remembered: "One mild April night, we were sitting near the Kamenny Bridge. The dome of the Cathedral of Christ the Savior floated in the dark water of the Moscow River like a gigantic golden boat. Infrequent cars skimmed over the bridge, eyes goggling and tires hissing. Waves beat their cold, glassy bodies against stone. I wanted to talk about unusual

things with uncommon words. I took a cobblestone and threw it into the
river, in the reflection of the dome. The golden boat shattered into sparks,
glittering fragments, and black dashes. Look! Gold solid and flat again
floated in the river. The cobblestone that had sliced through it was forgotten and left no trace."[15] The metaphor was transparent: it was impossible to destroy the cathedral or to wreck the spirit of the city.

The abandoned structure remained a symbol of Moscow and continued
to dominate the skyline. It appeared in every photograph of the city center,
along with the Kremlin, the Pashkov house, the river, and the bridges. It
was mentioned often without a thought, as people mention familiar things
they pass every day. But the city was living the last years of its "normal" life.
The brief era of NEP was coming to an end.

One of the most striking sequences in Eisenstein's film *October*, released
in 1929, was the demolition by revolutionary workers and soldiers of the
gigantic statue of Alexander III. The figure of the seated monarch is encased in ropes, like Gulliver, and then slowly — hands, legs, and finally
head — it topples over. Later in the film, when the city of Petrograd and the
fate of the revolution are threatened by General Kornilov's army, the ruined
colossus comes back to life, as the destruction of the monument is shown
in reverse.

This statue of the czar that plays such an important role in the film wasn't
in Petrograd at all. It was in Moscow, near the cathedral, and it was destroyed in 1917. Eisenstein exercised artistic license by moving it — actually,
a papier-mâché copy — to the former capital so he could film its destruction
by the revolutionary masses.[16] The sequence was staged in August 1927,
after most of the film had been shot in Leningrad. According to an article
published in the newspaper *Kino* in July, the remains of the original monument had been found in the cathedral cellars and were used to make plaster molds for the papier-mâché monarch, who was erected in his original
place.[17]

In the film, the bronze czar and gigantic cathedral in the background
symbolize the rotten autocracy, and the destruction of the statue, the revolution. In his memoir of the events of 1917, Eisenstein recollected another
monument to Alexander III, which stood in Petrograd, near the Moscow
railway station on Znamenskaia Square. "At that time Kerensky was roar-
ing against those who wanted to see a guillotine erected on Znamenskaia

Square. I took it as a personal offence. How often, in passing the monument to Alexander III, I had tried to imagine the 'widow' — Dr. Guillotin's
machine standing on its basalt pedestal. . . . I was anxious to be a witness of
history. But what kind of history is possible without a guillotine!"[18] Eisenstein's wish came true. He saw the guillotine of Russian history in action
and escaped it himself only by luck. However, in the late 1920s, when his
avant-garde cinema was still widely acclaimed, the demolition of the czar's
monument seemed like the realization of the young radical's dream on the
eve of the October revolution.

Eisenstein wasn't the first who gave symbolic value to the destruction
of the czar's monument. In March 1927 Alexander Rodchenko designed a
cover for the third issue of *Novy LEF* (New Left Front), edited by Vladimir Mayakovsky, featuring a photograph of workers preparing to dismantle
the bronze czar; another photo was published inside the magazine. This
image on the cover of the country's major radical avant-garde publication
was more than appropriate. The issue opened with Mayakovsky's poem
addressed to the youth corrupted by NEP who believed that the revolution
had failed. Mayakovsky insisted it wasn't true. The destruction of the idol
of autocracy was a metaphor for the revolutionary values that were sorely
needed in 1927, the tenth anniversary of the revolution. Avant-garde radicals had to remind the NEP men, the new soviet bourgeoisie, that the force
of revolutionary iconoclasm was still alive.[19]

But the cathedral, symbol of the hated monarchy, still stood in the center
of Moscow, capital of the proletarian state, even if the monarch was gone.
Its days were numbered. Like the bronze czar, it was destined for ritual
destruction.

Chapter Twenty-five

By 1931, when the first Five Year Plan ended, the face of the country
had been changed, for good or ill. Gigantic projects on the scale of the
Dnieper Hydroelectric Station had been realized, about fifteen hundred
factories had been constructed, and agriculture was now collectivized. At
this moment, it was decided that the fantastic palace Kirov had called for
in 1922 at the First Congress of Soviets — his symbol of the growing might
and triumph of Communism — would be constructed. A special body

was formed to realize the task, called the Council on Construction of the Palace of Soviets of the Presidium of the Central Executive Committee of the USSR. It included a number of important officials—Molotov, Voroshilov, Yenukidze—and was granted legislative powers. The Construction Administration, led by Mikhail Krukov, was responsible for management. This complex bureaucratic structure was put in place before it was decided what to build or where.[1]

Soviet officials decided against holding an open competition for the project because the task was unprecedented. Instead, they organized a closed preliminary contest intended to define the project more precisely and to pick a site for the new structure. Twelve architects and architectural groups were invited to participate, including the rationalist Nikolai Ladovsky, the constructivist Alexander Nikolsky, the eclectic Boris Iofan, and such associations as the Union of Contemporary Architects (OSA), the Union of Urban Architects (ARU), and ASNOVA. Sixteen projects were submitted, because one participant entered two plans and three unsolicited plans were received.[2] The projects reflected a broad stylistic spectrum, from classical revivalism to radical constructivism. But, according to Alexey Shchusev, the renowned architect and designer of the Lenin Mausoleum, none was adequate. The contest, in his opinion, did not yield enough "mature" proposals.[3]

One important idea emerged, however. The ASNOVA group wanted to construct the palace on the site of the Cathedral of Christ the Savior, opposite the Kremlin. Balikhin's cube, which had been shown to the Comintern delegates in 1924, was now put forth again as a proposal for the Palace of Soviets. Still dreaming of world revolution, Balikhin and his ASNOVA colleagues envisioned the gigantic cube as a living organism, alive with demonstrations and revolutionary mass festivals. On one facet of the cube would be a list of members of the World Union of Soviet Socialist Republics, to which the names of new republics would constantly be added. Topping the list would be the date of the establishment of the World Union of Soviet Socialist Republics, in red electric lights.[4]

The Acting Technical Council for the Construction of the Palace of Soviets was entrusted with picking the site, and after long discussion it endorsed the ASNOVA proposal. Some of the competing architects preferred Okhotny Ryad, because they thought it would be difficult to build a gigantic palace on the cathedral site, but Balikhin found an unexpected supporter at the very top of the Soviet hierarchy. Boris Iofan later remembered that Stalin himself inspected the site, together with the Council on Construction and its head, Molotov. On that day, Iofan wrote, the site of the cathedral was chosen. Stalin liked its beautiful setting, its proximity to the Kremlin, and its location in the center of the city on the bank of the Moscow River. With great attention, he analyzed the opinions of the architects, many of whom criticized the configuration of the site and its relatively small size. It was possible, Iofan thought, that some of them opposed the destruction of the cathedral, though they could not defend its architectural qualities.[5]

Lazar Kaganovich, the all-powerful head of the Moscow party organization and the moving spirit behind the reconstruction of the capital, remembered at the end of the 1980s how the site for the palace was chosen: "Various proposals were made to the Moscow Committee, among others my proposal to construct it on Lenin's Mountains [the former Sparrow Hills]. Everybody agreed that the place was good, but it was far from the Kremlin, and it was necessary to construct it close to the Kremlin. Then the Moscow Committee suggested that it be constructed where Manezh Square is now."[6] But there were objections that the Manezh might be damaged. Then, Kaganovich continued, the proposal was made to demolish the building housing the Comintern, but this idea was unacceptable because the immense structure to be built would overwhelm the Rumyantsev Museum (later the Lenin Library).

Finally, the site of the Cathedral of Christ the Savior came up for discussion. "The resolution of this question was neither quick nor easy," Kaganovich claimed. "The Moscow Committee and I personally had objections. I can say frankly that we believed such a step would offend the religious part of the population. The Moscow city council and, as I remember, especially its head, Comrade Ivanov, supported the idea of constructing the Palace of Soviets on the site of the Cathedral of Christ the Savior. The question was discussed many times during meetings of the 'Council on Construction of the Palace' called by the government and chaired by Vyacheslav Molotov, the head of the Council of People's Commissars. Finally, in 1931, the decision was adopted to construct the Palace of Soviets near the Kremlin, on the bank of the Moscow River, in the area of Volkhonka and Saimonovsky Passage, by demolition of various buildings, including the Cathedral of Christ the Savior."[7]

Molotov reported the decision to the government, and Stalin agreed with it. Kaganovich added that a number of architects believed the cathedral to be of no great aesthetic value. Kaganovich, probably the only survivor of Stalin's circle who lived from the beginning to the end of the Soviet Union, tried to exculpate himself in his late memoirs, but it is clear from his account that the decision, which was backed by Stalin, was not open to debate. The cathedral was doomed.

Stalin supported Balikhin's site proposal without sharing his aesthetic utopianism. Although Stalin wasn't interested in memorial cubes or futuristic light projections, he did appreciate the symbolism of erecting a monument to the new order on the site of a memorial to the old regime. The first Five Year Plan had coincided with the last assault against the church, and the demolition of the cathedral would symbolize the party's victory over the last anti-Soviet entity in the country.

On July 18, 1931, *Izvestia* published a decree concerning the architectural competition. It stated that "the Palace of Soviets must be specially designed to accommodate congresses and large public assemblies. It must be easily accessible to great multitudes of demonstrating laborers and workers. The palace should be fitted out with the best equipment to provide the technical apparatus needed for revolutionary events, including theatrical and musical productions."[8] And, the decree continued, it would be constructed on the site of Christ the Savior.

On December 3, 1931, the famous children's writer Kornei Chukovsky found himself unexpectedly detained in Moscow when a baggage porter failed to deliver a promised black-market ticket for the Red Arrow train to Leningrad. The next day Chukovsky witnessed a historic event, which he recorded in his diary that night.

> The day was sunny and frosty, with a silver and azure sky. The Number 10 tram took me not to Kamenny Bridge but to Zamoskvoretsky, because the Cathedral of Christ the Savior was being blown up in the vicinity. A cannon shot three times, and five minutes later—no sooner—the bluish smoke so beautifully lit by the sun floated up. Boys with red noses (because of the frost) sitting on fences and heaps of earth and talking:
> "Look at the green light—it's a signal."

"Two signals already."

"Pigeons, pigeons!"

"Those are carrier pigeons!"

"The second shot. Oh, it was loud!"

"Two shots already!"

"Three."

They are chewing bread in the frost.

"There won't be any more shots."

"You're lying. There will be."

Another explosion, and smoke, and the middle tower becomes very short.

A woman looks and weeps.

I walked along the other shore of the Moscow River, and when I had almost reached the Kamenny Bridge, I was stopped by a patrol.

Where are you going? Didn't you see that the church has been demolished! I turned back.[9]

Chukovsky finally reached the apartment of his friend Mikhail Koltsov, the well-known political journalist (executed by Stalin in 1940), who lived in the House of Government, better known as the House on the Embankment, a huge constructivist structure inhabited by members of the political and cultural establishment. It was on the river, opposite the slowly disappearing cathedral. The two had a long talk, exchanging gossip and telling stories. They discussed everything but the destruction of the cathedral. But Chukovsky noted in his diary: "During the conversation, the explosions in the Cathedral of Christ the Savior continued."[10] The blasts made the house shake.

Andrei Kozarzhevsky, a professor at Moscow State University, who was a schoolboy at the time, later remembered that before demolition began a plank fence was erected around the church and gardens. And then one morning, passing on his way to school, he saw that a small square of gilded copper had been stripped from the church's central dome, revealing the iron framework beneath. Little by little, the copper facing disappeared, reminding him of the Chinese torture of cutting off small pieces of skin. "It would be better," he thought, "if they razed everything to the ground more quickly, with one blow."[11] After the most powerful explosion, an arch decorated with images of saints reared up against the December sky. It was surrounded by rubble. Each morning, Kozarzhevsky would approach the site expecting to see the golden domes and instead stumble on a gigantic heap of broken bricks, statues, and bent iron. It took a long time for the rubble to be removed.

International reaction to the destruction of the largest church in Russia was muted. Even those who deplored the action considered it an internal Soviet affair. On December 5 the Associated Press reported from Moscow: "Dynamite was exploded in the old Cathedral of the Redeemer today to complete the work of demolition started some time ago. The blasts were set off with intervals of an hour and by mid-afternoon almost the entire side of the great granite structure facing the river had been torn away." The *New York Times*, which published the report on December 6, added no editorial comment, showing more concern with the situation in Germany, where "Herr Hitler" had announced that he would not run for the chancellorship. Virtually the only international organization that protested the destruction was Roerich's Pact, organized by the Russian émigré artist and mystic Nicholas Roerich. However, despite his efforts to convince the governments of the world to ratify a convention protecting architectural and cultural monuments and to protest their demolition, public opinion was not aroused.[12]

It was the Russian people who suffered. Many among the intelligentsia shared Chukovsky's indifference to the cathedral's ruin, but the common people reacted very differently. There was nothing they could do except weep, like the woman Chukovsky saw in the street. Allan Monkhouse, an Englishman who spent more that twenty years in Moscow, wrote in his memoirs that the cathedral's destruction was a "cruel shock to the people of Moscow. On the site where it stood, the central portion of the palace of Soviets will rise. . . . I had looked upon the heap of blasted masonry which had been the Cathedral of the Savior with deep regret, but when I beheld a score of labourers shoveling the dust of this most sacred shrine into motorlorries, my feeling of regret became one of horror and disgust at this unnecessary act of sacrilege."[13]

Monkhouse understood the significance of the church's destruction: "I appreciated then for the first time that the U.S.S.R. is no longer a Christian country. The majority of its citizens to-day are not to be numbered amongst those who belong to the Christian Churches. Time is a wonderful healer, however, and flies fast in the U.S.S.R. . . . The children of Moscow in 1943 will know as little regarding Christianity as the youth in Great Britain to-day know of Buddhist rites in Thibet."[14]

An international competition for the Palace of Soviets was announced, although the leadership had already decided that the winner would be a Soviet architect. The original deadline for submission of projects, October 10, 1931, was extended to December 1. Some Politburo members were against inviting foreign architects to participate. "It will impose a very high responsibility, which Comrade Krukov isn't taking into account," Molotov wrote to Yenukidze.[15] But Comrade Krukov prevailed. The government did not want to advertise its course toward cultural isolationism.

The specifications were detailed and complicated. The palace was to have four main complexes within a single tall building. Group A was to include an auditorium large enough to hold 15,000 people, as well as other public spaces (totaling 15,720 square meters). Group B would consist of a small auditorium for 5,900 people, a library, and exhibition halls (16,280 square meters). Group C was to comprise two auditoriums for 500 people each and two smaller ones for 200 people each (2,800 square meters). Group D would house the executive and administrative offices (2,000 square meters). The total floor space was initially set at 36,800 square meters, but in September the figure was raised to 38,800. The palace was to be connected to the city center by a projected "Avenue of Ilyich," extending from Sverdlov Square to "the place of the former cathedral of the savior." (The word *savior* wasn't capitalized.)[16]

The competition attracted wide international attention: of the 160 projects submitted, twenty-four were foreign entries: eleven from the United States, five from Germany, three from France, two from Holland, and one each from Italy, Switzerland, and Estonia. The entrants included such international stars as Walter Gropius, Le Corbusier, and Erich Mendelsohn, designer of the striking Einstein Tower observatory in Potsdam. The constructivist artist Naum Gabo, who had no formal architectural training, also submitted a plan.

Le Corbusier was inspired to share his rapturous vision of the role of the future palace with Lunacharsky. "The Palace of Soviets is the crowning glory of the Five-Year Plan. What is the Five-Year Plan? It is a heroic attempt and truly majestic decision to create a new society and to provide conditions for life in complete harmony. At the core of the Five-Year Plan

lies an idea. What idea? Simply to make mankind happy. The USSR has
already struck the light of dawn over the whole world. All sincere hearts
are turned toward you. That is a victory. Architecture expresses the spirit
of the age. Consequently the majestic proportions and perfection of the
Palace of Soviets will express the goals you have been pursuing since 1918.
It must be there for the whole world to see."[17]

Le Corbusier expressed the excitement of all the foreign architects involved in the competition, who saw the USSR as a futuristic social experiment as well as a leading patron of modern art and architecture. At the
end of the 1920s, numerous Western architects, including Le Corbusier,
were involved in the rapid urbanization that accompanied the first Five
Year Plan, designing and building important projects in Soviet cities. A few
radical practitioners, including Hannes Meyer, director of the Bauhaus,
even moved to the USSR.[18] These Western architects saw Bolshevism as
the political analogue of artistic modernism, and, like their colleagues of
the Russian avant-garde, they mistakenly interpreted the beginnings of in-
dustrialization and the start of the Stalinist cultural revolution as a return
to the radicalism of the early revolutionary years. Like Ilya Ehrenburg, they
believed that France still lived in the nineteenth century and Germany in
the twentieth, but the Soviet Union had leaped ahead to the twenty-first.[19]

To Russian avant-garde architects, the competition offered an opportunity to win their battle with the traditionalists, who controlled many important architectural offices in the country. Among the Soviet participants
were the Vesnin brothers, Nikolai Ladovsky, Moisei Ginzburg, Ilya Golosov, and the ASNOVA group. The classicist camp was represented by Ivan
Zholtovsky, Boris Iofan, Alexey Shchusev, Dmitry Chechulin, and Anatoly
Zhukov, among others. One important name was not on the list. Tatlin,
creator of the Monument to the Third International, didn't enter the competition, but when the entries were exhibited publicly, he found them all
wanting and wrote to Yenukidze that they reflected "bourgeois ideology.
Our Soviet form is absent." Instead, he proposed a "building of absolutely
novel structural design," but nobody was interested any longer in the great
utopian's ideas.[20]

When the submitted projects were examined, it became clear that some
of the participants were confused by the specifications or had simply

chosen to ignore them. Although a single building was called for, some entrants submitted plans for a complex, with large and small auditoriums connected by corridors and surrounded by courtyards. They envisioned a place perfect for mass demonstrations, although this was not among the requirements. A bold high-rise had been called for, but too many of the entries were low, stocky buildings. Few of the architects incorporated towers into their projects. If dominating vertical elements were used at all, they were secondary and decorative, with little practical function.

Not only renowned architects sent in entries, however. As a true socialist phenomenon, the competition was open to everybody, and enthusiastic amateurs — students, cooks, doctors, accountants, laborers, and even a twelve-year-old schoolgirl — responded with designs and descriptions for a monument. Activists submitted their imaginative if naively symbolic designs, one proposing a building that had the same contours as the map of the USSR, topped with a gigantic statue of a proletarian brandishing a torch. Another suggested a building in the form of a tractor.[21] The nonprofessionals did, however, give the competition committee some good advice. A cook pointed out that one could not feed six thousand delegates without a kitchen. Another activist sent in an ingenious design for collapsible chairs that disappeared into storage in the floor.[22]

The professionals submitted 160 projects, and amateurs sent in about 150.[23] The commission was obliged to examine this flood of unprofessional entries seriously, even knowing that most of them were no more than daydreams. The professionals were willing to learn from the amateurs, but the lesson was strictly ritualistic in character. In the new Soviet culture, professionalism was not an unquestioned value. Ultimate truth belonged not to the *spets* ("specialist," usually preceded by the epithet "bourgeois") but to the proletarian, who was armed not with book learning but with the highest virtue: class consciousness.

The results of the competition delivered a mortal blow to radical architecture in the USSR and bitter disappointment to the international architectural community. The decision of the Council on Construction of the Palace of Soviets of the Presidium of the Central Executive Committee, dated February 28, 1932, stated that none of the designs was completely satisfactory.[24] The first prize of twelve thousand rubles was awarded to the projects of Ivan Zholtovsky, Boris Iofan, and Hector Hamilton, a twenty-eight-year-old unknown architect from New Jersey.[25] If Zholtovsky's project was in a style that recalled the Romantic version of classicism, Hamilton's was coldly symmetrical, and Iofan's close to Art Deco.

The committee's decision provoked numerous protests abroad. Le Corbusier couldn't believe it. In a letter to Lunacharsky, he warned of dire consequences: "People are enraptured by royal palaces, but it is the task of elected minds to lead the masses. We expect a masterful and lofty gesture from the USSR. Should this not come, the USSR will be no more, there will be no truth, no mystical belief." He applied to the International Congress of Modern Architecture, hoping that this organization's interference might save the situation; the congress obliged by sending two letters of protest directly to Stalin, calling Iofan's design "the most bourgeois expression of academic thoughts" and labeling Hamilton's project an "arrogant transfer of pompous procedures from the age of kings."[26] These protests remained unanswered.

Western criticism was not reflected in the Soviet press, where the results of the competition were widely discussed. Writers, art historians, and other members of the intelligentsia were too busy spinning visions of the global future of Soviet architecture to pay serious attention to the actual entries. Perhaps the most striking vision was conceived by Alexey Tolstoy, the famous writer who had fled to the West after the revolution and returned to the motherland in 1923. Tolstoy, who was nicknamed the Red Count, stated that the end of history was at hand. The hour was near, he predicted, when "History—fierce, insane, dressed in bloody rags after the eternal battle of class against class, would be tamed and yoked like the horses of Hercules."[27] The construction of the Palace of Soviets would be a sign of the end of history—the establishment of the classless society.

According to Tolstoy, just as the mountains of Pamir had been called the "Roof of the World," the Palace of Soviets would be called the "House of the World." So what should the House of the World look like? The Red Count didn't give a direct answer, undertaking instead an excursion into the history of civilization, with the aim of distinguishing traditions worthy of emulation from those inimical to proletarian society. He idealized antiquity—with the exception of Egypt. "The heavy colonnade and semi-darkness of the crypt typical of the mystical Egyptian temple was transformed into light with the marble Parthenon, open to the winds and to the

sun. . . . The idea is clear—human reason is the creator of being, the harmony of moderation is the highest aesthetic law, to which even the denizens
of heaven, drawn down from the clouds to be placed on the friezes and
facades of buildings, are subordinated."[28]

But ancient Greece is just a prelude to ancient Rome, which Tolstoy believed was the best historical example for the Soviet Union: "The classical
architecture of Rome is closer to us than anything else because many of its
elements correspond to our demands. Its openness, its purpose to serve the
masses, the impulse of grandiosity neither threatening nor oppressive, but
grandiosity as a manifestation of universalism—all these can be adopted by
our construction."[29]

Tolstoy rejected architecture that he considered "alienating, expressing
oppression," including "Gothic, American skyscrapers and Corbusier-
ism."[30] He concluded his article with this grandiose statement: "In ancient
times, Seven Wonders of the World were known. Let the Palace of Soviets
be the Eighth Wonder!"[31] His manifesto sounded the familiar note of Russian great-power chauvinism: the Bolshevik Third Rome would be the last
one because the end of history was at hand.

Tolstoy was not the only proponent of Roman revivalism. The renowned architect Ivan Zholtovsky, who had participated in the competition, wrote that it was necessary to create new architecture on the base of
the rich cultural heritage of antiquity, specifically Greece and—"the highest moment"—Rome.[32] The liberal Lunacharsky, who was rapidly losing
his influence, countered that ancient Rome wasn't the right example for
the Soviet Union. "We must rely more on classical architecture than on
bourgeois—to be precise, on the achievements of Greek architecture, because Marx's attitude to Rome was completely different from his attitude to
Greece."[33]

Although the architects, intellectuals, and cultural hierarchs disagreed
about whether democratic Athens or imperial Rome offered a more correct
example for Moscow, they agreed on what was not suitable. One of the critics of the competition, Nikolai Beker, wrote with satisfaction that formalism had been defeated. The primitive symbolism of the formalist projects
and their use of pyramids and other "deformed" elements were proof to
Beker of architectural illiteracy and feebleness. The ideology of formalism,
he continued, fed on "Menshevik idealism." But he considered construc-

tivism an even greater danger. "The representatives and begetters of this movement are gradually diluting the class essence of proletarian architecture."[34]

Le Corbusier's words were prophetic. The Soviet Union was no longer a country where political experimentation was matched by radical aesthetic practice. The Stalinist cultural revolution meant not a return to cultural radicalism but its demise. Lenin's statement that proletarians must take the best from the culture of the past was used to justify a new retrospective cultural fetishism, which would characterize Stalin's epoch. The world's most futuristic country had started to ossify. The Palace of Soviets competition was an important step toward the creation of the new proletarian Rome, where Caesar had the last word.

Boris Iofan's project had a motto: "Liberated Labor." It was a reference to the monument that Lenin had planned to erect on the base of the destroyed sculpture of Alexander III, near the Cathedral of Christ the Savior. With this motto, Iofan added a symbolic overtone to the idea of constructing the Palace of Soviets on the site of the destroyed cathedral, suggesting that it was the realization of Lenin's forgotten plan. Iofan wanted to create a complex of buildings framing a square built on the Moscow River embankment, with porticos and galleries connecting large and small auditoriums. Near the large auditorium he planned to erect a tower in the form of a spiral, crowned with a figure of a proletarian holding a torch — Liberated Labor.

Criticizing Iofan's project, Shchusev wrote that the tower, although it was aesthetically necessary to Iofan's plan, would interfere with mass demonstrations by blocking the entrance to the auditorium. Moreover, it would remind people of American skyscrapers, "which, of course, doesn't help to improve the project."[35] Shchusev didn't know that Stalin himself had already selected Iofan's tower as a prototype of the future palace.

Boris Mikhailovich Iofan, who was destined to become one of the leading architects of the Stalin era, was born in Odessa in 1891. He graduated from the Odessa School of Art and, after a short stay in St. Petersburg, went to Italy in 1914 to continue his architectural education at the Regio Istituto Superiore di Belle Arti in Rome. An eclectic historicist, Iofan combined his passion for the stones of Rome with the political leftism typical of liberal Jewish circles in prerevolutionary Russia. He was interested in construction engineering and spent his free time designing fantastic projects for gigantic buildings suitable for imperial Rome or Hellenistic Alexandria. One of Iofan's favorite teachers was Armando Brasini, an architect who belonged to an old Roman family of stonemasons. Brasini's atelier was an interesting place for the young Odessa native because he was a classicist, involved in constructing churches and cathedrals all over Italy. Brasini taught Iofan to make three-dimensional models as the basis for his projects.[36]

In 1916 Iofan began his career as a practicing architect, constructing villas, schools, power stations, and other buildings around Italy. He welcomed the Russian Revolution and in 1921 joined the newly formed Italian Communist party. He was even involved in sabotage: when the Fascists held a congress in Rome, Iofan, who had worked as an engineer on the Tivoli electric station, shut off the power, leaving the capital — and the congress — in the dark.[37]

Iofan returned to revolutionary Russia in 1924. In Italy he had designed buildings in an anonymous classical style, but in Russia he adopted constructivism, which was dominant there. A gifted chameleon, he forgot for the moment the glorious Renaissance palaces that had inspired him. His major commission (shared with his brother Dmitry) before the Palace of Soviets competition was the House of Government (1928–30), later nicknamed the House on the Embankment, at the time the largest construction in the city and a symbol of the might of the Soviet state as it was completing the first Five Year Plan. Like so many constructivist projects, it was not free of revolutionary idealism: its five hundred apartments for high-ranking Soviet officials offered a standard of comfort unavailable elsewhere in the country. They were equipped with hot water, gas, trash chutes — luxuries most Muscovites couldn't even dream of — as well as furniture designed by the architect. Shared facilities included food stores, a laundry, a theater, a sports hall, dining halls, and even a bank. It was like a fortress whose residents never needed to leave its shadowy courtyards to face the reality of the city outside. In 1931, however, Iofan realized that pure constructivism was no longer the favored style, and in his project for the Palace of Soviets he returned to the fantastic architectural dreams of his youth.

To Iofan's surprise, his old teacher Brasini also submitted a project, a strange fairy-tale castle replete with towers and spires. But it had one prophetic element, a statue of Lenin crowning one of the towers. If anyone

noticed it, there was no comment, and Brasini's project provoked no serious discussion. A few years later he was participating in the competition
for construction of the Fascist Forum in his native Rome.[38]

There was one other person who shared Iofan's vision of a tower—not
an architect by profession but a vastly more influential figure than any of
the competition participants or the judges. That person was Joseph Stalin,
who was the real creator of the Palace of Soviets. If Balikhin had given him
the site for the palace, Iofan's monument to Liberated Labor gave Stalin
a hint of how the palace should look. On August 7, 1932, Stalin wrote to
Kaganovich, Molotov, and Voroshilov: "Of all the projects for the 'Palace
of Soviets,' Iofan's plan is the best. Zholtovsky's project resembles 'Noah's
Ark.' Shchusev's project is just like the Cathedral of Christ the Savior, but
without a cross (for the moment). It's possible that Shchusev hopes to
'supplement' it with a cross later."[39]

Stalin asked Iofan to make some changes, the most important being the
height of the building. He wanted the Palace to soar "high into the air in the
shape of a tall column" like the column Iofan had used in his first project.[40]
On top of the column Stalin wanted a hammer and sickle that would be lit
electrically from within. If technical reasons made it impossible to erect the
column on top of the palace, then he wanted it nearby. As for its height, it
was to be, if possible, "as high as the Eiffel Tower, or a little bit higher."[41] In
front of the palace three monuments were to be placed—to Marx, Engels,
and Lenin. These few phrases written by Stalin were more important than
all the projects supplied by Soviet and international architects. The only
problem was to capture Stalin's vision in architectural blueprints. The
highly professional and highly flexible Iofan was the perfect candidate for
the task.

The plan underwent one very important change. Stalin decided to replace the electrified hammer and sickle on top of the tower with a statue
of Lenin. After Lenin's death, in 1924, his "closest comrade" had encour-
aged the establishment of the departed leader's ersatz religious cult. The
mummification of Lenin's body and the construction of the Mausoleum,
the establishment of countless memorials and museums, the ritualization
of everything connected with Lenin's life, from his birthday to the date of
his death, helped the all-powerful Central Committee secretary consoli-

THE TOWER OF BABEL

date his own power, using the name of the deceased godlike figure in the struggle against his enemies. Lenin was dead, but Stalin became "Lenin today," the only true prophet of the teaching of Leninism.[42] The Palace of Soviets was to become the pinnacle of this cult, the symbol of Stalin's victory over all false prophets.

On February 28, the day the awards were announced, the Council on Construction issued a decree setting forth specifications for the final design. The Palace of Soviets had to be a single building.[43] And, despite the constant statements in the press that American skyscrapers were alien to proletarian culture, the decree stated that it was a "bold high-rise composition" that was wanted, not "stocky buildings."[44] Another important correction was that demonstrations didn't have to be accommodated.[45]

This time the competition wasn't open to all. The committee chose the artists it wanted to submit projects, releasing them from all other work for three months to complete their designs as quickly as possible. Finally, after two rounds of closed competition, the choice was announced on May 10, 1933. The Council on Construction had decided to accept the project of Comrade Iofan as the basis of the Palace of Soviets.[46] And following the proposal of Comrade Stalin, the palace would be crowned by a gigantic statue of Lenin, fifty to seventy-five meters high.[47] In this matter, Stalin didn't hide his creative role in shaping the future construction.[48] It was, after all, only appropriate that Lenin's best pupil and most devoted follower should be responsible for elevating his teacher's gigantic image to the top of the tallest building in the world. The true creator of the palace must have been satisfied: his conception of the tallest building in the world was to be realized. On the site found by Balikhin, the monstrously enlarged column designed by Iofan would be erected and crowned by the immensely inflated statue of Lenin borrowed from Brasini's project.

Boris Groys, the contemporary Russian philosopher, has defined Socialist Realism as "the total work of art born of the will of its true creator and artist—Stalin."[49] Groys describes Stalin as a demiurge creating a *Gesamtkunstwerk*—"a kind of artist whose material was the entire world and whose goal was to 'overcome the resistance' of this material and make it pliant, capable of assuming any desired form."[50] In the case of the Palace of Soviets, however, Stalin proved to be not only the demiurge-artist creating a brave new world but the true designer of the most important construction in the country. More than a monument to the end of history, the palace was a manifestation of Stalin's own pompous taste. Only after he conceived the building could the professionals transform his vision into reality.

Iofan was supplied with two assistants, Vladimir Gelfreikh and Vladimir Shchuko. On June 4, 1933, the Council on Construction announced that Iofan had been appointed chief architect for the final development of the project. He was to produce a design by the beginning of the next year; the blueprints necessary for construction to begin were due by May 1934.[51] A new board, the permanent architectural-technical conference, was established to consult on the final development of the project and its construction.[52] It was a blue-ribbon group, which included, along with architects and engineers, such advisers as Maxim Gorky, Konstantin Stanislavsky, and Vsevolod Meyerhold; the painters Isaak Brodsky, Kuzma Petrov-Vodkin, and Ilya Mashkov; the art historian Igor Grabar; the Old Bolshevik Leonid Krasin; and the official Lunacharsky.[53] Not all of these advisers actually participated in the council's meetings. Some, like Meyerhold, were doomed to vanish during Stalin's purges. Others, including Lunacharsky and Gorky, died soon afterward.

The final stage of the project's development was not without conflict. Gelfreikh and Shchuko had been appointed because the project had to be completed very quickly and there was an immense amount of work to do, but it was widely believed in establishment architectural circles that Iofan had been judged too young and inexperienced for the job and needed the help of older hands.[54] From the start, the trio disagreed. Gelfreikh and Shchuko wanted to place the colossal figure of Lenin on the vertical axis, turning the building itself into a gigantic pedestal. Iofan objected. He wanted to place the statue on a column composed of cylindrical drums diminishing in circumference, whereas the other two introduced rectangular elements. The Council on Construction rejected the rectangular plan, but it adopted the idea of placing the sculpture on the vertical axis of the building. This decision dictated an increase of one hundred meters in the building's height. Finally, in 1934, the project designed by the trio of architects was adopted, and preparation of the site where the Cathedral of Christ the Savior had once stood could begin.

In his book on the formation of Stalinist culture, Vladimir Paperny wrote about the rejection of all the submitted projects at the Seventeenth Party Congress: "No project can be accepted. The natural competition hierarchy of first, second, and third prizes now seems insufficient." Although Zholtovsky, Hamilton, and Iofan had received the top prizes, their buildings seemed terribly remote from the ideal, not good enough for the central building in the capital of the world. Paperny believes that none of the final projects produced in the late 1930s by Iofan, Shchuko, and Gelfreikh would have been accepted for construction if they had been offered at the beginning of the competition. "One open competition is too 'uniform' a path to perfection" for Stalinist culture. "After the second open competition . . . there were several closed ones. Then Iofan's project prevails; but this does not mean that the project is approved for construction—the process of perfecting it continues."

According to Paperny, the hierarchy of the competitions "mirrored" the hierarchical structure typical of Stalinist culture. The final project for the Palace of Soviets repeated the same structure: "a sequence of ascending, gradually narrowing tiers crowned with a human figure, one representing not merely the highest tier (100 m) but the transition to another level of representation."[55]

The final project supplied by Iofan and his colleagues was based on a single element of the initial plan, the tower crowned by a monument to Liberated Labor, which Stalin had liked so much. Of Iofan's initial project, only the tower was left, the colossus of Lenin having replaced the figure of the proletarian. Scorn for bourgeois skyscrapers was conveniently forgotten. The Palace of Soviets was going to be the world's tallest building, dwarfing all monuments ever built.

The combination of high-rise tower and gigantic sculpture was praised as both a brave artistic decision and a successful solution to a difficult technical problem. Endless discussions were dedicated to the size of the sculpture. "However, the proportion was found one day after long experiment when a figure fastened to the model of the palace seemed to take root in it, grow out naturally from the proportions of the Palace and unite with it. This then was the second mass composing the grandeur of the palace—a colossus as high as a house of twenty-five stories, the index finger of the outstretched hand measuring 20 feet, shoulders 105 feet. Heel to toe measurement 46 feet. The engineering problem of building the statue alone is equal to the erection of a whole skyscraper."[56]

The realization of the gigantic figure was entrusted to Sergei Merkurov, the sculptor who had cast Lenin's death mask. It would be Merkurov's job to re-create Lenin's image on an unheard-of scale.[57] He had to be posed with outstretched arm and pointing finger — "Lenin's typical gesture" that expressed the "vitality of the Socialist Revolution."[58]

The palace was to be an engineering marvel as well as an artistic one — the largest framed building in the world. The chief engineer, Andrei Prokofiev, proudly reported: "The frame of the Empire State Building in New York contains 57,000 tons of steel. The greatest bridge in the world connecting San Francisco with Oakland contains 190,000 tons. The framework of the Palace of Soviets will take 360,000 tons of steel."[59]

Frescoes and ornamental panels were to cover an interior wall area of twenty-seven thousand square meters and mosaics another four thousand square meters. Two hundred and fifty sculpture groups had to be cast. Even this decoration was not enough: "In addition, the Palace of Soviets will be ornamented with wood carvings, bronzes, and stone-work. The adornment of the Palace of Soviets will occupy a whole army of artists, Ukrainian embroiderers, Daghestani embossers, Turkman carpet weavers and Eskimo carvers. The Palace will be draped with hundreds of tapestries. Soviet potteries will contribute thousand-piece services. The complete Palace of Soviets will be endowed with all the comforts and amenities of modern civilization."[60]

Like a medieval cathedral, the Palace of Soviets would be a model of the world and house all its wonders. Its complicated hierarchical and artistic program reflected the vision of the Stalinist version of Communism, which was rapidly being transformed into a quasi-religion. The whole program was a manifestation of the simplified idea of the synthesis of arts, that very idea Tatlin had fought against in 1919.

In 1937, while the architects were working on the details of the future palace and excavation of the foundation in the Volkhonka Street area had begun, Frank Lloyd Wright visited the Soviet Union. Soviet architects treated him royally, but he was observant enough to notice that Soviet architectural policy had changed, and he expressed his disappointment to his Moscow hosts. Many Soviet architects at this time expected further changes in political direction and answered Wright by remarking, "Never mind — we'll tear it down in ten years." Wright pointed out that it would take nearly that long to finish the Palace of Soviets. " 'Never mind,' said they; 'we may tear that down too — even before we complete it.' "[61] This cynical remark sums up the relations between the architects and power, but it was strikingly prophetic as well. The palace wasn't torn down in ten years; it was simply abandoned before construction had progressed very far.

Wright visited the studio of Iofan, whom he had already met in 1934, when Iofan, Gelfreikh, and Shchuko had been sent to the United States to study American skyscraper construction. Although Wright disliked the Palace of Soviets project, his meeting with Iofan was relatively mellow. "Said young Iofan, not yet quite disillusioned concerning his highly decorative Palace of Soviets: 'Never mind, Mr. Wright. It will improve as we go along. We are studying it continually.' And I saw proofs of that statement in Iofan's studio (Napoleon's old residence in Moscow by the Kremlin wall)."62

Wright saw the roots of the problem not in Iofan's project but in the Soviet leadership's rejection of the legacy of Russian avant-garde architecture. "I found that in Russia, as in the United States long ago, the masses who had nothing and to whom the landed Aristocracy appeared to have everything, now have their turn to be pleased. Nothing pleases them so much as the gleam of marble columns under high ceilings, glittering chandeliers, the unmistakable signs of luxury as they looked up to it when it decided their fate, when they ate out of luxury's hand if they ate at all."63 Wright made a mistake that was typical of foreign interpreters of Soviet culture during this period when he assumed that the purpose of all this luxury was to gratify the masses. It was to some extent a reflection of the personal taste of the Soviet leaders, but to a much greater extent it was the paradigm of the new style of Socialist Realism.

From 1937 through 1939, Iofan worked on the so-called technical project of the Palace of Soviets. Construction was progressing; the immense foundation capable of supporting the colossal building was completed in 1939. The huge base of the structure—two reinforced concrete rings linked by massive beams—looked like a spaceship that had landed in the center of Moscow. The steel forest of the framework rose higher day by day. By the beginning of the summer of 1941, thirty-two pairs of steel columns that would encircle the amphitheater of the great hall had been installed in massive concrete shoes.

And then came June 22, 1941. An anonymous photograph has preserved

for us the expressions on the faces of workers standing in front of the tower-
ing foundations of the palace and listening to Molotov's speech, broadcast
over loudspeakers, telling them of the Nazi invasion of the USSR.

A few days later, most of the laborers, with their foremen and engineers,
led by chief engineer Andrei Prokofiev, were sent to the outskirts of Moscow to construct fortifications. Some of the workers, with their equipment,
were dispatched to the Urals to build a munitions factory. More than six
hundred workers, engineers, and architects of the Palace of Soviets joined
the fifth division of the Moscow militia — poorly armed troops, lacking even
elementary military training, who were used as a living shield against elite
Nazi divisions. The people who had dreamed of constructing the largest
building in the world were doomed to die in snow-covered trenches to save
Moscow. Very few who were sent to fight survived.

The steel elements that had been forged for the construction were used
instead in the production of tank traps. In 1942, when the Donbass, the
heart of the Soviet coal industry, was occupied by the Nazis, part of the
steel skeleton of the palace was cut out, and the steel was used to construct
railway bridges along the route connecting the center of the country to the
coal mines of the north. Iofan and his staff were gone by then: selected architects, artists, and engineers, along with their blueprints and the project
archive, had been evacuated to Sverdlovsk, the designated seat of government if the enemy occupied Moscow.

Even as the Germans advanced to the outskirts of the capital, the Soviet
government was planning the city of the future. In December 1942 Iofan
was ordered to continue working on the Palace of Soviets, and by fall 1943
a new version of the project had been completed, which was known as the
Sverdlovsk version. Iofan's job had changed: the building envisioned originally as a monument to the end of history was now a monument to victory
in the Great Patriotic War.

This victory was by no means certain, but the architects, sculptors,
and artists were obliged to create a plaster model of the future monument to Soviet triumph and to work on a gigantic watercolor perspective
of the palace in their inadequately heated studio. The role of sculptural
decoration in the Sverdlovsk version was more important than in previous projects, and the sculptor Merkurov rose to second in command. The
lower tier of the skyscraper was to be decorated with gigantic sculptures in-

stalled in niches between the pylons. The statues were to represent "titans of the October socialist revolution, the construction of socialism, civil and patriotic wars."[64] The titans were to be fifteen meters high and placed on platforms one hundred meters high, making them visible from all over the city.

A new suite of halls for official receptions, decorated with frescoes depicting great battles, was added to the interior. At both ends were gigantic murals, one depicting the storming of the Winter Palace and the other the Battle of Stalingrad—events now treated as equally important in the heroic history of the Soviet Union. Another new feature was a Communist pantheon, a memorial hall dedicated to heroes of the Soviet epoch. It was to be located in the third tier, high enough to command a breathtaking view of Moscow.

As if this weren't enough, Merkurov, who had been appointed director of the Pushkin Museum after his return from evacuation, proposed to Mikhail Khrapchenko, head of the Arts Committee of the Council of People's Commissars, that a museum of world art should be added to the complex to house the cultural trophies that the victorious Red Army would capture in occupied Europe. "All valuables received from the Axis countries must be concentrated in one place and can play the role of a perfect memorial dedicated to the glory of Russian arms," Merkurov wrote.[65] The place, of course, was the Palace of Soviets.

By the end of the war, the palace had become a symbol of victory as well as a sign of the regime's stability. At the end of 1944, when it was clear that the Allies would win the war, new blueprints, a model, and perspective drawings were exhibited in St. George's Hall in the Kremlin. A year later they were shown to the deputies of the first postwar session of the Supreme Soviet of the USSR.

Chapter Twenty-six

With the end of the war, everything changed. The government ordered the architects to develop a new plan reducing the size of the building. In 1941 the projected height of the palace was 416 meters. In the 1947–48 version, it was reduced to 320 meters, though this did not satisfy the leaders. By 1950 the building had grown again, to 411 meters, and then orders were given to reduce it yet again. In 1953 it was diminished to a height of 353 meters.[1] That same year, on March 5, Stalin died.

These changes reflected Stalin's loss of interest in the project of the century. The reason for his abandonment of an idea that had been so important to him at the end of the 1930s is a matter for speculation. It was perhaps that the monument to Lenin had been transformed into a monument to the victory in the Great Patriotic War—but this victory had been Stalin's and his alone. Did Stalin at the end of his life become jealous of the god he had helped create?

Stalin's death did not signal the end of Iofan's labors. Between 1947 and 1956 the architect produced plans for six versions of the palace; in the last, the Lenin colossus finally stepped down from the summit of the building to a small pedestal near the entrance.[2] But in that year the Council on Construction and the Union of Architects announced a new competition for the Palace of Soviets. A very important specification had changed. It was now proposed—irony of ironies—to erect the palace in the Lenin Hills (formerly the Sparrow Hills), on the original site of the Cathedral of Christ the Savior.

In a book dedicated to the competition, it was claimed that a new project was needed because the first one had been inferior. "Was the true image of the Palace of Soviets created in that project? Formerly this question was answered in the affirmative. In reality it was more a sculptural than an architectural creation. The image of that monument, which exceeded the pyramids of the ancient Egyptian pharaohs several times over, would be foreign to the ideology of Soviet man."[3]

Although Iofan was held responsible for Stalin's architectural daydreaming, he participated in the new competition, submitting probably the only project for a high-rise structure. But the competition ended without positive results, and at the beginning of the 1960s the whole idea was abandoned. There would be no Palace of Soviets. Like his German counterpart Albert Speer, Boris Iofan remained a paper architect. Most of his creative life was wasted on a project that would never be built.

The Soviet architectural establishment was shaken to the core. Khrushchev's fierce attack on "architectural excesses" and "embellishment" brought a sudden end to the era of Stalin Empire style. The same architects who had been designing colonnades and arches straight out of Piranesi were busy planning new districts of five-story apartment buildings made of prefabricated concrete blocks and deprived of any architectural individuality. In this new situation, the future of the gigantic excavation in the center of the capital had to be decided. It was clear that nobody was going to construct an architectural extravaganza on the site: the time for extravaganzas had passed.

Where the world's tallest building was to have stood there was nothing but a hole in the ground. The huge foundation pit, stripped of steel during the war, had filled with rainwater and become a swamp. In 1958 the Moscow city council resolved that a swimming pool would be built there, and Dmitry Chechulin, an orthodox Stalinist architect who had just constructed the House of Radio in Beijing, was entrusted with the design. This project, too, would be the biggest — the biggest swimming pool in the Soviet Union and the whole of Europe.[4]

The water surface covered thirteen thousand square meters, large enough for two thousand swimmers at a time and capable of accommodating thirty thousand to thirty-five thousand people a day. The architect wanted to incorporate a heating system, but it was not clear whether keeping the pool open all year long would be possible, even with heat. Chechulin then proposed that Europe's largest swimming pool could easily be converted in winter into Europe's largest skating rink. But these utilitarian functions weren't enough for him; he suggested that for holidays the pool could be turned into a gigantic fountain, which, "combined with artistic spotlighting, would create an enchanting sight." On the foundation of the unrealized Palace of Soviets he envisioned an ephemeral palace of water jets.[5]

In 1960 the swimming pool was completed and proudly named "Moscow." To crown their joy, officials discovered that it was not only the largest pool in Europe but the largest in the world. It was destined for the *Guinness Book of Records* and instantly became a Moscow landmark. The pool was never transformed into a skating rink because the water was heated all year long, and it never became a fountain because that idea violated the Khrushchev-era creed of "democratic practicality." The "place of mass swimming and sport exercises," as it was officially called, became a metaphor for the period of the thaw. Now it was so warm in Moscow that it was possible to play in water even during the winter.

Chechulin, an experienced member of the Soviet architectural elite, knew well that trends in political leadership had a tendency to change. In 1958 he stated that the reinforced concrete bases and especially the circular foundations constructed for the Palace of Soviets were well made and would serve for the swimming pool.[6] But these structural supports had another advantage that Chechulin didn't mention. His biographer noted that the pool "preserved the reinforced concrete construction so that it could be used in the future for the possible erection of a large public building."[7] Chechulin had the gift of prophecy, but it is unlikely that in saving the Palace of Soviets foundation he imagined it being used for the reconstruction of the Cathedral of Christ the Savior.

PART FIVE

The Concrete Cathedral

Chapter Twenty-seven

A member of the Moscow intelligentsia recently commented that during the Communist era intellectuals passing the Moscow swimming pool would whisper to each other, "There was once a famous cathedral here, but the government destroyed it and built the swimming pool." Now they tell each other, "There was once a famous swimming pool here, but the government destroyed it and built the cathedral."[1]

He was right. Our generation remembers the swimming pool that took the place of the old Cathedral of Christ the Savior. It was the largest in the world, a blue-green lake thirteen thousand meters square that sparkled invitingly in the sweltering heat of the Moscow summer. Tourist buses crowded around it, the guides shouting out statistics about this wonder of the Soviet world. In winter a cloud of steam rose over the water, and the people rushing by in their fur hats and sheepskins could see swimmers bobbing in the mist as snowflakes swirled in the air. At night the scene was brightly illuminated, and one could see the portico of the Pushkin Museum through a luminous cloud dotted with the swimmers' colorful rubber caps. Students of our generation hurried to the pool after classes in the old building of Moscow University. Like all pools, it smelled of chlorine. But it was different. The invisible cathedral towered over it.

The memory of Christ the Savior was alive during the 1960s through the 1980s. Old Moscow babushkas, diehard churchgoers who weren't intimidated by the twists and turns of antireligious campaigns by the government, whispered that the swimming pool was a gigantic baptistery where unwitting atheists were converted without their knowledge to the true faith. Another version of the pool mythology was not so optimistic. From time to time rumors spread that a mysterious illness was affecting swimmers. It was, of course, heaven's punishment for the blasphemy of cavorting in the holy ruins.

Dissident intellectuals had their own interpretations of the cathedral's destruction. From the 1970s, the fate of Christ the Savior was an element of dissident thinking. Liberals as well as conservatives exploited it as a symbol of the Soviet regime's crimes and were equally devoted to this symbol of Old Russia.

On December 26, 1962, the young nationalist artist Ilya Glazunov gave a speech during the conference of the Ideological Commission of the Communist Party Central Committee in Moscow calling for the protection of historical monuments and the reconstruction of the Cathedral of Christ the Savior. His courage was offset by his criticism of "modernist" art. The meeting, in fact, had been convened because at the beginning of December Khrushchev had attended an exhibition in the Manezh where he had been outraged by the creations of "formalist" artists. Although Glazunov's extravagant proposal was ignored by officials, he was not punished. He had influential supporters in both the Central Committee and the Komsomol (Young Communists League). Russian nationalism was becoming a secret passion of certain Communist apparatchiks.[2]

Khrushchev's days were numbered. A year later he was overthrown by the Politburo. Leonid Brezhnev, who replaced him, put an end to the liberal spirit of the 1960s.

After 1968, when Soviet tanks rolled into Prague, crushing hopes for a reformed socialism, intellectual opposition to the regime drifted rightward. Young intellectuals whose parents had dreamed of careers as geologists or nuclear physicists no longer believed that Soviet society could be transformed. The only possibilities for them were opposition and escape. A generation of highly educated street sweepers and night watchmen replaced the optimistic scientists of the thaw epoch.

Unlike their fathers, who had aspired to return to Lenin and had idealized the true revolution before its face was disfigured by the cult of personality, the intellectuals of the 1970s and 1980s rejected revolution entirely. A characteristic of the time was the strong interest in religion and the occult as an alternative to the official materialist philosophy. The intense mysticism of the era of stagnation, as the Brezhnev period came to be called, was in some ways similar to the spiritual climate in Russia between the two revolutions of 1905. Esoteric teachings were fashionable, as they had been in the West in the 1960s, and scores of young intellectuals twisted themselves into the lotus position in the kitchens of their concrete apartment blocks.

Others took to Christianity. The turn-of-the-century religious philosophers Vladimir Solovyov and Nicholas Berdyaev were required reading.
The revival of interest in the Orthodox Church was part of the upsurge of
nationalist feeling, which was supported by both conservative dissidents
and the official writers of the "village" school, such as Valentin Rasputin,
who celebrated the ideal of village life untainted by urban corruption. The
interest in Orthodoxy drew also from the translation of Jesus-rock into the
Russian language. The dark-faced Christ of Russian icons and the Jesus
Christ Superstar of American album covers morphed into a symbol of
spiritual opposition. Young Jewish intellectuals converted to the Orthodox
faith and persistently tried to enroll in seminaries, refusing to understand
that these institutions were as likely to admit them as the famously anti-
Semitic Kiev University or the KGB academy.

The rediscovery of the church was reflected not only in literature, both
official and unofficial, but even in such state-controlled media as cinema.
Andrei Rublev, Andrei Tarkovsky's film about the canonized icon painter,
became a cult movie. In the visual arts, Christian connotations were exiled
to the underground or were exploited by such "official dissidents" as
Glazunov. By the middle of the 1970s sentimentalized Christian content—
ruined churches, crosses, saints, and themes from Dostoevsky—became
standard for some unofficial artists, who succeeded in establishing by the
end of the decade a kind of religious mannerism that was anti-Soviet in
content but saccharine and surrealistic in form.

The first serious revelations about the destruction of the cathedral came
from oppositional artistic circles. In 1988 the Paris-based dissident art
magazine *A-Ya* published dozens of photographs of the explosion.[3] Their
appearance in a magazine dealing with contemporary art forms prohibited in the Soviet Union was at first sight paradoxical, since the cathedral's
official Russian Revival architecture could hardly be imagined as a source
of inspiration for the radical dissident artists linked to the publication. If
some of them flirted with Christian spirituality, most were producing modernist artworks having nothing in common with Orthodox values. The
general trend of the 1980s, however, made the publication of these pho-
tos explicable. They expressed the point that the regime wasn't just the
enemy of modernism but the enemy of culture as such. The ironic period
of underground culture, when both Soviet and anti-Soviet values would

be rejected, had not yet begun.[4] In this atmosphere of struggle against a common enemy, a certain eclecticism of views among allies didn't bother anyone.

A few months later, the same photographs made their appearance in a very different context: an album dedicated to the destruction of the cathedral that was issued by a London-based publishing house.[5] Irina Ilovaiskaia-Alberti, the longtime leader of the Paris émigré community and editor of the Russian-language newspaper *Russkaia Mysl* (Russian Thought), wrote the introduction to the album and stressed a different side of the story. For the readers of this publication, the demolition of the cathedral was equivalent not to the destruction of culture but to the destruction of religion.

Mention of the vanished cathedral was generally banned from the pages of official publications, but the Byzantine style of Soviet censorship during the seventies and eighties left certain loopholes. These, of course, were not for ordinary mortals but for the immortals of Soviet culture. The old proverb "What is permitted to Jupiter is not permitted to the ox" was as true in Brezhnev's Moscow as in ancient Rome. In 1979 the famous writer Valentin Kataev, recipient of numerous state awards, published his fictionalized memoir, *Almaznyi moi venets* (My Diamond Diadem), which is devoted to Soviet literary circles of the 1920s and early 1930s. Kataev created colorful if not always accurate portraits of dozens of writers and poets whose books were either prohibited or semiprohibited, though he did not name them. All of them, from the officially canonized Mayakovsky to the semipermitted Mandelshtam and the completely prohibited Vladimir Narbut, were given friendly nicknames. The trick worked. Censors were not obliged to black out the names of the ostracized poets, and the mysterious nicknames provoked readers' curiosity.

One of the themes of the memoir is the Cathedral of Christ the Savior, which still dominated the skyline in Kataev's youth. Its golden dome was the first thing he and his friends saw as their train from Odessa approached the capital. The writer recollects his love affair with the sister of Mikhail Bulgakov and how on one occasion the young couple wandered around Moscow all night long and found themselves in the morning on the steps of the cathedral. Kataev transformed it into a nostalgic symbol of Moscow in the days of Mayakovsky, and of his own lost youth. The demolished cathedral and the murdered writers belonged in this melancholy book about the *temps perdu* of Russian literature: "Dawn was near. The city was empty and dead. Only the sound of an invisible airplane could be heard from somewhere very distant and very high. It seemed to me that an irreversible catastrophe had occurred, that the world war had started; and that the city around us had already been killed by some silent chemical or physical weapon. We—neither she nor I—was still alive; our souls flew away, and only two immobile bodies remained pressed to one another in eternal sleep on the basalt steps of the dead cathedral, deprived of God. But its dead, gilded dome continued to shine brightly over dead Moscow, the lifeless forests on the outskirts of the city—that same legendary dome of the Cathedral of Christ the Savior that we had seen from the train windows."[6]

Kataev's contemporaries didn't share his nostalgia. A few years before the publication of *Almaznyi moi venets,* Viktor Shklovsky, the well-known literature historian and theoretician of the avant-garde, had published a book about Sergei Eisenstein. Like many books written during the 1970s, it contained blasphemy sweetened by flat pro-Soviet statements inserted to please the censor. Shklovsky's explication of the radical Soviet cinema of the 1920s and of the montage method coexisted with pages of anti-American slogans and other patriotic nuggets stuck into the mix to make the text publishable. At the beginning of the book, Shklovsky describes a visit to Moscow by Eisenstein's mother, a middle-class housewife from Riga. The radical son is showing the city to his bourgeois mother.

"This is the Cathedral of Christ the Savior," Eisenstein said. "It was built, Mother, in memory of the war of 1812; it is a mediocre work by Ton; the architect wanted to restore the tradition of Russian five-domed cathedrals, but he did not understand it."

"You young people believe that you will remake everything [she replied]; you believe that you know everything and understand everything. I think it is a perfect construction. Technically speaking, perfect. Stones are even connected by iron as the ancient Romans did it. This building will stand for eternity if we don't blow it up."[7]

Kataev's nostalgic description of the gigantic golden dome corresponded more closely to the mood of a later generation of intellectuals. In the years immediately following the revolution, artists, writers, and film directors were not interested in the discredited past; but to their counterparts in the 1970s and 1980s the past was much more appealing than the future. The cathedral's golden dome belonged to an ideal past populated by Akhmatova and Mandelstam, avant-garde painters and merchant patrons, murdered czars, and all the other martyrs of the revolution.

Chapter Twenty-eight

In 1985, cracks finally appeared in the Soviet monolith. Mikhail Gorbachev tried to patch them, but the country could not be reformed. Gorbachev was typical of his time in that he had two obsessions: he adored the intelligentsia and he admired the West. These obsessions were shared by the middle class. Professors and schoolteachers, army officers and minor officials, scientists and engineers, diplomats and journalists, yearned for social change. These people respected education and wanted to live like normal people in the West. They were sick of party rhetoric, senseless rituals, and all the other trappings of the ossified state.

One of Gorbachev's important ideological steps was the establishment of the Culture Fund in 1986. The purpose of the foundation, led by Raisa Gorbachev, was to stress the new regime's enlightened character. The academician Dmitry Likhachev, a respected literature historian whose works had moderate nationalistic overtones and who had been imprisoned in the late 1920s in the legendary Solovki camp, was appointed president of the foundation. From its inception, the Culture Fund promoted a new trend: yearning and nostalgia for the past. The fund published the works of prohibited prerevolutionary writers and poets, organized exhibitions of forgotten avant-garde artists, and sought out the archives of Russian cultural figures who had emigrated to the West after the revolution. Articles dedicated to ruined monuments and to writers and philosophers who had vanished into the gulag began to appear in *Nashe Nasledie* (Our Heritage), the Culture Fund's magazine. Inevitably, in this context, the fate of Christ the Savior became a topic of discussion.

The first public mention of the destroyed cathedral came not from the academics grouped around Raisa Gorbachev but from the Leningrad underground rock group Akvarium, which was finally allowed to perform openly. In 1987 the group released a video of a song called "This Train Is on Fire." Its lyrics told of a Colonel Vasin, who went to the front line:

And brought his young wife along;
Colonel Vasin rallied his corps
And told them, "Let's go home."
We fought this war for seventy years;
We were taught that life is a battle;
But intelligence has just reported
We have been fighting ourselves all this time.[1]

The allusion to Gorbachev was transparent. In the video the group is dressed in paramilitary uniforms of the civil war period and is riding in a steam engine, a scene based on many Soviet movies about the first postrevolutionary years. Then came a surprise. Clips of the detonation of Christ the Savior were run backward so that heaps of bricks grew on the screen into the gigantic construction crowned by the carcass of the dome. The group could hardly have imagined how prophetic their vision was.

For an older generation, the film *Repentance,* by the Georgian director Tengiz Abuladze, became their emblem of perestroika. The Communist Party Central Committee allowed its release in 1987, after a discussion led by Gorbachev, and it was shown first in provincial towns to test audience reaction. Despite its heavy symbolism and dense intellectual allusions, the film became a blockbuster, seen by almost 14 million people. In a memorable scene, the protagonist, endowed with the features of Lavrenty Beria, chief of Stalin's secret police, cuts and eats a cake in the form of a church. At the end, when all enemies of the state and all churches have been smashed, an old woman passing by asks him an absurd question: "Please tell me, does this road lead to the cathedral?" Those words became a motto of the Gorbachev era, appearing frequently as newspaper headlines and quoted in various contexts.

Liberal intellectuals mourned the political and architectural victims of the Soviet regime and wrote about the new spirituality, but at the beginning of the 1990s the initiative was taken by a group with a different political agenda. The former participants of the "soil" movement in literature turned from their idealizations of village life and began to attack "Westernizers," very often taking an ultranationalist stand. In 1990 a group of nationalist writers associated with the magazine *Nash Sovremennik* (Our Contemporary) fomented a popular movement for the rebirth of the cathedral. The group included such well-known figures as Vladimir Soloukhin, Valentin Rasputin, and Viktor Krupin, who by this time openly associated themselves with the so-called patriotic opposition affiliated with the Pamyat (Memory) Society and the newspaper of the same name.

Anti-Semitic and radically anti-Western, these new Slavophiles created a strange ideology that was later dubbed "red-brown." They idealized prerevolutionary Holy Russia, mourned the martyred czar, and deplored the destruction of the Orthodox Church by the Bolsheviks. At the same time they revered Stalin and the powerful Soviet state, which they saw as inheritor of the glorious Russian empire. Because it was Stalin who had ordered the demolition of the cathedral, they had to transfer the blame to someone else. They chose Lazar Kaganovich, who was responsible for the reconstruction of the Soviet capital in the 1930s and who was a Jew. Thus Stalin was relieved of guilt.

The new opposition found supporters within the Orthodox Church, which started to play an active political role at the end of the Gorbachev period under the leadership of a new patriarch, Aleksei II. The church's first tentative steps into the political arena—its requests for the return of property confiscated after the revolution—became more confident with the rise of nationalism after the collapse of the Soviet Union and the Yeltsin government's adoption of nationalistic rhetoric. Yesterday's party members, whose religious observances had been limited to excessive consumption of vodka on Easter Sunday (widely celebrated in Orthodox-dominated parts of the country, despite overwhelming antireligious propaganda), began to appear publicly in church. High-ranking government officials were televised ostentatiously holding candles at Christmas or Easter services, their stiffness betraying their discomfort in these unfamiliar surroundings.

Yeltsin wanted to steal for himself the support of the Moscow patriarchy, which controlled a substantial part of the electorate, especially in rural areas. His flirtation with the church had another goal. With Communism dead, Russia needed an ideology. Russians had suddenly become losers, deprived of their superpower pride. The former satellites were planning their return to Europe. The former republics were building new identities based on nationalism and, in some cases, strong anti-Russian sentiment. In Tallinn and Vilnius, Lviv, Almaty, and Tbilisi, yesterday's rulers had turned into pariahs. Thousands of ethnic Russians who had lived all their lives in the Baltic states or Central Asia immigrated to a country that was foreign to them. The Russian government could not afford to take care of these penniless refugees and tried to keep them as far as possible from the major cities.

This huge, roiled country had no clear identity. The Communist ideology that had held it together for more than seventy years had died with the Soviet Union. The dream of living the way people lived in the West was forgotten. Most people were much worse off than they had been before, and they believed that it was Westernizers led by Gorbachev who had ruined the country. Slowly the vacuum left by Soviet ideology started to fill with officially sanctioned nationalism mixed with the new capitalist slogans.[2]

The Orthodox Church was destined to fill the vacancy left by the Central Committee's ideology department. The patriarchy granted Yeltsin the support he wanted, but he had to pay for it, with economic as well as political power: the duty-free status the government gave to the patriarchy transformed it into a major importer of Western cigarettes. The patriarchy's business arm became a huge and extremely profitable enterprise. Somehow the separation of church and state mandated by the constitution was forgotten. The presence of the patriarch at presidential inauguration ceremonies became standard protocol.

Chapter Twenty-nine

In 1990, a year before the fall of the Soviet Union, the Moscow priest Georgy Dokukin received the blessing of Bishop Arseny to establish the Brotherhood of the Cathedral of Christ the Savior. It was registered that year as a nongovernmental organization (NGO). Three years later, the enterprising priest succeeded in attracting the support of some influential businessmen and, with their help, founded the Bank of the Cathedral of Christ the Savior, of which he became director. His intention was to use the bank to administer contributions to a construction fund; special collection brigades were established with this intent.[1] But a conflict arose, and some of the brigades, unhappy with Dokukin's leadership, defected from the brotherhood and formed a new group, the Community of Christ the Savior, which was blessed by the patriarch himself. The community constructed a little wooden chapel decorated with placards stating that the cathedral would be rebuilt on this place, near the empty, dilapidated swimming pool. But the victory of the Community of Christ over the Brother-hood of the Cathedral was short-lived. The reconstruction of the cathedral was too big a job for religious activists. More powerful forces decided to appropriate the initiative, and in August 1994 the patriarch abolished the community.

In September a new group assembled in Moscow: the Public Council for Control of the Reconstruction of the Cathedral of Christ the Savior, headed by Aleksei II. President Yeltsin addressed the assembly by letter: "Today Russia needs the Cathedral of Christ the Savior," he wrote. He pledged his support and assured the assembly that the Russian government on all levels would treat its construction as a state priority.[2] Regional authorities were expected to fall into line immediately.[3] The patriarch found a powerful ally in Moscow mayor Yury Luzhkov, Yeltsin's ally who had begun to act more independently by this time. The mayor, whose corpulent figure and trade-mark leather cap were already familiar to every TV viewer, was establishing his image as a competent, no-nonsense politician. From the beginning of the cathedral reconstruction project, he thought not so much about the future kingdom of God as about his own future kingdom.

The announcement of the reconstruction of the cathedral provoked a wave of public outrage. People did not understand why millions of rubles should be spent on a concrete replica when hundreds of thousands of poor and homeless people desperately needed help. Many did not believe that private donations would cover even a fraction of the cost. Art historians and architects expressed their doubts about the artistic value of Ton's origi-nal structure. Why rebuild it when thousands of historically important churches and monasteries all over the country were crumbling (and are still crumbling). Aleksei Komech, director of the Research Institute of Art History, calculated that the cathedral reconstruction cost would be equiva-lent to the federal budget for restoration of architectural monuments for a hundred years.[4]

Voices of protest sounded inside the church as well. Archpriest Mikhail Ardov spoke for many when he objected that it was unwise and morally in-defensible to spend billions on a new cathedral when the devastated coun-try, a spiritual desert rife with "criminality, pornography, and active satan-ism," lacked hospitals and orphanages, even prisons. He reminded his superiors of King Solomon's words: "Except the LORD build the house, they labour in vain that build it."[5]

Otto Latsis, then the editor of *Izvestia,* one of the most influential newspapers of the time, wrote: "A child who accidentally broke an expensive vase tries to put the pieces together, hoping that his parents won't notice the loss, as if it never happened. Can society behave like a naughty kid and pretend that nothing happened? Everything happened, and nothing lost can be returned—not cathedrals nor people nor the spiritual impulse of the past."[6]

Latsis, of course, was right, but the country at this time was caught up in a fever of renaming, as if giving back their prerevolutionary names to streets, cities, and regions could change reality. In the early years after the revolution, Bolshevik radicals had not only tried to rename every street in every village but to adopt a new calendar and even produce a new language. They had done it in the name of the future. Now it was being done in the name of the past.

And then of course there were the protests of those who did not want to lose their favorite swimming pool. Surprisingly, the Orthodox newspaper *Bytie* (Existence) supported them, asking why it was necessary to destroy a rare amenity for the sake of creating something else.

Moscow radical artists contributed their bit to the chorus of outrage. A group of young conceptualists appeared one day on Volkhonka Street and started to measure the pool and draw blueprints. They told curious passersby that they were preparing an important architectural document for the future: if, in the course of the next revolution, the new cathedral would be blown up, architects could use their blueprints to reconstruct the swimming pool.[7]

The only government figure who supported the enemies of reconstruction was Yevgeny Yasin, the newly appointed finance minister. In his first television interview, in November 1994, he declared that the state could not fund such projects.[8] Luzhkov and the patriarch immediately sent letters to Yeltsin attacking Yasin and promising that the cathedral would be reconstructed without state support. The Moscow city government and the donations of believers would finance it. Nevertheless, the project's adherents continued to demand state support. The "state program of national self-consciousness" would be realized visually in church architecture, wrote one commentator, in an article called "Christ Is Crucified Again."[9]

The Pontifical Synod, which gathered at the end of 1994, took a similar position, calling on everyone—"bishoprics, monasteries, and curacies of the Russian Church, the Orthodox and all other Christians all over the world, organs of state power, enterprise collectives, new merchants, all our brothers and sisters"—to offer their donations. Every person should "use his skills and offer his mite for this holy deed."[10] The language of this epistle—archaic Church Slavonic mixed with Soviet-style newspeak—reflected the stylistic cacophony typical of Yeltsin's Russia. The new rich, generally known as New Russians, received the antiquated-sounding sobriquet "new merchants." But the epistle made the point that the reconstruction was an obligation of "church, state, and people." The state would open its coffers.

There followed an extraordinary public relations effort, which seemed to be equally concerned with collecting donations and stating the new cathedral's ideological program. There was the story—aimed at the government—of the poor old woman who sacrificed her last ruble for the reconstruction of the cathedral.[11] There were the articles in nationalistic newspapers reporting the multimillion-ruble donations made by corporations, which accompanied a campaign of pressure to extract donations from private and foreign companies in Moscow. City officials scrutinized enterprises that refused to donate and found irregularities in their activities until everybody got the message that it was better to follow the examples of unselfishness lauded in the patriotic press. Rendering unto God was at the same time rendering unto Caesar.[12]

The third PR wave of 1997–98 featured incessant TV ads stressing the role of the cathedral as the "unifying symbol of the nation's rebirth," as Luzhkov defined it. One ad showed a group of Russian tourists standing near the cathedral, its domes surrounded by scaffolding and cranes. A bus of French-speaking tourists stops near the group, and one of the foreigners, a silver-haired man, joins the Russian group as the guide repeats the cliché about the cathedral as "symbol of the renaissance of new Russia." The foreigner interrupts the guide in perfect, highly cultivated Russian. "Don't divide Russia into old and new!" he says. "Russia is united! And it will live as long as the cathedral stands." He is, we understand, a noble Russian émigré, symbolizing the old Russia. The creators of the new cathedral state their conception of history and announce themselves the heirs of the ancien régime. The second clip showed a little boy asking his grandfather where the heart of Russia was. Grandfather predictably answers that the heart of Russia is in the cathedral.[13]

The sharpest reaction to the advertisements appeared not in the press but in literature. The writer Viktor Pelevin dedicated his novel *Generation P* to the state of mind of the new Russia in general and the important role of advertising in particular. The hero of his novel, a copywriter working for an advertising agency, is composing his own ad for the reconstructed cathedral. In his ad, a long white limo stops near the cathedral and the door opens. We see a sandaled foot and a hand on the open door. Everything else is invisible because of the radiance streaming from the car. A slogan appears on the screen: "Christ the Savior. The respected Lord for gentlemen of respect!" (a euphemism for a New Russian or a mafioso, or often both).[14] Pelevin's vision was well grounded: "Gentlemen of respect" paid attention to the cathedral in the early stages of reconstruction, though it wasn't clear whether their aim was to please the Lord or to gain entry into Luzhkov's office.

Some donors were attracted by the opportunity to have their names included on the memorial plaques that were to be installed inside the cathedral, alongside plaques bearing the names of officers and soldiers who fell in the Napoleonic Wars. The names of these wealthy benefactors, however, were sometimes enveloped in scandal. One was Alexander Smolensky, the head of the SBS-Agro Banking Group, who in 1995 donated, on behalf of the group, a hundred kilos of gold. For this saintly deed, the patriarch decorated him with the order of Holy Prince Daniil of Moscow. The Holy Prince, however, could not save Smolensky's banks from default in 1998. SBS-Agro was declared bankrupt, and hundreds of depositors lost their entire savings. In 1999 Smolensky was arrested for the illegal transfer to Austrian banks of $32 million.[15]

Another donor who attracted public attention was Josef Kobzon, the Soviet-era pop singer turned successful businessman. Kobzon—member of the Duma, member of the Russian Humanities Academy, head of a foundation supporting families of police killed in the line of duty, and Luzhkov's close friend—was said to be linked to the Russian mafia. (He was repeatedly denied a visa to enter the United States.) A Jew, he donated 875 million (predefault) rubles to the cathedral fund, claiming to be an admirer of all religions.[16]

But it wasn't only babushkas, businessmen, and gentlemen of respect who contributed money to the cathedral fund. Ten large metallurgical factories donated metal valued at more than three billion rubles. Another

industrial enterprise, the Moscow Karacharovsky Factory, donated elevators it had produced, a gift valued at more than 1.5 billion rubles. Vladimir
Pozner, the liberal journalist and TV host, visited the site and got stuck in
one of the elevators, which convinced him that it would be cheaper to buy
Western products than to accept such gifts.[17]

Luzhkov was determined that the building would be finished on time
at any price. Soon the construction site was a gigantic anthill crowded
with laborers and soldiers from construction battalions (draftees who had
served as a free labor force in Soviet times and are still used today). The
rumor spread that Turkish construction companies active in Russia had
been invited to participate, but the Moscow administration angrily denied
these allegations. Godless Turks would never be invited to reconstruct the
symbol of Russia's rebirth![18]

The decision to build the cathedral on the foundation of the Palace of
Soviets dramatically cut the cost and also made possible the use of the vast
underground space for a small church, a fifteen-hundred-seat auditorium
for Orthodox synods, a refectory, and an office for the patriarch. The ex-
cavators found that the space had been used before. Sixty meters down,
they came upon a bunker constructed for the Politburo, with working telephone lines and warnings on the telephones: "Remember, comrade, the
secrecy of telephone communications is not guaranteed." The equipment
was removed and the bunker encased in concrete.[19] But the most agitated
discussion was provoked by the decision to build an underground garage,
which led opponents to dub the new Christ the Savior the Cathedral on the
Garage.[20]

The speed of the rebuilding was miraculous, thanks to the "shockworkers of Orthodox labor," as the liberal press called them. Construction
began in 1994, and the last brick was proudly placed in the wall in 1996.
The domes were gilded in time for Easter and, perhaps more important,
the presidential election. The Communists were leading in opinion polls,
and Luzhkov did what he could for Yeltsin's campaign by plastering the
city with billboards proclaiming "Cathedral of Christ the Savior—Symbol of Russia's Renaissance." The cathedral's role in the anti-Communist
campaign of the president and the mayor was to represent the rebirth of
Russian values under their leadership.

According to a report by Flore de Préneuf, there was in the last stage of
the reconstruction "a widespread willingness to believe that all that glit-

ters is gold." When it came time to gild the domes, Luzhkov yielded to the patriarch. "Luzhkov went to the patriarch with two pieces of golden metal, asking him to select the one covered with a layer of authentic gold. The patriarch, fallible after all, chose the wrong piece, which was titanium nitrate sprayed over with golden lacquer. 'See! Even you can't tell the difference!' exclaimed the mayor."[21]

The choice of titanium nitrate sprayed with golden lacquer was typical for the whole project. Bronze was often replaced by plastic, and a thin skin of marble covered thick concrete walls. Missing here was the quality of restoration that brought back to life the ruined imperial palaces outside St. Petersburg after World War II — the exact replication, by hand, of every destroyed element in materials similar to the originals. The mayor's inspiration might have been Las Vegas; it certainly wasn't the academic reconstructions of architectural restorers.

There were, to do him justice, time pressures. The need to finish parts of the cathedral for various political occasions dictated the use of contemporary materials, and justifications could be found for them. The architect Mikhail Posokhin, the head of the reconstruction project appointed by Luzhkov, said that domes were traditionally covered with gold leaf, but it was "lemon" colored and not durable. "In five-six years it will fail and every bird can scratch it with its claws. . . . We achieved very good results using new technologies."[22] Vladimir Osin, manager of the financial support group, gave an even better explanation. "The cathedral is already standing. It is of course wondrous to construct a cathedral from nothing. In earlier days, it would have been called a heroic deed of labor. In one year, our Russian construction workers and not foreigners erected such an enormous bulk of a building."[23]

Chapter Thirty

By 1996 Mayor Yury Luzhkov had taken the reconstruction completely under his control. The project's first architect, Igor Pokrovsky, was dismissed because he rated the patriarch's wishes higher than the mayor's. Predictably, when awarding the commission for the crosses, Luzhkov called on his friend, the sculptor Zurab Tsereteli, who had already carried out a number of major projects. The commission for the fourteen bells went to the near-bankrupt car factory ZIL, which the Moscow city administration was committed to helping.[1]

Victory over Communists in the presidential election of 1996 was achieved not because of the symbolism of the cathedral but thanks to the millions of dollars the oligarchs had poured into Yeltsin's campaign. For Luzhkov, however, this victory wasn't the end. He aimed higher than helping Yeltsin win reelection, and the cathedral had a role in helping him realize his ultimate goal.

In 1997 the Moscow government announced plans for the 850th anniversary of the city's foundation. This expensive extravaganza, masterminded by the mayor, was intended to be the beginning of his presidential campaign. The construction (but not interior decoration) of the cathedral had to be finished by September, before the celebration, to prove that Luzhkov could achieve the impossible. According to the *Daily Telegraph*, "Laborers have been working day and night on the cathedral, which is as big as St. Paul's. Mr. Luzhkov had made it clear that the contractors would never lay a brick in Moscow again if the exterior was not finished in time for the anniversary celebration."[2]

The scale of the celebration impressed international observers as well as the Muscovites themselves. "Miracles will also be laid on," the *Daily Telegraph* commented. Luzhkov paid for military aircraft to seed clouds with pellets of silver iodide so that any rain would fall before the festivities started. "To cap the celebrations, a closing ceremony at the newly roofed Olympic stadium will feature a laser vision of the Virgin Mary projected onto artificial mist, while white swans swim below. The aim is to show the world that Moscow has shed its dour, gray visage and is now, in the words of Mr. Luzhkov, becoming a 'normal civilized capital.'"[3]

There had been nothing like it since the centenary of Lenin's birth in 1970. The main event was a concert on the steps of the illuminated cathedral, where the world's largest chorus—more than two thousand singers sent by local officials from all over Russia—performed Tchaikovsky's *1812 Overture*. Chorus and audience then joined in singing "My Beloved Capital," by Isaak Dunaevsky, the Stalinist composer whose marches had been wildly popular in the 1930s. The grandeur of it all was such that Russian journalists dubbed Luzhkov "the pharaoh."

The last stage of the reconstruction started in 1998. The interior of the immense building had to be decorated with murals, a commission that the

painter Ilya Glazunov had expressed an interest in since the project's outset. This former semidissident who had strong nationalist and Orthodox
sentiments had become an official artist in Yeltsin's time and even had his
own museum. But Tsereteli, who preferred to forego Glazunov's assistance,
cut him out. The "desperate struggle of artistic groups for the commission
of the century," as one writer called it, was settled by a competition. Both
camps showed their works in the Academy of Arts, where, the writer said,
"Yesterday's champions of Socialist Realism easily transformed Lenin into
Christ."[4]

"Is it a good thing that the saints look like partisans and the archangels
look like the women with machine guns decorating the dome of the pavilion in the Komsomolskaia metro station?" the writer asked. This rhetori-
cal question didn't bother the academy presidium, which selected fifteen
"creative collectives," bringing together seventy painters led by recognized
Socialist Realists such as Nikolai Solomin, Sergei Repin, Valentin Chelom-
biev, and others. "We can begin work in the cathedral tomorrow," said the
satisfied Tsereteli. The interior decoration had to be completed before the
millennium.

The re-creation of the original murals and paintings in Ton's cathedral was even more problematic than the reconstruction of the building.
Most of the decorations had been destroyed and had to be copied from
nineteenth-century black-and-white photographs. Architectural furnishings had also been lost. A strange rumor circulated in the Russian press
that the Stalin government had sold a gigantic marble baptismal font saved
from the cathedral to Eleanor Roosevelt, who in turn had given it to the
Vatican, though the Holy See denied having any such object.[5]

While the scaffolding for the painters was going up, Luzhkov asked
UNESCO to put the unfinished building on its list of international heritage sites — along with the Pyramids, the Great Wall of China, and Cologne
cathedral.[6] UNESCO turned him down. But in Russia Luzhkov's activities
as a master builder were imitated by regional administrative heads all over
the country. In St. Petersburg, a competition was announced to build a
cathedral that would be dedicated to the memory of the first church built in
the city. "Every capital has to have its own Cathedral of Christ the Savior,"
one journalist commented.[7] The most striking "reconstruction" was in
Kaliningrad, the former Königsberg, where the Soviets had destroyed no
Orthodox churches because there weren't any to begin with, Königsberg

having been a German city until the end of World War II. Today Kalinin-grad is cut off from Russia proper by the Baltic states, but it is still a cru-cial base for the Russian fleet, and the construction of a smaller replica of Christ the Savior on Victory Square was a blatant assertion of who owned the city.

The reconstruction frenzy extended to secular monuments as well. The Assembly of Russian Nobility, which became active in the 1990s, estab-lished a charitable foundation, Repentance and Renaissance, to collect funds both in Russia and abroad for the reconstruction of czarist monu-ments destroyed during the Communist epoch.[8] Their first project was the huge seated figure of Alexander III situated near the cathedral. The most conservative of the czars, Alexander became a cult figure during Yeltsin's late years. From the post-Soviet perspective, the reign of this true Russian czar seemed ideal. Ruling over a powerful empire in a time of relative social peace, he imposed his will on the Balkans and completely repressed politi-cal opposition at home. Not least, his support of Russian values encour-aged the stability so desired by the citizens of Yeltsin's Russia. Who could lead with a strong hand, as Alexander III had? Clearly, not Yeltsin.

The man who created a cathedral from nothing was a better candi-date to become the new Alexander III. Christ the Savior was associated most strongly with Luzhkov; it was part of his image and even the foun-dation of a personality cult that recalled Soviet days. The sculptor Meru-zhan Mkheian, who took part in the reconstruction, created a bronze work called *Renaissance,* depicting the mayor and the patriarch standing over the ruins of the old Christ the Savior and holding a small model of the new cathedral.[9]

By 1999 it was clear that Luzhkov's Moscow, with its gigantic monu-ments, its new old cathedrals, its lavish underground shopping malls, and its museums dedicated to such court artists as the sentimental realist Shilov and the nationalist Glazunov, was a reflection of postperestroika Russia. "The Russian heritage industry is thriving, nowhere more so than in Mos-cow of the powerful mayor, Yury Luzhkov," reported an English journalist. "The new/old cathedral is the epitome of the new Russian Zeitgeist — pro-foundly conservative, backward-looking, and hugely controversial."[10]

To the art critic Andrei Kovalev, Luzhkov had proved himself the real artist of the New Russian Moscow. He showed his power of artistic innova-tion when he poured concrete in the form of the ghost cathedral. "His real predecessor, of course, wasn't the architect Ton, who never succeeded in finishing his ill-fated construction, but Joseph Stalin, whose name is associated not only with Stalin's repressions but also with Stalin's style."[11]

Meantime, the decoration of the interior was in full swing. Tsereteli and his crew used acrylic and fluorescent paints for the murals, which had originally been executed in oils. But the priest Leonid Kalinin, head of the Coordination Council for the Reconstruction of the Artistic Decoration, found an excuse for the modern materials: "The church accepts with pleasure scientific innovations that do not contradict the canons nor lower quality."[12]

A chain of ritual ceremonies accompanied the interior decoration. In the spring of 1998 Luzhkov himself climbed to the gallery of the cathedral to execute a symbolic brushstroke on the ornamentation, and in May 1999, on Luzhkov's initiative, members of the Federation Council, the upper house of the Duma, did the same. Vladimir Platonov, deputy head of the Federation Council, Ivan Sklyarov, governor of the Nizhny Novgorod region, and other regional statesmen donned construction helmets and applied their brushes to the cathedral walls, using only the colors of the Russian flag — blue, white, and red. The ceremony symbolized "the participation of all of Russia in the reconstruction of the cathedral."[13]

By September 1999 the decoration of the main dome of the cathedral was completed. More than a quarter of a century had been required for the task in the original cathedral, but "in our century one year was enough for the decoration," a typical press report boasted.[14] In true Soviet fashion, Tsereteli "reported that work on the painting of the dome of 4,235 square meters was completed substantially ahead of the schedule approved by the mayor and patriarch Aleksey II." This feat was celebrated in a ceremony in which the patriarch and the mayor climbed to a platform forty-three meters above the ground and with a symbolic spanner unscrewed a symbolic nut to begin the process of disassembling the scaffolding.[15]

The triumphant Tsereteli announced: "Yury Luzhkov entrusted us with creating a school of fresco painting. We had to create it anew (because during the years of Soviet power the knowledge was lost)."[16] Tsereteli's self-congratulation was not entirely warranted, because the paintings in the new cathedral were not frescoes — and the knowledge of fresco painting had never been lost — but this kind of general anti-Soviet rhetoric was popular with the new Russian officialdom. If the painters who decorated the cathedral belonged to any tradition, it was Socialist Realism. All of them had been trained in the most conservative Soviet art schools. The only thing that was new to them was the subject matter.

The project of the century allowed an army of official realist painters whose skills were no longer in demand after the end of the Soviet Union to return to their role of aesthetic priests. Now they marched not under the red banner but with cross in hand, and immediately they began to dictate their own aesthetic canon. Father Leonid Kalinin, who supervised the decoration, expressed his preferences in art: "If I go to New York and see some of that stuff they call modern art, I want to take a shower. There are no artistic criteria there at all. It is false, lying, repulsive work. You need to wash it all away."[17]

Both the mayor and the patriarch were ready to celebrate a victory. The decoration was scheduled for completion in November 1999 because the cathedral was opening to the public on January 7, 2000, for the first Orthodox Christmas of the new millennium. The patriarch proudly stated that critics had been silenced. "Many asked if it was necessary to build cathedrals in our difficult times. But when was it ever easy to build cathedrals in Russia?" The new cathedral became the trademark of the Moscow patriarchy and of the patriarch himself. Visiting the Krasnoyarsk region in 1999, he gave the governor, General Lebed, a porcelain vase decorated with his monogram and the image of the cathedral, "the symbol of Russia and faith." Touched, the general promised to send the vase to the local museum to commemorate this historical event.[18]

In 2000, the first year of the Putin presidency, the Cathedral of Christ the Savior was the scene of two important political events. On January 30, in a televised ceremony, Patriarch Aleksei decorated General Anatoly Kvashnin, head of the general staff, and his deputy, Colonel General Valery Manilov, with the church order of Holy Prince Daniil of Moscow. Both generals played instrumental roles in the second Chechen war, which was in full swing at the time. According to the religious writer Alexander Nezhny, the ceremony and the patriarch's speech in support of the war demonstrated that the Russian Orthodox Church had once again become an official state church.[19]

The final step was to solve the problem of the last czar and his family. They had been canonized by the Orthodox Church Abroad, but the patriarch didn't attend their burial service in St. Petersburg in 1998 because the most conservative bloc in the synod refused to recognize the remains as those of the royal family. Despite this unwillingness, two years later Nicholas and Alexandra achieved sainthood. The patriarch was concerned that the issue might prove to be socially divisive, because most Russians did not support canonization, but the Synod of Bishops, which convened on August 13, 2000, went ahead with it. The reaction the patriarch feared did not materialize. The truth was, according to one newspaper report, that the "overwhelming majority of Russian citizens don't care if the family of the last Russian emperor is canonized or not."[20] But the circle had been completed. The ruined cathedral was resurrected and the murdered czar sanctified.

Many members of the Russian intelligentsia who had supported the church during the 1960s through the 1980s became disillusioned with the new official Christianity of the 1990s. Liberal observers of the Moscow Patriarchy compared the role it played to that of the Central Committee Ideological Department in the Soviet Union. The romance of the Orthodox Church with the state in the new Russia led to a new ideological function for the church; it became a foundation of the official nationalism established during Yeltsin's reign and enforced under Putin. Once prosecuted and repressed, the church was associated at best with officialdom and at worst with the dark nationalist forces that destroyed contemporary art exhibitions, fought for the prohibition of Western movies, and distributed anti-Semitic literature. The image of the honest priest pursued by the KGB was replaced by the public figure of the church hierarch calling for religious censorship or asserting that human rights did not correspond to the teachings of Christianity.

"The intelligentsia wanted faith," noted one commentator sadly. "It got the Cathedral of Christ the Savior. . . . The intelligentsia doesn't like it. So what? The intelligentsia never likes the world. The idea of an intelligentsia that is happy with the state of the world is nonsense."[21]

Notes

Chapter One

1. "Zalozhenie Khrama vo imia Khrista Spasitelia," 5–11.
2. Sokolov, *Istoricheskoe opisanie torzhestva*, 1–2, 16.
3. Herzen, *Zapiski Vitberga*, 380.
4. Iakubovskii, *Karlik Favorita*, 97–98.
5. Alexander, who didn't want to be known as the ruler of a nation of savages, hurriedly denounced Napoleon as the arsonist, calling him "the new Atila." Two opposing views of who started the Moscow fire coexist in the Russian consciousness to this day. How these views were affected by political trends is described by Lapin in *Rossiia v XIX–XX vv.*
6. Pushkin, *Eugene Onegin*, chap. 10: "A Fragment." General Mikhail Barclay de Tolly was the author of the plan of retreat for the Russian army.
7. Bartenev, "Rasskazy kniazia A. N. Golitsyna," 91.
8. Lotman, *Besedy*, 319.

Chapter Two

1. [Kikin], "O postroenii khrama Spasitelia," 228.
2. Ibid.
3. Ibid., 229.
4. Eikhenbaum, "S. P. Zhikharev," 653.
5. Lotman, *Karamzin*, 523.
6. Zorin, *Kormia dvuglavogo orla*, 157–186.
7. [Kikin], "O postroenii khrama Spasitelia," 230.
8. Ibid., 230–231.
9. *Polnoe sobranie zakonov Rossiiskoi Imperii* (1885), 296.
10. Shishkov, *Dvenadtsat' sobstvennoruchnykh pisem*, 16.
11. Viazemskii, *Stikhotvoreniia*, 239.
12. Czartoryski, *Besedy*, 85.
13. Bogdanovich, *Istoriia*, 516.
14. Zorin, *Kormia dvuglavogo orla*, 248–249.
15. Geller, *Istoriia Rossiiskoi imperii*, 282.
16. Kliuchevskii, *Sochineniia*, 424.
17. Geller, *Istoriia Rossiiskoi imperii*, 290.
18. Troinitskii, *Aleksandr I i Napoleon*, 284.
19. Kersnovskii, *Istoriia Russkoi armii*, 6.
20. Mironenko, *Samoderzhavie i reformy*, 209.

Chapter Three

1. Kersnovskii, *Istoriia Russkoi armii*, 11.
2. After the foreign campaign began, Shishkov and his supporters were gradually removed from the ideological leadership of the society, and in August 1814 he was dismissed as secretary of state. Zorin, *Kormia dvuglavogo orla*, 254.
3. [Kikin], "O postroenii khrama Spasitelia," 231.
4. Kirichenko 1992, 18–24. Kirichenko was the first art historian who not only analyzed the materials relating to the competition for the cathedral project but also researched the history of its construction.
5. Voronikhin is believed to have been the illegitimate son of Alexander Stroganov, president of the Academy of Arts.
6. Grimm, *Arkhitektor Voronikhin*, 95–99.
7. Kirichenko 1992, 22.
8. The architectural historian Vladimir Snegirev, Vitberg's first biographer, was referring to Voronikhin's classical heritage when he said that "Voronikhin's ideas were the foundation of Vitberg's architectural creativity." Snegirev, *Vitberg*, 34.
9. Herzen, *Zapiski Vitberga*, 380.
10. Ibid., 382.
11. Ibid., 385.
12. For Herzen's description of Vitberg's design, see *Zapiski Vitberga*, 387–388.
13. Mostovskii, in *Khram* 1996b, 10–12.
14. Kirichenko 1992, 29.

Chapter Four

1. Herzen, *Zapiski Vitberga*, 401.
2. His favor to Baroness Krudener came about because at the moment he was informed of her desire to see him, he was reading these lines in Revelation 12:1: "And there appeared a great wonder in heaven; a woman clothed with the sun, and the moon under her feet, and upon her head a crown of twelve stars."
3. For Vitberg's autobiography, see *Russkaia starina*, 1876, no. 9: 109–126; no. 10: 267–296; no. 12: 759–770; Herzen, *Zapiski Vitberga*. For additional information, see Serkov, *Russkoe masonstvo*, 184–185.
4. Labzin's role in the history of Masonry is described by Sokolovskaia, "Rannee Aleksandrovskoe masonstvo," 154–155. For Labzin's biography and further bibliography, see Serkov, *Russkoe masonstvo*, 454–455; for the Dying Sphinx lodge and lists of its members, 1106–1108.
5. Billington, *Icon and Axe*, 255; Smith, *Working the Rough Stone*, 162.
6. For Novikov and the Martinists, see Smith, *Working the Rough Stone*, and Serkov, *Russkoe masonstvo*, 594–595.
7. Sokolovskaia, "Rannee Aleksandrovskoe masonstvo," 167–168; Serkov, *Russkoe masonstvo*, 1122, 1124.

8. Sokolovskaia, "Rannee Aleksandrovskoe masonstvo," 154–155, 178.

9. Pypin, *Religioznye dvizheniia pri Aleksandre I,* 148, noted that "Labzin renewed old Masonic legends with the latest discoveries of mysticism."

10. Serkov, *Russkoe masonstvo,* 1106.

11. According to Billington, *Icon and Axe,* 285, Labzin "became a kind of coordinator-in-chief for publications of the new supra-confessional church."

12. Shilder, *Imperator Aleksandr Pervyi,* 267; Serkov, *Russkoe masonstvo,* 454.

13. Zhikharev, "Petr Iakovlevich Chaadaev," 203.

14. In 1821 Runich, the trustee of the St. Petersburg academic district, accused certain professors at the university of attacking religion and the government in their lectures. One professor was accused of not believing that the Bible was a "sufficient historical source." Some professors were forced to resign. Runich believed that he was fighting the godless Enlightenment and acting in the spirit of Alexander's universalist ideology.

15. Bartenev, "Rasskazy kniazia A. N. Golitsyna," 61.

16. Billington, *Icon and Axe,* 282–283; Georgii Florovskii, *Puti,* 130–131, notes that Alexander consciously created the legend that his spiritual enlightenment was a consequence of the burning of Moscow. Florovskii believes that the czar became interested in mysticism much earlier and that the war was merely a catalyst to intensify his mystical passion. In any case, in Alexander's mind his moral transformation was connected to the miraculous salvation of Russia in 1812.

Chapter Five

1. Zorin, *Kormia dvuglavogo orla,* 265. Two other friends of Golitsyn, Koshelev and Lenivtsev, were known among the Rosicrucian-Martinists as radical mystics. In 1806 they, together with Golitsyn, Labzin, and Runich, were members of the mystic People of God lodge. They induced ecstatic states in which they talked to God and prophesied. Sokolovskaia, "Rannee Aleksandrovskoe masonstvo," 172; Serkov, *Russkoe masonstvo,* 1051.

2. Billington, *Icon and Axe,* 282.

3. Filaret, *Pis'ma k rodnym,* 166–167.

4. Sokolovskaia, "Rannee Aleksandrovskoe masonstvo," 84.

5. A court counselor held the seventh rank in the civil service, corresponding to the military rank of lieutenant-colonel. Most officials received the Order of St. Vladimir, fourth (lowest) class, after thirty-five years of "constant and blameless civil service." Vitberg was only thirty-five years old when he received this decoration, third class. Shepelev, *Tituly, mundiry, ordena,* 116, 195.

6. Herzen, *Zapiski Vitberga,* 422.

7. Novitskii, "Masonstvo i russkoe tserkovnoe zodchestvo," 61–72. The problem was recently taken up by Medvedkova, "Solomonov khram — dom premudrosti," 459–468.

8. Serkov, *Russkoe masonstvo,* 1106.

9. Pypin, *Russkoe masonstvo,* 120.

10. Runich, director of the Moscow post office, managed the secret correspondence of the Masons, including Novikov's. He wrote to Novikov about Vitberg's wish to meet him. Novikov agreed and answered Runich in the Aesopian language typical of his correspondence: "I await Karl Lavrentievich with impatience, especially after reading in your letter everything you wrote about him. I will be happy to be useful to him and to the cause. If I find appropriate earth, I'll be happy to sow it with everything my Master gave to me for such a purpose." [Novikov], "Pis'ma N. I. Novikova k D. P. Runichu."

11. Lotman, *Karamzin,* 34.

12. Herzen, *Zapiski Vitberga,* 444.

13. The architecture historian Evgenia Kirichenko for some reason changed the meaning of Vitberg's words in her book (Kirichenko 1992, 27). She attributed his words to Novikov and also changed the expression "exterior cathedral" to "people's cathedral." The Russian words for exterior, "naruzhnyi," and people's, "narodnyi," sound alike. This mistake led to the replacement of Vitberg's ardent defense of the Masonic essence of the cathedral with the "democratic" Novikov's politically correct statement.

Chapter Six

1. Sokolovskaia, "Rannee Aleksandrovskoe masonstvo," 102.

2. Smith, *Working the Rough Stone,* 121.

3. Herzen, *Zapiski Vitberga,* 386.

4. Ibid.

5. Sokolovskaia, "Rannee Aleksandrovskoe masonstvo," 88.

6. Pypin, *Religioznye dvizheniia pri Aleksandre I,* 148; Ridley, *Freemasons,* 23.

7. Serkov, *Russkoe masonstvo,* 1106.

8. Goldovskii, *D. G. Levitskii,* 28.

9. Mel'gunov and Sidorov, *Masonstvo v ego proshlom i nastoiashchem,* vol. 1 (Moscow 1914): 96, 107, 183.

10. In 1813 Vitberg became master of rituals of the lodge. Serkov, *Russkoe masonstvo,* 1106.

11. Herzen, *Zapiski Vitberga,* 438.

12. Merzliakov, *Pesn'.*

Chapter Seven

1. Pipes, *Russia under the Old Regime,* 159.

2. The Holy Alliance was established on Christmas Day, 1815.

3. Mironenko, *Samoderzhavie i reformy,* 36, 41, 209.

4. Vitberg ("Avtobiografia") didn't consider Arakcheev his enemy. He thought Arakcheev wanted to win him over in the struggle with Golitsyn for control of the construction.

5. Arakcheev, traditionally considered a bit of a blockhead as well as a petty tyrant, was Alexander's only minister who was a high school graduate. He reformed the Russian artillery on the eve of the Napoleonic War. Kersnovskii, *Istoriia Russkoi armii*, 10; Mironenko, *Samoderzhavie i reformy*, 40.

6. At his country estate, Gruzini, Arakcheev adopted the most progressive methods of agriculture and even established a kind of credit bank. He freed all his peasants in his will.

7. Vitberg's only achievement was to liberate the serfs who participated in the cathedral construction; in 1829 they received from Nicholas the right to "move up to another estate." Snegirev, *Vitberg*, 67.

8. Mironenko, *Samoderzhavie i reformy*, 103.

9. Ibid., 157.

10. Ibid., 46.

11. Ibid., 140–141.

12. According to Kliuchevskii's incisive observation (*Kurs russkoi istorii*, 416), Alexander, "who wanted to become the peacemaker of Europe, found himself its dictator."

Chapter Eight

1. Many of Magnitsky's ideas later flowed into the theory of Russian exceptionalism, from Nicholas's "official nationalism" to the Eurasianist theory of the first half of the twentieth century that Russia's role was to be a bridge between East and West.

2. Herzen, *Zapiski Vitberga*, 429.

3. As a number of historians have noted, Vitberg had another source of inspiration, French classicism, which had nothing in common with the idea of Russian uniqueness. Medvedkova ("Solomonov khram—dom premudrosti," 446) has called Vitberg's cathedral project "one of countless 'paper' projects in the style of the architectural fantasies of the French pensioners in Rome." Semyon Mikhailovskii ("Mechta o khrame," 8) has pointed out the striking resemblance of the later version of the cathedral project, with its side porticoes and dome, to Étienne-Louis Boullée's visionary design of 1791 for a monument to the supreme being. Just as the French revolutionaries hoped to replace Roman Catholicism with a new quasi-religion, Alexander dreamed of establishing a universal European religion.

Chapter Nine

1. A number of private landowners had utopian dreams; one of the best known was the liberal Nikolai Turgenev, who tried to establish a kind of peasant republic on his estate. It failed because the elected leaders treated the peasants more harshly than the overseers appointed by the master. Arkhangelskii, *Aleksandr I*, 310.

2. The main corpus of documents on the construction of Vitberg's cathedral is held

in TsIAM, f. 243, op. 1-8. A detailed description of the construction is given in "Case of the Investigative Commission," OPI GIM, f. 132, d. 549.

3. Mostovskii, in *Khram* 1996b, 18.

4. TsIAM, f. 243, op. 12, d. 2, l. 423.

5. Ibid., ll. 130-140, 146-148.

6. Herzen, *Byloe i dumy*, 151.

7. OPI GIM, f. 132, d. 549, l. 748.

8. Mostovskii, in *Khram* 1996b, 19.

Chapter Ten

1. The Decembrist uprising was led by a group of army officers who belonged to a secret society advocating the introduction of a constitution, the abolition of serfdom, and other reforms. The occasion was the death of Alexander I on November 19, 1825. His brother Constantine refused to assume the throne, and Nicholas, the third brother, had to be persuaded to accept it. Taking advantage of the confusion, the officers, commanding about three thousand men, assembled in Senate Square on December 14 and refused to swear allegiance to Nicholas. The revolt was quickly suppressed, five leaders were publicly hanged, and many others were exiled. Nicholas, who personally participated in the interrogations of the leaders, was convinced that the uprising resulted from Alexander's liberal policies.

2. The unsuitability of the site is disputable. Snegirev (*Vitberg*, 65-66) was convinced that the committee's decision was engineered to discredit the architect. Kirichenko, who didn't refute Snegirev, wrote: "It is hard to believe in the dishonesty or professional incompetence of truly authoritative members of the expert commission." Kirichenko 1992, 37.

3. Gordin, *Mistiki i okhraniteli*, 197.

4. For information about the investigation, see "Delo sledstvennoi komissii po obvineniu Aleksandra Lavrentievicha Vitberga v zloupotrebleniakh pri postroike Khrama Khrista," OPI GIM, f. 132, d. 549.

5. Mostovskii, in *Khram* 1996b, 21.

6. Dmitriev, *Vospominania*, 318.

7. Gordin, *Mistiki i okhraniteli*, 18.

8. Herzen, *Byloe i dumy*, 148-153.

9. Billington, *Icon and Axe*, 297.

10. Vitberg's surviving blueprints are scattered among the State Museum of Architecture, Tretiakov Gallery, State Historical Museum, and the Alexander Herzen Memorial Museum, Moscow; the State Russian Museum and Research Museum of the Academy of Arts, St. Petersburg; and the Vasnetsov Regional Art Museum, Kirov.

11. Geller, *Istoriia Rossiiskoi imperii*, 30.

12. Uvarov was as paradoxical a figure as Magnitsky, whose ideological blueprints he recycled. The historian Sergei Soloviev (*Zapiski*, 58-59) provided the best description of this father of the Russian national idea, writing that Uvarov "contrived the words 'Orthodoxy, Autocracy, Nationality.' 'Orthodoxy,' being an atheist; 'autocracy,' being a liberal; 'nationality,' having read not one Russian book in the course of his life and always writing in French or German."

Chapter Eleven

1. Slavina, *Ton*, 36-38. Ton's completed project was approved by the czar on April 10, 1832.
2. Zhukovskii, *Proizvedenia*, 5; Stasov, *Izbrannie sochineniia*, 505.
3. Slavina, *Ton*, 149.
4. For the Ton brothers' Masonic activities, see Serkov, *Russkoe masonstvo*, 804.
5. Slavina, *Ton*, 106-107.
6. Ibid., 149.
7. Vrangel', "Iskusstvo i gosudar Nikolai Pavlovich," 53-64.
8. Norman, *Hermitage*, 79.

Chapter Twelve

1. Senator Aleksandr Bashilov, head of the Moscow Construction Commission, wrote: "What a wonderful idea, worthy of Nicholas I, who wants the new monument to face the ancient Kremlin." OR RPB, f. G/4, d. 691, l. 66ob.
2. Kirichenko, in *Khram* 1996a, 28-32.
3. Ibid., 24, 31; "Arkhitekturnye ansambli Moskvy, 1830-60 godov," 8.
4. Shmaro, "Khram Khrista Spasitelia," 14.
5. Kirichenko, in *Khram* 1996a, 51.
6. Sirotkin, *Napoleon i Rossiia*, 250.
7. Passek, *Iz dalnikh let*, 146.
8. Golitsyn, "Zapiska," 105, 107-109.
9. During the 1830s the Russian army numbered almost one million soldiers and was equal to the armies of Great Britain, France, and Prussia combined. Kennedy, *Rise and Fall of the Great Powers*, 154. Officially, half of the state budget was spent on the army. In the end, militarization overstrained the country's resources. Gordin, *Mistiki i okhraniteli*, 198.
10. Golitsyn, "Zapiska," 295-296, 442-444.
11. Kuzmichev (pseud.), *Torzhestvo zakladki khrama vo imia Khrista Spasitelia*, 5.
12. Mostovskii, in *Khram* 1996b, 29.
13. Billington, *Icon and Axe*, 314.
14. Veresaev, *Pushkin v zhizni*, 64.
15. F. I. Tiutchev, *Lirica*, vol. 1, ed. K. V. Pigarev (Moscow: Nauka, 1965), 210.
16. Bezatosnyi, "Rossiskii titulovannyi geniralitet," 20.

17. Pypin, *Kharakteristiki literaturnikh mnenii,* 192.

18. Mostovskii, in *Khram* 1996b, 48, 55.

Chapter Thirteen

1. Florovskii, *Puti,* 166–184.

2. When Labzin fell into disgrace, the usually extremely cautious Filaret was one of the few who continued to correspond with him and support him financially. Laikevich, "Vospominaniia," 174, 195.

3. "Iz zapisnoi knizhki Russkogo Arkhiva," 93.

4. Educated Russians preferred to read the Bible in European languages. The czar always used the French version of Lemaistre de Sacy, the famous Jansenist who, accused of heresy, translated the Bible in 1666 while imprisoned in the Bastille.

5. Arkhangelskii, *Aleksander I,* 364.

6. Herzen, *Zapiski A. L. Vitberga,* 394.

7. "Iz pis'ma N. V. Berga," 222–223.

8. Florovskii, *Puti,* 163, 166.

9. The translation of the Bible into Russian began in 1858. The Gospels were published in 1860, the entire New Testament in 1862, and the Old Testament in installments from 1868 to 1875.

10. The situation of 1825 was repeated. Shortly after the Decembrist uprising, Filaret made known the testament of Alexander I, in which Nicholas was named as his successor over Constantine. Nicholas, tainted by the questionable legality of the document and by the fratricidal carnage that accompanied his accession, urgently needed the church to legitimize him and to justify the bloodshed. The spectacle of Filaret solemnly removing Alexander's testament from a shrine concealed in the altar had the desired effect on the crowds.

11. Florovskii, *Puti,* 203.

12. Mostovskii, in *Khram* 1996b, 29.

13. Lotman, *Karamzin,* 25.

14. Mostovskii, in *Khram* 1996b, 48, 55.

15. Mostovskii, "Khram Khrista Spasitelia v Moskve," 23.

16. In Shishova, *Khram Khrista Spasitelia,* published by the Russian Academy of Arts, the relief sculptures are illustrated in clockwise sequence. As a result, each facade looks separate and unconnected to the others. The academy's leaders, former Soviet functionaries who traded their "Communist values" for nationalreligious ones, showed their misunderstanding of their new faith.

17. Mozgovaia, "Skul'ptury Khrama Khrista Spasitelia," 49–50.

Chapter Fourteen

1. Because all Russian czars after Alexander I and Nicholas I were called either Alexander or Nicholas, the symbolism of heavenly support for the house of Romanov

never lost its topicality. Saints Alexander Nevsky and Nicholas also symbolized the unity of church and state. According to Filaret's program, the major historical protagonists were a holy prince and a saintly hierarch. This topic was also tied to the hidden meaning of the decoration.

2. Along with these transcendent ideas, Filaret was aware of the issues of the day. The right corner relief justifies the liberties Nicholas took in executing his older brother's construction; the left corner relief supports Nicholas's right to succeed to the throne. According to the Bible, David declared Solomon his successor, bypassing his older sons (1 Kings: 1–2).

3. The image of the Virgin, like the image of Christ, symbolized the theme of divine protection and appeared on every wall of the cathedral except the western wall, where Christ appeared. On the southern facade was the Virgin of Smolensk; on the eastern wall, the Virgin of Vladimir; on the northern wall, the Virgin of Iver. All these icons were connected to accounts of miraculous salvation. All were Byzantine in origin, stressing Russia's inheritance of the true faith of the first and second Romes.

4. Bartenev, "Rasskazy kniazia A. N. Golitsyna," 95.

5. The icon of the Virgin of Vladimir is the most honored in Russia. According to legend it was painted by Saint Luke himself. In 1395 the icon saved Russia from the invasion of Timur. But it failed to save the Russian parliament when President Yeltsin shelled it in 1993, although it was taken from the Tretiakov Gallery and carried in procession around Moscow during the conflict.

6. An iconographic prototype for these reliefs can be found among the illustrations in *Zhivopisnyi Karamzin.*

7. Stalin became the true heir of Filaret and Nicholas a hundred years later when he turned to the heroic Russian past to support the ideology of national bolshevism. He ordered Eisenstein to create the films *Alexander Nevsky* and *Ivan the Terrible,* which exploited victories symbolizing the triumph of Russia over both the West (Teutonic knights) and the East (Tatars).

8. Because Russian troops didn't participate in the battle of Waterloo or other battles of 1815, these events were excluded from the Russian version of the victory over Napoleon. The famous Hundred Days didn't exist in official Russian historiography, nor did the pre-1812 Napoleonic Wars in which Russia and its allies were consistently defeated.

9. Kirichenko, in *Khram* 1996a, 33.

10. For an enlightened mystic like Alexander, civilization united Enlightenment and Christianity.

11. Another ideological pair of this sort existed: the Kremlin Palace designed in the Byzantine revival style by Ton in 1838 and the "western" Winter Palace in St. Petersburg, reconstructed in record time after the fire of 1837.

12. In 1652 the future patriarch Nikon had Philip's relics transferred to Moscow. It was

an impressive demonstration of the humiliation of state power by the church. Czar Aleksei placed in the martyr's coffin a letter of repentance begging forgiveness for the sins of his ancestor. Later Nikon carried through church reform and tried to establish the superiority of church power. He was defeated, but his ideas strongly influenced Filaret.

Chapter Fifteen

1. "Materialy dlia istorii russkoi tserkvi," 132-146. After Filaret's death, Metropolitan Inokenty, Archbishop Leonid of Yaroslavl, and Bishop Amvrosy of Dmitrov completed the program of painterly decoration. All proposed subjects were approved by the Construction Commission, but the last word belonged to Nicholas I and, after his death, to Alexander II. Mostovskii, in *Khram* 1996b, 56.
2. Mostovskii, in *Khram* 1996b, 56.
3. Ibid.
4. Ibid.
5. The gallery was Ton's version of the war museum Vitberg had planned for his cathedral.
6. Different interpretations of the iconostasis can be found in Kirichenko, in *Khram* 1996a, 39-40; Kirichenko, *Zapechatlennaia istoriia Rossii*, 252-253; and Sergeev, "Mitropolit Filaret i tserkovnaia arkhitektura," 27-31.
7. Filaret emphasized the importance of the unusually grand iconostasis in a letter of 1813. "Pis'ma mitr," 153-154.
8. Semyon Dmitriev, an architect and Ton's assistant, wrote, "The idea of the iconostasis canopy in the form of a chapel belonged to Emperor Nicholas I. The chapel over the tomb of Christ in the New Jerusalem monastery inspired this thought of the Sovereign. Architect Ton developed the idea." OR RGB, f. 90, k. 2, d. 8, p. 23. Dmitriev mentioned the "copy" of the tomb of Christ erected in the New Jerusalem monastery situated in Istra near Moscow.
9. For the second cathedral Filaret borrowed many ideas from his former opponent Shishkov: nationality, the unique character of Orthodoxy, and the history of Russia.
10. Pogodin, "Pis'mo k Gosudaru Tsesarevichu," 10-11.
11. Mostovskii, in *Khram* 1996b, 31.
12. "Kratkie svedeniia o sooruzhenii v Moskve Khrama vo imia Khrista Spasitelia," *Zhurnal Ministerstva Vnutrennukh Del*, pt. 29, no. 8 (1838): 185.
13. Sergei Mironenko, "Nikolai I," in *Rossiiskie samorderzhtsy* (Russian autocrats), ed. N. M. Maslova (Moscow: Mezhdunarodnye otnoshenniia, 1993), 158.

Chapter Sixteen

1. Mostovskii, in *Khram* 1996b, 22, 113-116.
2. Serfdom was abolished in 1861. The state budget was published for the first time in

1862. On April 17, 1863, the sovereign's birthday, corporal punishment was abolished. Court reform and the introduction of the jury system came in 1864.

3. Maiorova, "Bessmertnyi Rurik"; RGIA, f. 207, op. 3; f. 789, op. 2.

4. Maiorova, "Bessmertnyi Rurik."

5. Wortman, "Rule by Sentiment."

6. Bokhanov, *Romanov*, 77.

7. Fedorov, *Velik Bog Zemli Russkoi;* Protopopov, *O tom kak Bog sokhranil zhizn Gosudaria; Chetvertoe aprelia 1866 goda i ego patrioticheskoe znachenie.*

8. Zakharova, "Aleksandr II," 195.

9. *Istoricheskoe opisanie*, 55.

10. TsIAM, f. 243, op., 9, d. 427.

11. The construction of Ton's cathedral cost 15,123,163 rubles. Vitberg's unfinished cathedral cost 4,132,560 rubles. Mostovskii, in *Khram* 1996b, 116, 122.

Chapter Seventeen

1. RGIA, f. 789, op. 1/2, d. 2873, l. 28. This file contains the most complete documentation of sculpture production for the cathedral. See also op. 14, d. 74-L (Loganovskii) and d. 4-R (Ramazanov).

2. Kargopolova, "Takie zvezdy svetiat narodu raz v stoletie," 171.

3. Most of the documentation of the painterly decoration is in OPI GIM, f. 235, d. 2, 3, 5, 14, 15. See also Klimov, "Zhivopisnoe ubranstvo khrama Khrista Spasitelia," 75-132.

4. Ton's blueprints are in the Research Museum of the Academy of Arts in St. Petersburg and in the Museum of Architecture in Moscow.

5. TsIAM, f. 243, op. 9, d. 224, l. 4.

6. Bernshtein, "Ivanov i slavianofilstvo," 58-66.

7. Botkin, *Aleksandr Andreevich Ivanov*, 156.

8. Allenov, *Aleksandr Andreevich Ivanov*, 63.

9. Most of Ivanov's sketches for his Resurrection are in the Tretiakov Gallery.

10. OPI GIM, f. 235, d. 14. l. 3; OR RGB, f. 90, k. 3, d. 15, ll. 30-31.

11. Although Ton signed it, the blueprint of the interior of the cathedral of 1854 was executed by the architect I. A. Riazantsev. It is in the Research Museum of the Academy of Arts in St. Petersburg.

12. OPI GIM, f. 235, d. 14, l. 25.

13. OR RGB, f. 90, k. 2, d. 8, l. 23.

14. A. N. Bogoliubov, "Akademia khudozhestv v gody vozrozhdenia 1859-64. Vospominaniia Khudozhnika," *Russkaia Starina* (Moscow, 1880), vol. 29, no. 10.

15. Vorobieva, "K istorii masterskoi religioznoi zhivopisi v Akdemii khudozhestv," 34.

16. OPI GIM, f. 235, d. 14, l. 90.

17. The list of subjects for the painterly decoration of the cathedral with a description

of the disposition of the frescoes is in the files of the Construction Commission OPI GIM, f. 235, d. 15, ll. 25-31. Another version with some changes is in the file of documents of Semyon Dmitriev, OR RGB, f. 90, k. 1, d. 5, ll. 39-400b.

18. OPI GIM, f. 235, d. 14. l. 239. The Cathedral of St. Vladimir in Sevastopol (1862-88) is a monument to the Crimean war. The heroes—admirals fallen during the siege of the city—are buried there.

19. Bogoliubov, *Vospominaniia o v Boze pochivshem Imperatore Aleksandre III,* 10.

20. OR RGB, f. 90, k. 2, d. 8, l. 23.

21. Ibid., k. 1, d. 20, l. 42.

22. Bogoliubov, "Zapiski moriaka-khudozhnika," 123-124, 181-183; Bogoliubov, "Akademia khudozhestv v gody vozrozhdenia 1859-64," 413-414.

23. OR RGB, f. 90, k. 9, d. 11. l. 10b.

24. Kramskoi, *Pis'ma i stat'i,* 27.

25. OPI GIM, f. 235, d. 2, l. 1.

26. Ibid., l. 132.

27. OR RGB, f. 90.

28. The correspondence about Bruni's murals can be found in OPI GIM, f. 235, d. 14, 15.

29. Klimov, "Zhivopisnoe ubranstvo khrama Khrista Spasitelia," 105.

30. Surikov remembered, "I needed money to become free and to resume my activities." Voloshin, *M. A. Surikov,* 54. Semiradsky felt the same: "Executing such commissions from time to time gave me a chance to paint my own paintings, not stinting on materials and not counting on the sales of such works." OR RGB, f. 498, k. 1, d. 17, l. 12.

31. This painting was exhibited for the first time on the day Alexander II was assassinated and became an icon of the revolutionary intelligentsia.

32. "Khudozhestvennie raboty v Kharame Khrista Spasitelia v Moskve."

33. Klimov, "Zhivopisnoe ubranstvo khrama Khrista Spasitelia," 103.

34. Kargopolova, "Takie zvezdy svetiat narodu raz v stoletie," 171.

35. OPI GIM, f. 235, d. 2.

36. Mostovskii, in *Khram* 1996b, 38.

37. Ibid., 99.

38. Ibid., 93.

Chapter Eighteen

1. Billington, *Icon and Axe,* 395.

2. RGIA, f. 1284, d. 78, l. 274.

3. Tolstaia, *Zapiski freiliny,* 77.

4. The sumptuous banner produced for the Cathedral of Christ the Savior illustrated this new intention. The dates of the "miraculous salvations of the czar" were embroidered on the banner. Mostovskii, in *Khram* 1996b, 87-88.

5. Some contemporaries even stated that they saw the design of the new empress's monogram, E III, Ekaterina (Catherine) III. The czar ordered that all documents related to the coronation of the first Russian empress, Catherine I, be collected in archives. According to Leonid Liashenko, "The composition of the scenario for the future solemn act was in full swing." *Aleksander II* (Moscow: Molodaia gvardia, 2002), 144. The diplomat Count Vladimir Lamsdorf noted in his diary (*Dnevnik,* 111), "Everybody was convinced that His Majesty was willing on this occasion (the Moscow celebration) to marry publicly his morganatic wife and to place on her head the crown of the empress."

6. Zaionchkovskii, *Krizis,* 449-472.

7. Ibid., 452.

8. Ibid., 465.

9. Vitte (Witte), *Vospominaniia,* 212-213, 250.

10. Pobedonostsev, *Sochineniia,* 22.

11. Ibid.

12. Florovskii, *Puti,* 410.

13. Wortman, *Scenarios of Power,* vol. 2, 202.

14. RGIA, f. 473, op. 3, d. 78, l. 33.

15. Ibid., f. 797, op. 53/3-4, d. 24, ll. 10-100b, 11-110b, 15-150b, 16.

16. Ibid., l. 15.

17. Ibid., l. 150b.

18. For the ceremony, see *Sviashchennoe koronovanie imperatora Aleksandra III.*

19. Ibid., 411.

Chapter Nineteen

1. Zummer, *Kniga Botkina,* 12; Herzen, *Byloe i dumy,* 149; Grabar, *Peterburgskaia Arkhitektura,* 283-284; Trubetskoi, *Izbrannoe,* 328.

2. RGIA, f. 797, op. 53/3-4, d. 24, ll. 34-35.

3. Ibid., l. 35.

4. TsIAM, f. 244, op. 1, d. 297.

5. OPI GIM, f. 235, d. 15, ll. 103, 114.

6. RGIA, f. 797, op. 53/3-4, d. 24, l. 35.

7. Belousov, "Ushedshaia Moskva," 344.

8. Slonov, "Iz zhizni torgovoi Moskvy," 211-212.

9. Kozlov, "Pravoslavnie traditsi chestvovania pamiati Otechestvennoi voiny 1812 goda v Moskve," 53-58.

10. The complex was to include a museum of the war of 1812, featuring a gigantic panorama by Franz Rubo of the battle of Borodino as well as a museum devoted to Kutuzov. Sirotkin and Kozlov, *Traditsii Borodina,* 37. The conflict over the museums is described in Sirotkin, *Napoleon I i Rossiia.*

11. The museum's collection was to include objects from the period of 1812 from the

private collections of Ivan Kolodeev, Pyotr Shchukin, and others, such as diaries, memoirs, newspapers, folk prints, and objects that had belonged to participants.

12. The Special Committee was established in 1907. *Godovye otchety Vysochaishe utverzhdennogo Komiteta po ustroistvu v Moskve Muzeia voiny 1812 goda.*

13. V. Lapin, "100 letnii ubilei Otechestvennoi voiny 1812 goda."

14. Gavriil Konstantinovich, *V Mramornom dvortse,* 110.

Chapter Twenty

1. Kandidov, *Kogo spasal khram,* 67.

2. Ibid.

3. Vostrishev, *Tikhon,* 85.

4. Kandidov, *Tserkov,* 24-25.

5. Kandidov, *Kogo spasal khram,* 51-52.

6. Ibid., 53.

7. Ibid., 54.

8. Kamchatsky, *Razstrel,* 32-46.

9. Okunev, *Dnevnik moskvicha,* 106.

10. Erenburg, "Sudnyi Den'," in *Stikhotvoreniia,* 306. He made a mistake. The patriarch had not yet been elected.

11. Regel'son, *Tragediia,* 33.

12. Okunev, *Dnevnik moskvicha,* 109.

13. Kandidov, *Kogo spasal khram,* 55.

14. Ibid., 56.

15. Martsinkovskii, *Zapiski,* 37-38.

16. Ibid., 101. The explosive political atmosphere heated up even more after the so-called miracle of the First of May. For the May Day celebration, the icon of St. Nicholas mounted over the Nicholas Gates of the Kremlin was hidden by a Soviet slogan. When columns of Red soldiers marched past the gates, the slogan fell, revealing the icon.

17. Ibid., 119.

18. Ibid., 112.

Chapter Twenty-one

1. Kandidov, *Kogo spasal khram,* 58.

2. *Khram* 1996b, 73.

3. Kandidov, *Kogo spasal khram,* 60-66.

4. *Khram* 1996b, 99.

5. Martsinkovskii, *Zapiski,* 127.

6. Ibid.

7. According to some sources, more than a thousand bloody clashes with the authorities took place. Regel'son, *Tragediia,* 285.

8. One such exhumation, which was filmed, was edited by the young Dziga Vertov, who had just resumed his career as a documentary filmmaker.

9. Regel'son, *Tragediia*, 265.

10. Martsinkovskii, *Zapiski*, 160.

11. *Khram* 1996b, 97.

12. Ibid., 96-97.

13. Regel'son, *Tragediia*, 262-264.

14. Maiakovskii, "O patriarkhe Tikhone," 16.

15. *Khram* 1996b, 97.

16. Ibid.

17. Soloviev, *"Obnovlencheskii" raskol.*

Chapter Twenty-two

1. A few months after this appeal to the government, Kalinovsky left the priesthood to become an atheist propagandist. Vostrishev, *Tikhon*, 239.

2. Ibid., 239-241.

3. Ibid., 241-242.

4. Krasnov-Levitin, *Trudi i dni*, 9.

5. Regel'son, *Tragediia*, 326.

6. Lentulova, *Lentulov*, 116.

7. Ibid., 116-117.

8. Kozarzhevskii, in *Khram* 1996a, 252.

9. Ibid.

10. Nikos Kazantzakis, *Report to Greco* (London: Faber and Faber, 1973), 411-412.

11. Vvedenskii, *Tserkov i revolutsiia*.

12. Ibid., 52.

13. Regel'son, *Tragediia*, 329.

14. Ibid.

15. Ibid.

16. Ibid.

17. Soloviev, *"Obnovlencheskii" raskol*, 320.

18. Regel'son, *Tragediia*, 330.

19. Ibid., 329.

20. *Khram* 1996b, 101-102.

21. Kataev, *Almaznyi moi venets*, 57.

Chapter Twenty-three

1. The Comintern replaced the Second (Socialist) International, which had ceased to exist at the beginning of World War I because many of the European Social Democratic parties had supported their governments' war efforts—a betrayal for which Lenin never forgave them.

2. Punin, *O Tatline*, 19–20.
3. Punin, "Tatlinova bashnia," 22.
4. Punin, *O Tatline*, 16.
5. Bowlt, "Tatlin und seine Antitisch," 188; Radlov, *O futurizme*, 48.
6. Teige, "Dnesni vytvarna," 174.
7. Ibid., 175.
8. Lizon, *Palace*, 66–67.
9. Ibid., 67.
10. Kogan, *Literatura*, 12.
11. Prokofiev, *Palace of Soviets*, 11.
12. *Dvorets Sovetov*, 6.
13. Kopp, *Town and Revolution*, 55.

Chapter Twenty-four

1. Krasin, "Arkhitekturnoe uvekovechivanie Lenina," 23. The article was first published in *Izvestia*, February 7, 1924.
2. Krasin, "Arkhitekturnoe uvekovechivanie Lenina," 24.
3. Kotyrev, *Mavzolei Lenina*, 67.
4. Ibid.
5. Khan-Magomedov, "K istorii vybora mesta," 21.
6. Malevich, "Lenin," 26.
7. Khan-Magomedov, "K istorii vybora mesta," 22.
8. Ibid.
9. Ibid.
10. Kataev, *Almaznyi moi venets*, 57.
11. Shklovskii, "Peterburg v blokade," in *Khod Konia*, 18–19.
12. Jacobson, *My Futurist Years*, 64.
13. Bulgakov, *Fatal Eggs*, 57.
14. Ibid., 132.
15. Mariengof, *Roman bez vran'ia*, 94.
16. Iurenev, *Eizenshtein*, 205.
17. The false monument aroused great excitement. Demian Bedny, the official Soviet fabulist, even wrote a poem about Eisenstein's reconstruction of the Alexander III monument: "Once it was a monument stupid and trivial,/Now when we need it—/A cheap cardboard 'model' is erected." Ibid.
18. Eizenshtein, *Memuary*, 50.
19. Maiakovskii, "Za chto borolis'?"

Chapter Twenty-five

1. Karine N. Ter-Akopyan, "Design and Construction of the Palace of Soviets of the USSR in Moscow," in Merkert and Revzin, *Naum Gabo and the Competition for the Palace of Soviets*, 185.

2. *Dvorets Sovetov,* 7.

3. Lizon, *Palace,* 76.

4. *Iz istorii sovetskoi arkhitektury,* 62–63.

5. Isaak Eigel, "K istorii postroeniia i snosa khrama Khrista Spasitelia," *Arkhitektura i stroitel'stvo Moskvy,* no. 7 (1988).

6. Kaganovich, *Pamiatnye zapiski,* 527–528.

7. Ibid.

8. Ter-Akopyan, "Design and Construction of the Palace of Soviets," 202–203.

9. Chukovskii, *Dnevnik,* 43.

10. Ibid., 44.

11. Andrei Kozarzhevskii, "Vospominaniia starogo moskvicha o khrame Khrista Spasitelia," in *Khram* 1996a, 253.

12. Nikolai Rerikh [Roerich], "Dukhovnye sokrovishcha: Komitetu Pakta Rerikha v Kharbine," in *Sviashchennii Dozor,* 122–127.

13. Monkhouse, *Moscow,* 231–232.

14. Monkhouse, *Moscow.*

15. *Sovetskoe rukovodstvo perepiska,* 158.

16. *Dvorets Sovetov,* 70.

17. Ter-Akopyan, "Design and Construction of the Palace of Soviets," 187.

18. Igor Kazus, "The Competition for the Country's Supreme Building," in Merkert and Revzin, *Naum Gabo and the Competition for the Palace of Soviets,* 213.

19. Erenburg, *Viza vremeni,* 31–32.

20. Ter-Akopyan, "Design and Construction of the Palace of Soviets," 190.

21. *Dvorets Sovetov,* 97–98.

22. Ibid., 96.

23. Ibid., 97.

24. Ibid., 53.

25. Igor Kazus, "The Great Illusion," in *Art and Power,* 189.

26. Helen Adkins, "International Participation in the Competition for the Palace of Soviets," in Merkert and Revzin, *Naum Gabo and the Competition for the Palace of Soviets,* 199.

27. *Dvorets Sovetov,* 105.

28. Ibid.

29. Ibid.

30. Ibid.

31. Ibid.

32. Ibid.

33. Ibid., 106.

34. Ibid., 105–106.

35. Ibid., 76.

36. Eigel, *Boris Iofan,* 19–34.

37. Andreeva, "Fashistskoe iskusstvo," 11.

38. Ibid.
39. *Stalin i Kaganovich*, 269.
40. Ibid.
41. *Stalin i Kaganovich.*
42. Tumarkin, *Lenin Lives!*
43. *Dvorets Sovetov*, 55.
44. Ibid., 56.
45. Ibid.
46. Ibid., 60.
47. Ibid., 59.
48. Prokofiev, *Palace of Soviets*, 15.
49. Groys, *The Total Art of Stalinism*, 53.
50. Ibid., 3.
51. *Dvorets Sovetov*, 59–60.
52. Ibid., 59.
53. *Dvorets Sovetov*, 60.
54. Eigel, *Boris Iofan*, 95.
55. Papernyi, *Kultura "Dva,"* 101–110.
56. Prokofiev, *Palace of Soviets*, 18.
57. Merkurov, *Zapiski skul'ptora.*
58. Prokofiev, *Palace of Soviets*, 19.
59. Ibid., 20.
60. Ibid., 26.
61. Wright, "Architecture and Life," 14–15.
62. Ibid., 14.
63. Ibid.
64. Eigel, *Boris Iofan*, 109.
65. Akinsha, Kozlov, and Hochfield, *Beautiful Loot*, 33–34.

Chapter Twenty-six

1. Eigel, *Boris Iofan*, 116–119.
2. Ibid., 117.
3. Ibid., 119.
4. Zhuravlev, *Dmitrii Chechulin*, 105.
5. Ibid.
6. Ibid.
7. Ibid.

Chapter Twenty-seven

1. Iarkevich, "Intelligentsiia i literatura."
2. Nikolai Mitrokhin, "Russkaia partiia" (Russian party), *Novoe literaturnoe obo-zrenie* 48 (2001). See also *Apparat TSK KPSS i kul'tura, 1958–1964: Dokumenty*

(Bodies of the CC, CPSU and culture, 1958-1964: Documents), ed. V. Iu. Afiani (Moscow: Rosspen, 2005).

3. *A-Ya, Unofficial Russian Art Review* 4 (Paris–New York–Moscow, 1982): 51.

4. Numerous film directors tried to use footage of the destruction of the cathedral. Yuri Beliankin, for example, included it in his documentary film about the writer Leonid Leonov. The film was immediately prohibited. Valentin Novikov, "Bitva za Moskvu: Oni vedali, chto tvorili" (Battle for Moscow: They knew what they were doing), *Parlamentskaia gazeta* 227, no. 1844 (December 22, 2005).

5. *The Destruction of the Church of Christ the Savior: Samizdat Photographs*, introduction by Irina Ilovaiskaia (London: Overseas Publications Interchange, 1988).

6. Kataev, *Almaznyi moi venets*, 57.

7. Viktor Shklovskii, *Eizenshtein* (Moscow: Isskustvo, 1973), 90.

Chapter Twenty-eight

1. Lyrics translated by Mikhail Morozov: www.planetaquarium.com/ discography/ trans/this_train665.

2. Kathleen E. Smith, in *Mythmaking in the New Russia,* has investigated the formation of the new Russian ideology during the Yeltsin period and the role of the cathedral in the nationalist ideological model.

Chapter Twenty-nine

1. Shusharin, "Vokrug khrama."

2. Smith, "An Old Cathedral for a New Russia."

3. "Obrashchenie Prizidenta Rossiiskoi Federatsii."

4. Komech, "Postroim dvorets Khrista Spasitelia."

5. Ardov, "U nas est' dela povazhnee chem snova stroit' khram Khrista Spasitelia."

6. Latsis, "Poddel'naia Rossia."

7. *Sotsialno-khudozhestvennaia aktsiya "Bassein Moskva" 27 maia 1994 g.* (Moscow-Berlin, 1995); Kovalev, "Bassein Moskva."

8. Tsiba, "Zachem Luzhkovu khram Khrista?"

9. Kalinina, "Khrista raspinaut vnov."

10. "Sobor prosit umnozhit' molitvu'."

11. Batalova, "I khram vostanet v svoei velichestvennoi krasote."

12. Lebedeva, "Udarniki pravoslavnogo truda."

13. Deriabin, "Russkii proekt."

14. Viktor Pelevin, *Generation P* (Moscow: Vagrius, 1999), 159.

15. Vybornov, "Zhulik-ordenonostes."

16. Borodai, "Parik Kobzona."

17. Pozner, "Karacharovskii Lift."

18. Viktor Belikov, "Pervaia sluzhba v khrame Khrista Spasitelia"; "Obrashchenie Prezidenta Rossiiskoi Federatsii."

19. Butkevich and Shevchenko, "Podrobnosti."

20. Ibid.
21. De Préneuf, "Façade of Glory."
22. Solntseva, "Na fundamente Dvortsa Sovetov."
23. "Interviu s Vladimirom Osinym."

Chapter Thirty

1. De Préneuf, "Façade of Glory."
2. Philips, "Cathedral Destroyed by Stalin Rises Again."
3. Philips, "Free-spending Yuri Heads for Tsardom."
4. Tumarkin, "Ne podkhodite blizko."
5. Andreeva, "Khram Khrista Spasitelia."
6. Mikhailov, "Domom bol'she, domikom men'she."
7. "Prizrak khrama Khrista Spasitelia na beregakh Nevy."
8. "Golitsin Andrei Kirilovich."
9. Azizian, "Skul'ptura 'Vozrozhdenie.'"
10. Traynor, "Moscow Cathedral Damned."
11. Kovalev, "Gorodskoi golova i gorodskaia skul'ptura."
12. Butkevich and Shevchenko, "Podrobnosti."
13. "Senatory krasiat khram."
14. "Glavnyi kupol khrama Khrista Spasitelia vossozdan."
15. Fominova, "Stroika veka."
16. Ibid.
17. Traynor, "Moscow Cathedral Damned."
18. "Patriarkh Moskovskii i vseia Rusi Alexii."
19. Vail, "Kakoe pravoslavie nuzhno gosudarstvennym i tserkovnym vlastiam?"
20. "Rossiiskie SMI o kanonnizatsii Nikolaia II."
21. Iarkevich, "Intelligentsia i literatura."

Bibliography

Abbreviations

Khram 1851. "Khram Khrista Spasitelia" (Cathedral of Christ the Savior). *Zhurnal dlia chteniia vospitannikov voenno-uchebnikh zavedenii* 396. St. Petersburg, 1851.
Khram 1996a. L. D. Polinovskaia, comp. *Khram Khrista Spasitelia* (Cathedral of Christ the Savior). Moscow: Moskovskii rabochii, 1996.
Khram 1996b. *Khram Khrista Spasitelia. Po knige M. S. Mostovskii, "Istoricheskoe opisanie khrama vo imia Khrista Spasitelia v Moskve"* (Cathedral of Christ the Savior. According to the book by M. S. Mostovskii, "History of the cathedral of Christ the Savior in Moscow"). Moscow: Stolitsa, 1996.
Kirichenko 1992. E. I. Kirichenko. *Khram Khrista Spasitelia v Moskve: Istoriia proektirovaniia i sozdaniia sobora: Stranitsy zhizni i gibeli, 1813–1931* (Cathedral of Christ the Savior in Moscow: History of its design and creation, existence and destruction, 1813–1931). Moscow: Planeta, 1992.
Kirichenko, in *Khram* 1996a. E. I. Kirichenko. "Khram Khrista Spasitelia—pamiatnik arkhitekturi 1830-1850-kh gg" (The Cathedral of Christ the Savior—the architectural monument of the 1830s-1850s). In L. D. Polinovskaia, comp., *Khram Khrista Spasitelia* (Cathedral of Christ the Savior). Moscow: Moskovskii rabochii, 1996.

Archival Sources

OPI GIM Division of Written Sources, State Historical Museum (Moscow) f. 132, d. 549; f. 235, d. 2, 3, 5, 14, 15.
OR RGB Manuscript Division, Russian State Library (Moscow) f. 90, karton 1, d. 20; karton 2, d. 8; karton 3, d. 15.
OR RPB Manuscript Division, Saltikov-Shchedrin Russian Public Library (St. Petersburg) f. G/4, d. 691.
RGIA Russian State Historical Archive (St. Petersburg) f. 207, op. 3; f. 473, op. 3, d. 394; f. 789, op. 1/2, d. 2873; op. 2; op. 14, d. 74-L (Loganovskii); d. 4-R (Ramzanov); f. 797, op. 53 /3-4, d. 24; f. 1284, d. 78.
TsIAM Central Historical Archive of the City of Moscow f. 243, op. 1-9, 12; f. 244, op. 1, d. 392.

Books, Articles, and Electronic Sources

Adkins, Helen. "International Participation in the Competition for the Palace of Soviets." In *Naum Gabo and the Competition for the Palace of Soviets in Moscow, 1931–1933.* Berlin: Berlinischer Galerei, 1993.

Afanasiev, K. N., ed. *Iz istorii sovetskoi arkhitektury, 1926–1932 gg. Dokumenty i materialy. Tvorcheskie ob'edineniia* (From the history of Soviet architecture, 1926–1932. Documents and materials. Creative associations). Compilation and texts by V. E. Khazanova. Moscow: Nauka, 1970.

Akinsha, Konstantin, Grigorii Kozlov, and Sylvia Hochfield. *Beautiful Loot: The Soviet Plunder of Europe's Art Treasures.* New York: Random House, 1995.

Alekseev, Nikita. "Stambul: Instruktsia k polzovaniu" (Istanbul: Survival instructions). *Inostranets,* April 22, 1998.

Allenov, Mikhail. *Aleksandr Andreevich Ivanov.* Moscow: Izobrazitel'noe Iskusstvo, 1980.

Andreeva, Ekaterina. "Fashistskoe iskusstvo Italii i Natsionalsotsialisticheskoe iskusstvo Germanii v Sovetskoi khudozhestvennoi kritike, 1934–35 godov" (Fascist art of Italy and National Socialist art of Germany in Soviet art criticism, 1934–35). *Mesto pechati 3* (1993).

Andreeva, Svetlana. "Khram Khrista Spasitelia: Vozrozhdenie prodolzhaetsia" (Cathedral of Christ the Savior: Reconstruction continues). Russian Culture Navigator: http/www.vor.ru/culture/cularch9_rus.html.

Ardov, Mikhail. "U nas est' dela povazhnee, chem snova stroit' khram Khrista Spasitelia" (We have more important things to do than to reconstruct the cathedral of Christ the Savior). *Izvestia,* July 13, 1994.

Arkhangelskii, Aleksandr. *Aleksandr I.* Moscow: Vagrius, 2000.

"Arkhitekturnye ansambli Moskvy, 1830–60 godov" (Architectural ensembles of Moscow, 1830–60). *Arkhitekturnoe nasledstvo* 24 (Moscow, 1976): 3–19.

Art and Power: Europe under the Dictators. Exhibition catalogue. Compiled by Dawn Ades. London: Thames & Hudson, in assoc. with Hayward Gallery, 1995.

Azizian, Rafael. "Skul'ptura 'Vozrozhdenie'" (Sculpture "Rebirth"). *Planeta diaspora,* December 6, 1999.

Bartenev, Iurii. "Rasskazy kniazia A. N. Golitsyna, zapisannye Iu. N. Bartenevym" (Tales of Prince A. N. Golitsyn, recorded by Iu. N. Bartenev). *Russkii arkhiv* 2 (1886).

Batalova, Natalia. "I khram vosstanet v svoei velichestvennoi krasote" (And the cathedral will rise in its solemn beauty). *Moskovskaia Pravda,* September 10, 1994.

Belikov, Viktor. "Pervaia sluzhba v khrame Khrista Spasitelia zaplanirovana na avgust" (The first service in the cathedral of Christ the Savior planned for August). *Izvestiya,* July 12, 1995.

Belousov, Ivan. "Ushedshaia Moskva" (Vanished Moscow). In U. N. Aleksandrov, ed., *Moskovskaia starina: Vospominaniia moskvichei proshlogo stoletia* (Old-time Moscow: Memoirs of Muscovites of the last century). Moscow: Pravda, 1989.

Bernshtein, Boris. "Ivanov i slavianofil'stvo" (Ivanov and the Slavophiles). *Iskusstvo* 3 (1959).

Bezatosnyi, Viktor. "Rossiiskii titulovannyi generalitet v 1812–1815 godakh" (Russian titled generals in 1812–1815). In *Ot Moskvy do Parizha (1812–1814gg): 185 leti Maloiaroslavetskomu srazheniu* (From Moscow to Paris [1812–1814]: 185th anniversary of the battle of Maloiaroslavets). Maloiaroslavets, 1998.

Billington, James H. *The Icon and the Axe: An Interpretive History of Russian Culture.* New York: Knopf, 1966. Reprint, New York: Vintage, 1970.

Bogdanovich, M. I. *Istoriia tsarstvovaniia Imperatora Aleksandra I i Rossii v ego vremia / sochininie avtora Istorii otechestvennoi voiny 1812 goda* (History of the reign of the Emperor Alexander I and Russia in his time / composed by the author of *History of the patriotic war of 1812*). Vol. 6. St. Petersburg: Tip. F. Sushchinskago, 1869–71.

Bogoliubov, A. N. "Akademia khudozhestv v gody vozrozhdenia 1859–64: Vospominaniia khudozhnika" (The Academy of Arts in the years of renaissance, 1859–64: Memoirs of an artist). *Russkaia starina* 29, no. 10 (1880).

————. *Vospominaniia o v Boze pochivshem Imperatore Aleksandre III* (Memoirs of the late emperor Alexander III). St. Petersburg: Tip. A. Benke, 1895.

————. "Zapiski moriaka-khudozhnika" (Notes of an artist). *Volga* 2–3. Saratov, 1996.

Bokhanov, A. N. *Romanovy: Serdechnye tainy* (The Romanovs: Secrets of the heart). Moscow: AST Press, 2000.

Borodai, Aleksandr. "Parik Kobzona" (Kobzon's wig). *Zavtra,* December 15, 1998.

Botkin, Mikhail. *Aleksandr Andreevich Ivanov: Ego zhizn' i perepiska, 1806–1858* (Alexander Ivanov: His life and correspondence, 1806–1858). St. Petersburg: Tip. M. M. Stasiulevicha, 1880.

Bowlt, John. "Tatlin und seine Antitisch" (Tatlin and his anti-table). In Jürgen Harten, ed., *Vladimir Tatlin: Leben, Werk, Wirkung* (Vladimir Tatlin: Life, work, influence). Cologne: DuMont, 1993.

Bulgakov, Mikhail. *Rokovye iaitsa* (Fatal eggs). In *Al'manach Nedra* 6 (Moscow, 1925). Reprint, *The Fatal Eggs and Other Soviet Satire.* Ed. and trans. Mirra Ginsburg. New York: Macmillan, 1965.

Butkevich, Dmitrii, and Maksim Shevchenko. "Podrobnosti o glavnom khrame strani" (Facts about the country's main cathedral). *Nezavisimaia Gazeta,* December 22, 1999.

Chechulin, Dmitrii, and Nikolai Vishnevskii. "Otkrytyi plavatel'nyi bassein 'Moskva'" (The "Moscow" swimming pool is open). *Stroitelstvo i arkhitektura Moskvy* (1960).

Chetvertoe aprelia 1866 goda i ego patrioticheskoe znachenie na Rusi (4 April 1866 and its patriotic meaning in Russia). Moscow, 1866.

Chukovskii, Kornei. *Dnevnik: 1930–1969.* (Diary: 1930–1969). Moscow: Sovremennyi pisatel', 1994.

Czartoryski, Adam. *Besedy i chastnaia perepiska mezhdu Imperatorom Aleksandrom I i kniazem Adamom Chartorizhskim, opublikovannyia kniazem Ladislavom Charto-*

rizhskim (1801–1823) (Conversations and correspondence of Emperor Alexander I and Prince Adam Czartoryski, published by Prince Ladislav Czartoryski [1801–1823]). Trans. from the French by S. Iavlenskaia. Moscow: Sfinks, [1912].

de Préneuf, Flore. "Façade of Glory: A Potemkin Cathedral for the New Russia." *Washington Post,* November 24, 1996.

Deriabin, Andrei. "'Russkii proekt': Konstruirovanie natsional'noi istorii i edentichnosti." (Russian project: Designing national history and identity). *Russkii Zhurnal,* April 2, 1998.

Dmitriev, Mikhail. *Glavy iz vospominanii moei zhizni* (Chapters from recollections of my life). Moscow: Novoe literaturnoe obozrenie, 1998.

"Doroga k khramu: povorot ili tupik?" (The road to the cathedral: Turn or dead end?). *Samarskoe obozrenie,* May 17, 1999.

Dvorets Sovetov SSSR (Palace of Soviets of the USSR). Moscow: Vsekokhudozhnik, 1933.

Eigel, Isaak. *Boris Iofan.* Moscow: Stroiizdat, 1978.

Eikhenbaum, Boris. "S. P. Zhikharev i ego dnevnik" (S. P. Zhikharev and his diary). In S. P. Zhikharev, *Zapiski sovremennika (*Notes of a contemporary). Edited, with text and commentaries, by B. M. Eikhenbaum. Moscow: Izd-vo Akademii nauk SSSR, 1955.

Eizenshtein, Sergei. *Memuary* (Memoirs). Vol. 1. Moscow: Red. gazety "Trud": Muzei Kino, 1997.

Erenburg, Il'ia. Stikhotvoreniia i poemy (Verses and poems). St. Petersburg: Akademicheskii proect, 2000.

———. *Viza vremeni* (Visa of time). Berlin: Skif, 1929.

Fedorov, Mikhail. *Velik Bog Zemli Russkoi* (The God of the Russian land is great). St. Petersburg, 1866.

Filaret (Mikhail Drozdov). *Pis'ma mitropolita Moskovskogo Filareta (v mire Vasiliia Mikhailovicha Drozdova) k rodnym ot 1800-go do 1866-go goda* (Letters of Metropolitan Filaret [Vasilii Mikhailovich Drozdov] to his family from 1800 to 1866). Moscow: Tip. A. I. Mamontova i Ko, 1882.

Florovskii, Georgii. *Puti russkogo bogosloviia* (Ways of Russian theology). Paris: YMCA Press, 1981.

Fominova, Galina. "Stroika veka: Rospis' khrama Khrista Spasitelia podkhodit k kontsu" (The construction of the century: The decoration of the cathedral of Christ the Savior is coming to an end). *Nezavisimaia Gazeta,* September 8, 1999.

Gavriil Konstantinovich, Grand Duke. *V Mramornom dvortse* (In the Marble Palace). St. Petersburg: Logos, 1993.

Geller, Mikhail. *Istoriia Rossiiskoi imperii* (History of the Russian empire). Vol. 2. Moscow: MIK, 1997.

"Glava doma Romanovykh ne priedet na tseremoniu kanonizatsii Nikolaia II" (The head of the house of Romanov will not attend Nicholas II's canonization ceremony). *Lenta Ru,* August 15, 2000. http://lenta.krasnet.ru/russia/2000/08/15/tsar/).

"Glavnii kupol khrama Khrista Spasitelia vossozdan" (The main dome of the cathedral of Christ the Savior reconstructed). *Sankt-Peterburgskie novosti,* September 3, 1999.

Glazychev, Viacheslav. "Salut, rodnaya Vizantiia!" (Salute, native Byzantium!). *Russkii Zhurnal,* July 20, 1998.

Godovye otchety Visochaishe utverzhdennogo Komiteta po ustroistvu v Moskve Muzeia voiny 1812 goda (Annual reports of the Imperial Committee on the establishment in Moscow of the Museum of the war of 1812). Moscow, 1908–16.

Golitsyn, Andrei. "Zapiska vitebskogo, mogilevskogo i smolenskogo general-gubernatora kniazia Golitsyna" (Note of Prince Golitsyn, the governor-general of Vitebsk, Mogilev and Smolensk territories). *Russkaia starina* 69 (January 1891): 105, 107–109.

"Golitsyn Andrei Kirilovich": 200 vidaushchikhsia deiatelei sovremennosti. Pt. 2, Kto est kto. (Andrei Kirilovich Golitsyn: Two hundred important contemporary people. Who's who). http://www.biograph.comstar.ru/bank/golitsyn.htm.

Gordin, I. A. *Mistiki i okhraniteli: Delo o masonskom zagovore* (Mystics and protectors: The case of the Masonic plot). St. Petersburg: Pushkinskii fond, 1999.

Grabar, Igor. *Peterburgskaia arkhitektura v XVIII i XIX vekakh* (Petersburg architecture in the eighteenth and nineteenth centuries). St. Petersburg: Lenizdat, 1994.

Grimm, German. *Arkhitektor Voronikhin.* (The architect Voronikhin). Leningrad: Gos. izd-vo lit-ry po stroitelstvu, arkhitekture i stroitelnym materialam, 1963.

Groys, Boris. *The Total Art of Stalinism: Avant-garde, Aesthetic Dictatorship, and Beyond.* Trans. Charles Rougle. Princeton, N.J.: Princeton University Press, 1992.

Herzen, Aleksandr. *Byloe i dumy* (My past and thoughts). In vol. 8 of *Polnoe sobranie sochinenii* (Collected works). Ed. V. P. Volgin et al. 30 vols. Moscow: Izd-vo Akademii Nauk SSSR, 1956.

———. *Zapiski A. L. Vitberga* (Memoirs of A. L. Vitberg). In vol. 1 of *Polnoe sobranie sochinenii* (Collected works). Ed. V. P. Volgin et al. 30 vols. Moscow: Izd-vo Akademii Nauk SSSR, 1954.

Iakubovskii, Ivan. *Karlik Favorita: Istoriia zhizni Ivana Andreevicha Iakubovskogo, karlika Svetleishego Kniazia Platona Aleksandrovicha Zubova, pisannaia im samim* (The favorite dwarf: The life of Ivan Andreevich Iakubovskii, the dwarf of His Highness Prince Platon Alexandrovich Zubov, written by himself). Munich: W. Fink, [ca. 1968].

Iarkevich, Igor. "Intelligentsiia i literatura" (Intelligentsia and literature). *Russkii Zhurnal,* July 14, 1997. http://www.russ.ru/journal/travmp/97-07-14/yarkev1.html.

"Informatsia." http://show.stars. ru/- sobor/info/index.htm.

"Interviu s Vladimirom Osinym, starshim menedzherom fonda finansovoi podderzhki vossozdania khrama Khrista Spasitelia" (Interview with Vladimir Osin, manager of the foundation for the financial support of the reconstruction of the cathedral of Christ the Savior). *Vetrograd-Inform,* April 1996.

Istoricheskoe opisanie postroennogo v Moskvie khrama vo imia Khrista Spasitelia (Historical description of the Cathedral of Christ the Savior constructed in Moscow). Moscow, 1869.

Iurenev, Rostislav. *Sergei Eizenshtein: Zamysly, filmy, metod. Chast' pervai, 1898–1929* (Sergei Eisenstein: Ideas, films, method. Part One, 1898–1929). Moscow: Iskus-stvo, 1985.

"Iz pis'ma N. V. Berga" (From a letter of N. V. Berg). *Russkaia starina* 7 (1872).

"Iz zapisnoi knizhki Russkogo Arkhiva: Mitropolit Filaret" (From the notebook of a Russian Archive: Metropolitan Filaret). *Russkii arkhiv 3* (1903).

Jakobson, Roman. *My Futurist Years.* Ed. Bengt Jangfeldt. Trans. Stephen Rudy. New York: Marsilio Publishers, 1997.

Kaganovich, Lazar. *Pamiatnye zapiski.* (Recollections). Moscow: Vagrius, 1996.

Kalinina, Lidia. "Khrista raspinaut vnov': K polemike vokryg Khrama Khrista Spasi-telia" (Christ is crucified again: Polemics around the cathedral of Christ the Savior). *Moskovskaia Pravda,* September 23, 1994.

Kamchatskii, Nestor, Bishop. *Razstrel Moskovskogo Kremlia (27 oktiabria–3 noiabria 1917g.)* (Shelling of the Moscow Kremlin [27 October–3 November 1917]). Moscow, 1917.

Kandidov, Boris. *Kogo spasal khram khrista spasitelia?* (Who saved the cathedral of Christ the Savior?). Moscow-Leningrad: Moskovskii rabochii, 1931.

———. *Tserkov i Fevral'skaia revolutsia: Klassovaia pozitsia pravoslavnoi tserkvi v period fevral'–avgust 1917 g* (Church and February revolution: The class position of the Orthodox Church during February–August 1917). Moscow: Gosudarstvennoe antireligioznoe izdatdelstvo, 1934.

Kargopolova, Natal'ia. "Takie zvezdy svetiat narodu raz v stoletie" (Such stars shine on people once in a century). In A. N. Antoshin et al., eds., *Moskva v nachale XX veka: Budni i prazdniki, Moskovskaia starina, novorusskii stil'* (Moscow at the be-ginning of the twentieth century: Everyday life and holidays, old-time Moscow, the new Russian style). Written and compiled by A. S. Fedotov. Moscow: Izd-vo obedi-neniia Mosgorarkhiv, 1997.

Kataev, Valentin. "Uzhe napisan Verter" (Werther is already written). *Novyi Mir* 6 (1980).

———. *Almaznyi moi venets* (My diamond diadem). Moscow: Sov. pistatel, 1979.

Kennedy, Paul M. *The Rise and Fall of the Great Powers.* New York: Random House, 1989.

Kersnovskii, A. A. *Istoriia Russkoi armii* (History of the Russian army). Vol. 2. Mos-cow: Golos, 1994.

Khan-Magomedov, Selim. "K istorii vybora mesta dlia Dvortsa Sovetov" (History of the site selection for the Palace of Soviets). In *Arkhitektura i stroitel'stvo Moskvy* 1 (1998).

Kharkevich, Vladimir. *Voina 1812 goda: Ot Nemana do Smolenska. Prichiny voiny. Pod-gotovka obeikh storon. Plany deistvii. Operatsii do soedineniia russkikh armii pod*

Smolenskom. (The war of 1912: From the Neman to Smolensk. Causes of the war. Preparation of both sides. Plans of operations. Operations before the joining of the Russian armies near Smolensk). Vilno: Nikolaevskaia akademiia General'nogo shtaba, 1901.

"Khram Khrista Spasitelia" (Cathedral of Christ the Savior). *Zhurnal dlia chteniia vospitannikov voenno-uchebnikh zavedenii* 93 (St. Petersburg, 1851): 396.

"Khudozhestvennye raboty v Kharame Khrista Spasitelia v Moskve" (Artistic works in the cathedral of Christ the Savior in Moscow). *Sankt-Petrburgskie vedomosti* 301 (October 31, 1887).

[Kikin, P. A.] "O postroenii khrama Spasitelia v Moskve: Pis'mo P. A. Kikina" (About construction of the cathedral of the Savior in Moscow: Letter of P. A. Kikin). *Russkii arkhiv* 2 (1880): 228–232.

Kirichenko, E. I. *Zapechatlennaia istoriia Rossii: Monumenty XVIII — nachal XX veka* (Print history of Russia: Monuments of the eighteenth–beginning of the twentieth centuries). Vol. 1. Moscow: Zhiraf, 2001.

Klimov, Petr. "Zhivopisnoe ubranstvo khrama Khrista Spasitelia" (Painterly decoration of the cathedral of Christ the Savior). In *Khram Khrista Spasitelia,* comp. L. D. Polinovskaia. Moscow: Moskovskii rabochii, 1996.

Kliuchevskii, Vasilii. *Kurs russkoi istorii* (A course of Russian history). Vol. 5. Moscow: Mysl', 1989.

———. *Sochineniia* (Works). Vol. 5. Moscow: Mysl', 1989.

Kogan, P. S. *Literatura etikh let 1917–1923* (Literature of the years 1917-1923). Ivanovo-Voznesensk: Osnova 1924.

Kolpakov, Aleksandr. "Khram, kotoryi postroil mer, ili dva slova o prestuplenii i pokaianii" (The cathedral the mayor built, or two words about crime and repentance). *Moskovskii Komsomolets,* September 23, 1994.

Komech, Aleksei. "Postroim dvorets Khrista Spasitelia" (Let's construct the palace of Christ the Savior). *Moskovskie Novosti,* November 13-20, 1994.

Kopp, Anatole. *Town and Revolution: Soviet Architecture and City Planning, 1917–1935.* New York: George Braziller, 1970.

Kotyrev, Andrei. *Mavzolei V. I. Lenina: Proektirovanie i stroitel'stvo* (Lenin Mausoleum: Design and construction). Moscow: Sov. khudozhnik, 1971.

Kovalev, Andrei. "'Bassein Moskva': Temperatura chuvstvilishcha" ("Moscow" swimming pool: Emotional temperature). *Segodnia,* June 1, 1994.

———. "Gorodskoi golova i gorodskaia skul'ptura ili Zurab Tsereteli kak zerkalo kapitalisticheskoi revolutsii" (The city father and the city sculpture, or Zurab Tsereteli as the mirror of the capitalist revolution). http://members.tripod.com/~kritizer/zeret.htm.

Kozlov, Vladimir. "Pravoslavnye traditsi chestvovania pamiati Otechestvennoi voiny 1812 goda v Moskve" (Orthodox traditions of celebration in honor of the memory of the Patriotic war of 1812 in Moscow). In E. G. Boldina et al., eds., *Moskva v 1812 godu: Materialy nauchnoi konferentsii posviashchennoi 180 letiu Otechestvennoi voiny 1812 goda* (Moscow in 1812: Materials from a scholarly conference dedicated to the 180th jubilee of the Patriotic war of 1812). Moscow: Izd-vo Obedineniia Mosgorarkhiv, 1997.

Kramskoi, Ivan. *Pis'ma i stat'i* (Letters and articles). Vol. 1. Moscow: Iskusstvo, 1965.

Krasin, Leonid. "Arkhitekturnoe uvekovechivanie Lenina" (Architectural memorialization of Lenin). In *O pamiatnike Leninu: Sbornik statei* (About the Lenin monument: Collection of articles). Leningrad: Gos. izd-vo, 1924.

Krasnov-Levitin, Anatolii. *Trudy i dni* (Works and days). Paris: Vestnik, 1990.

Krautheimer, Richard. "Introduction to an Iconography of Medieval Architecture." *Journal of the Courtauld and Warburg Institutes* 5 (1942): 1–33.

Kuzmichev, Fedot (pseud.). *Torzhestvo zakladki khrama vo imia Khrista Spasitelia 10 sentiabria 1839 goda: Pis'mo k drugu v Parizh* (Celebration of the laying down of the foundation of the cathedral in honor of Christ the Savior on September 10, 1839: Letter to a friend in Paris). Moscow, 1840.

Laikevich, Sofia. "Vospominaniia" (Memoirs). *Russkaia starina* 124, no. 10 (1905).

Lamzdorf, V. N. *Dnevnik (1894–1896)* (Diary [1894-1896]). Moscow: Mezhdunarodnye otnosheniia, 1991.

Lapin, Vladimir. "100 letnii ubilei Otechestvennoi voiny 1812 goda i politicheskaia borba" (One hundredth anniversary of the Patriotic war of 1812 and political struggle). In A. A. Fursenko, ed., *Rossiia v XIX–XX vv.: Sbornik statei k 70-letiiu so dnia rozhdeniia Rafaila Sholomovicha Ganelina* (Collected articles dedicated to the seventieth birthday of Rafail Sholomovich Ganelin). St. Petersburg: DB, 1998.

Latsis, Otto. "Poddel'naia Rossia ne pomozhet dukhovnomu vozrozhdeniu obschestva" (A fake Russia will not help the spiritual rebirth of the fatherland). *Izvestia,* November 24, 1994.

Lebedeva, Elena. "Udarniki pravoslavnogo truda" (Shockworkers of Orthodox labor). *Moskovskie Novosti,* August 4–11, 1996.

Lentulova, Marianna. *Khudozhnik Aristarkh Lentulov* (The artist Aristarkh Lentulov). Moscow: Sov. khudozhnik, 1969.

Lizon, Petr. *The Palace of the Soviets: The Paradigm of Architecture in the USSR.* Colorado Springs: Three Continents Press, 1995.

Lotman, Iu. M. *Besedy o russkoi kul'ture.* Cologne: Böhlau, 1997.

———. *Karamzin.* St.Petersburg: Iskusstvo-SPB, 1997.

Maiakovskii, Vladimir. "O patriarkhe Tikhone: Pochemu sud nad milost'u ikhnei?" (About Patriarch Tikhon: Why is his worship on trial?). In *Polnoe sobranie sochinenii* (Complete works). Vol. 5. Moscow: Gos. izd-vo khudozh. lit-ry, 1957.

———. "Za chto borolis'?" (What did we fight for?). *Novy LEF* 3 (March 1927).

Maiorova, Ol'ga. "Bessmertnyi Rurik" (Immortal Rurik). *NLO* 43 (March 2000): 137–165.

Malevich, Kazimir. "Lenin." In D. V. Sarabianov et al., eds., *Sobranie sochinenii* (Collected works). Vol. 2, *Statii i teoreticheskie sochineniia, opublikovannie v Germanii, Polshe i na Ukraine, 1924–1930* (Articles and theoretical works published in Germany, Poland and Ukraine, 1924–1930). Moscow: Gilea, 1998.

Mariengof, Anatolii. *Roman bez vran'ia* (Novel without lies). In *Bessmertnaia trilogiia* (Immortal trilogy). Moscow: Vagrius, 1998.

Martsinkovskii, V. F. *Zapiski veruiushchego* (Notes of a believer). Prague: Izd. avtora, 1929.

Maslova, N. M., ed. *Rosiisskie samoderzhtsy* (Russian autocrats). Moscow: Mezhdunarodnye otnosheniia, 1993.

"Materialy dlia istorii russkoi tserkvi: Perepiska Moskovskogo mitropolita Filareta otnositel'no Khrama Khrista Spacitelia" (Materials for the history of the Russian church: Correspondence of Moscow Metropolitan Filaret about the cathedral of Christ the Savior). *Chtenia v Moskovskom obshchestve lubitelei dukhovnogo prosveschenia* (May 1882): 132–146.

Medvedkova, Olga. "Solomonov khram—dom premudrosti: K istorii neosuschestvlennogo proekta khrama Khrista Spasitelia arkhitektora Vitberga" (The temple of Solomon—the house of wisdom: History of the unrealized project of the cathedral of Christ the Savior by the architect Vitberg). *Revue des études slaves* 64, pt. 3 (1992): 459–468.

Merkert, Jorn, and Vladimir Revzin, eds. *Naum Gabo and the Competition for the Palace of Soviets, Moscow, 1931–1933.* Berlin: Berlinische Galerie; Moscow: Shchusev Museum, 1993.

Merkurov, Sergei. *Zapiski skul'ptora* (Notes of a sculptor). Moscow: Izd. Akademii khudozhestv.: SSSR, 1953.

Merzliakov, Aleksei. Pesn' na torzhestvennoe zalozhenie khrama Khrista Spasitelia v Moskve. Proiznesena v Obschestve lubitelei rossiskoi slovesnosti pri Imperatorskom Moskovskom Universitete deistvitel'nym chlenom Obshchestva, professorom Alekseem Merzliakovym (Song about the solemn placement of the cornerstone of the cathedral of Christ the Savior in Moscow read aloud in the Society of Lovers of Russian Literature of Imperial Moscow University by a member of the Society, Professor Aleksei Merzliakov). Moscow: Universitetskaia tip., 1817.

Mikhailov, Konstantin. "Domom bol'she, domikom men'she: Vlasti tseniat tu starinu, kotoruu sami postroili" (One house more, one house less: The officials appreciate the antiquity they constructed themselves). http://online.rbc.ru/documents/vek/9819/191403.html.

Mikhailovskii, Semyon. "Mechta o khrame" (Dream of the cathedral). *Pinakoteka* 3–4 (1999).

Mironenko, S. V. *Samoderzhavie i reformy: Politicheskaia borba v Rossii v nachale XIX v.* (Autocracy and reforms: Political struggle in Russia at the beginning of the nineteenth century). Moscow: Nauka, 1989.

Monkhouse, Allan. *Moscow, 1911–1933.* London: V. Gollancz, 1933.

Mostovskii, M. S. *Istoricheskoe opisanie khrama vo imia Khrista Spasitelia v Moskvie* (Historical description of the cathedral of Christ the Savior in Moscow). Moscow: Tip. S. Orlova, 1883.

———. "Khram Khrista Spasitelia v Moskve" (Cathedral of Christ the Savior in Moscow). In Svetlana Romanova, ed., *Khram Khrista Spasitelia* (Cathedral of Christ the Savior). Moscow: Profizdat, 2001.

Mozgovaia, Elena. "Skul'ptury Khrama Khrista Spasitelia" (Sculptures of the cathedral of Christ the Savior). In *Khram Khrist Spasitelia*, L. D. Polinovskaia, comp.

"Na Arkhireiskom Iubileinom Sobore, prokhodivshem v Moskve 13–16 Avgusta 2000 goda v khrame Khrista Spasitelia, byilo priniato Deianie o kanonizatsii Novomuchenikov i ispovednikov Rossiskikh" (Decision on the canonization of new Russian martyrs and confessors taken at the Bishops' Jubilee Synod in Moscow, August 13–16, 2000, in the cathedral of Christ the Savior). *Nezavisimaia gazeta*, March 28, 2001.

Norman, Geraldine. *The Hermitage: The Biography of a Great Museum*. London: Jonathan Cape, 1997.

[Novikov, N. I.] "Pis'ma N. I. Novikova k D. P. Runichu" (Letters of N. I. Novikov to D. P. Runich). *Russkii arkhiv* 7 (1871).

Novitskii, Aleksei. "Masonstvo i russkoe tserkovnoe zodchestvo v 18 i 19 vekakh" (Masonry and Russian church architecture). *Stroitel'. Vestnik arkhitektury, domovladenia i sanitarnogo zodchestva* 2 (Moscow, 1905): 61–72.

"Nu i denek" (What a day). Ekho Moskvi radio, January 7, 2000.

"Obrashchenie Prizidenta Rossiiskoi Federatsii k chlenam Obshchestvennogo nabliudatelnogo soveta po vossozdaniu Khrama Khrista Spasitelia" (Address of the President of the Russian Federation to the members of the public observers' council on the re-creation of the Cathedral of Christ the Savior). *Rossiiskaia Gazeta*, September 7, 1994.

Okunev, N. P. *Dnevnik moskvicha, 1917–1924* (Diary of a Muscovite, 1917-1924). Paris: YMCA-Press, 1990.

Ot Moskvy do Parizha (1812–1814gg): 185 let Maloiaroslavetskomu srazheniu (From Moscow to Paris [1812-1814]: 185th anniversary of the battle of Maloiaroslavets). Maloiaroslavets, 1998.

"Pamiati Konstantina Tona" (In memory of Konstantin Ton). *Strannik* 2 (1881).

Papernyi, Vladimir. *Kul'tura "Dva"* (Culture "Two"). Ann Arbor: Ardis, 1985.

Passek, T. P. *Iz dal'nikh let* (From years long past). Vol. 2. Moscow: Gos. izd-vo khudozh. lit-ry, 1963.

"Patriarkh Moskovskii i vseia Rusi Aleksii zakonchil svoi vizit v Krasnoiarskii krai" (Alexii, patriarch of Moscow and all Russia, ended his visit to Krasnoiarsk). *RIA "Press-Line,"* December 12, 1999.

Philips, Alan. "Cathedral Destroyed by Stalin Rises Again." *Electronic Telegraph*, September 4, 1997.

————. "Free-spending Yuri Heads for Tsardom." *Electronic Telegraph*, August 31, 1997.

Pipes, Richard. *Russia under the Old Regime*. New York: Charles Scribner's Sons, 1974.

"Pis'ma mitr. Filareta k ego roditelu" (Letters of Metropolitan Filaret to his father). *Russkii arkhiv* 2 (1882): 153–154.

Pobedonostsev, Konstantin Petrovich. *Sochineniia* (Works). St. Petersburg: Nauka, 1996.

Pogodin, Mikhail. "Pis'mo k Gosudaru Tsesarevichu, Velikomu Kniazu Aleksandru Nikolaevichu" (Letter to the Crown Prince Grand Duke Alexander Nicholaevich). In *Sochineniia M. P. Pogodina (Works of M. P. Pogodin)*. Vol. 4. Moscow: Tip. V. M. Frish, 1874.

Polnoe sobranie zakonov Rossiiskoi Imperii (Laws of the Russian empire). Collection 3, vol. 1, no. 118. St. Petersburg: Gos. Tip., 1885.

Polnoe sobranie zakonov Rossiiskoi Imperii (Laws of the Russian empire). Collection 32. Petrograd: Gos. Tip., 1915.

Pozner, Vladimir. "Karacharovskii Lift" (The Karachev elevator). *Druzhba narodov* 12 (1997).

"Prizrak khrama Khrista Spasitelia na beregakh Nevy" (The ghost of the cathedral of Christ the Savior on the banks of the Neva). http://www.kga.neva.ru/press/christ .html.

Prokofiev, Andrei. *The Palace of Soviets*. Moscow: Foreign Languages Publishing House, 1937.

Protopopov, Nikolai. *O tom ka Bog sohranil zhizn' Gosudaria* (How God saved the Sovereign's life). Moscow, 1866.

Punin, Nikolai. "Tatlinova bashnia" (Tatlin's tower), *Vesch* 1–2: 22.

————. *O Tatline* (About Tatlin). Moscow: RA, 1994.

Pypin, A. N. *Kharakteristiki literaturnykh mnenii ot dvadtsatykh do piatidesiatykh godov: Istoricheskie ocherki* (Characteristics of literary opinions from the twenties to the fifties: Historical essays). St. Petersburg: Kolos, 1909.

————. *Religioznye dvizheniia pri Aleksandre I* (Religious movements under Alexander I). St. Petersburg: Gumanitarnoe agentstvo "Akademicheskii Proekt," 2000.

————. *Russkoe masonstvo: XVIII i pervaia chetvert' XIX v.* (Russian Masonry: The eighteenth and first quarter of the nineteenth century). Petrograd: OGNI, 1916.

Radlov, Nikolai. *O futurizme* (On futurism). Petrograd: Akvilon, 1923.

Regel'son, Lev. *Tragediia russkoi tserkvi, 1917–1945* (The tragedy of the Russian church, 1917–1945). Paris: YMCA-Press, ca. 1977.

Ridley, Jasper. *The Freemasons*. London: Constable, 1999.

"Rossiiskie SMI o kanonnizatsii Nikolaia II" (Russian news media on the canonization of Nicholas II). *NTV*, August 16, 2000. http://www.ntv.ru/religy/16Aug2000/ sngru.html.

"Senatory krasiat khram" (Senators are painting the cathedral). http://www.russ.ru/ politics/nes/1999/05/18.html.

Sergeev, Pavel. "Mitropolit Filaret i tserkovnaia arkhitektura" (Metropolitan Filaret and church architecture). *Moskovskii zhurnal* 7 (1996): 27–31.

Serkov, A. I. *Russkoe masonstvo, 1731–2000: Ientsiklopedicheskii slovar* (Russian Masonry, 1731–2000: Encyclopedic dictionary). Moscow: Rosspen, 2001.

Shepelev, Leonid. *Tituly, mundiry i ordena v Rossiiskoi imperii* (Titles, uniforms, and orders of the Russian empire). Leningrad: Nauka, 1991.

Shilder, N. K. *Imperator Aleksandr Pervyi: Ego zhizn i tsarstvovanie* (Emperor Alexander I: His life and reign). Vol. 4. St. Peterburg: A. S. Suvorin, 1897–98.

Shishkov, Aleksandr. *Dvenadtsat' sobstvennoruchnykh pisem* (Twelve personal letters). St. Petersburg, 1841.

Shishova, Liubov'. *Khram Khrista Spasitelia, vossozdannoe skulpturnoe i zhivopisnoe ubranstvo.* (Cathedral of Christ the Savior, reconstruction of sculptural and painterly decoration). Moscow: Fond Skul'ptor, 2002.

Shklovskii, Viktor. *Khod konia* (Knight's move). Berlin: Gelikon, 1923.

Shmaro, Aleksander. "Khram Khrista Spasitelia" (Cathedral of Christ the Savior). *Nauka i religia* 9 (1987): 14.

Shugaikina, Alla. "Khram, pariashhii nad Moskvoi?" (A cathedral, soaring over Moscow?) *Vecherniaia Moskva,* August 22, 1994.

Shusharin, Dmitrii. "Vokrug khrama" (Around the cathedral). *Segodnia,* October 1, 1994.

Sirotkin, Vladlen. *Napoleon i Rossiia.* (Napoleon and Russia). Moscow: OLMA-Press, 2000.

Sirotkin, V. G., and Vladimir Kozlov. *Traditsii Borodina: Pamiat' i pamiatniki* (Traditions of Borodino: Memory and memorials). Moscow: Znanie, 1989.

Slavina, Tatiana. *Konstantin Ton.* Leningrad: Stroiizdat, 1989.

Slonov, Ivan. "Iz zhizhni torgovoi Moskvy" (From the lives of Moscow merchants). In U. N. Aleksandrov, ed., *Moskovskaia starina: Vospominaniia moskvichei proshlogo stoletia* (Old-time Moscow: Memoirs of Muscovites of the last century). Moscow: Pravda, 1989.

Smith, Douglas. *Working the Rough Stone: Freemasonry and Society in Eighteenth-Century Russia.* DeKalb: Northern Illinois University Press, 1999.

Smith, Kathleen E. "An Old Cathedral for a New Russia: The Symbolic Politics of the Reconstituted Church of Christ the Savior." In *Religion, State and Society* 25, no. 2 (1997): 163–175.

———. *Mythmaking in the New Russia: Politics and Memory in the Yeltsin Era.* Ithaca: Cornell University Press, 2002.

Snegirev, Vladimir. *Arkhitektor A. L. Vitberg: Zhizn' i tvorchestvo* (Architect A. L. Vitberg: Life and creative work). Moscow: Izd-vo Vsesoiuznoi Akademii arkhitektury, 1939.

"Sobor prosit umnozhit' molitvu" (The synod is asking for an increase in prayers). *Kuranty,* December 7, 1994.

Sokolov, Petr. *Istoricheskoe opisanie torzhestva, proiskhodivshego pri zalozhenii khrama Khrista Spasitelia na Vorobievykh gorakh pri Vysochaishem prisutstvii Ego Imperatorskogo Velichestva Gosudaria Imperatora Aleksandra Pavlovicha* (Historical description of the ceremony of laying the cornerstone of the cathedral of Christ the Savior on the Vorobiev Mountains in the Most High presence of His Imperial Majesty the Emperor Alexander Pavlovich). Moscow, 1818.

Sokolovskaia, Tira. "Rannee Aleksanrovskoe masonstvo" (Aleksander's early Masonry). In Mel'gunov and Sidorov, eds., *Masonstvo v ego proshlom i nastoiashchem* (1915), 2: 154–155.

Solntseva, Alena. "Na fundamente Dvortsa Sovetov: Beseda s rukovoditelem proekta vossozdania khrama Mikhailom Posokhinim" (On the foundation of the Palace of Soviets: Conversation with Mikhail Posokhin, head of the project of reconstruction of the cathedral). *Ogonek,* April 1996.

Soloviev, I. V., comp. *"Obnovlencheskii" raskol: Materiali dlia tserkovno-istoricheskoi i kannonicheskoi kharakteristiki* (The "Renovationist" schism: Materials for historical and canonical church reference). Moscow: Izdatel'stvo Krutitskogo podvor'ia, 2002.

Soloviev, Sergei. *Zapiski Sergeia Mikhailovicha Solovieva: Moi zapiski dlia detei moikh, a esli* mozhn, i dlia drugikh (My notes for my children and perhaps for other people). Petrograd: Prometei N. N. Mikhailova, 1915.

Sovetskoe rukovodstvo perepiska, 1928–1941 (Soviet leadership correspondence, 1928–1941). Moscow: Rosspen, 1999.

SSSR. Prague: CIN, 1926.

Stalin i Kaganovich: Perepiska (Stalin and Kaganovich: Correspondence). Moscow: Rosspen, 2000.

Stasov, V. V. *Izbrannye sochineniia v trekh tomakh* (Collected works in three volumes). Vol. 2. Moscow: Iskusstvo, 1952.

State Russian Museum. *D. G. Levitskii, 1735–1822: Sbornik nauchnykh trudov* (Collected scientific works). Ed. G. N. Goldovskii. Leningrad: GRM, 1987.

"STR: Vse na referendum!" (STR: Everyone to the referendum!) October 7, 1997. http://www.cityline.ru/politika/str/97071 Om.html.

Sviashchennii Dozor (Holy patrol). Harbin, 1931.

Sviashchennoe koronovanie imperatora Aleksandra III i imperatritsy Marii Fedorovny (The holy coronation of Emperor Alexander III and Empress Maria Fedorovna). Moscow: Gos. Tip., 1883.

Teige, Karel. "Dnesni vytvarna prace sov. Ruska" (Creative work in Soviet Russia today). In *SSSR.* Prague: CIN, 1926.

Tolstaia, A. A. *Zapiski freiliny: Pechal'nyi epizod iz moei zhizni pri dvore* (Memoirs of a lady-in-waiting: A sad episode in my life at court). Moscow: Entsiklopedia rossiiskikh dereven', 1996.

Traynor, Ian. "Moscow Cathedral Damned All Over Again." *Guardian,* October 25, 1999.

Troinitskii, Nikolai. *Aleksandr I i Napoleon* (Alexander I and Napoleon). Moscow: Vysshaia shkola, 1994.

Trubetskoi, Evgenii. *Izbrannoe* (Selected works). Moscow: Kanon, 1995.

Tsiba, Tatiana. "Zachem Luzhkovu Khram Khrista?" (Why does Luzhkov need the cathedral of Christ?). Interview with Yuri Luzhkov. *Argumenty i fakty,* November 1994.

Tumarkin, Mikhail. "Ne podkhodite blizko: Ozhidaemoi katastrofi ne proizoshlo" (Don't come close: The expected catastrophe didn't occur). *Ogonek,* April, 1996.

Tumarkin, Nina. *Lenin Lives! The Lenin Cult in Soviet Russia.* Cambridge: Harvard University Press, 1983.

Vail', Petr. "Kakoe pravoslavie nuzhno gosudarstvennym i tserkovnym vlastiam?" (What kind of Orthodoxy do state and church powers need?). *Liberty Live,* Radio Liberty, January 31, 2000.

Veresaev, V. V. *Pushkin v zhizni: Sistematicheskii svod podlinnykh svidetel'stv sovremennikov* (Pushkin in life: A systematic collection of the true testimonies of contemporaries). Vol. 3. Moscow: Nedra, 1928.

Viazemskii, Petr. *Stikhotvoreniia* (Verses). Moscow: Sovetskaia Rossiia, 1978.

Vitberg, Aleksandr. "Avtobiografiia" (Autobiography). *Russkaia starina* (1876) 9: 109–126; 10: 267–296; 12: 759–770.

Vitte (Witte), Sergei. *Vospominaniia* (Memoirs). Vol. 2. Moscow-Petrograd: Gos. izd-vo, 1923.

Voloshin, Maksimilian. *Surikov: Publikatsiia, vstupitel'naia stat'ia i primechaniia V. N. Petrova.* (Surikov: Publication, introduction and annotation by V. N. Petrov). Leningrad: Khudozhnik RSFSR, 1985.

Vorobieva, Tatiana. "K istorii masterskoi religioznoi zhivopis'i v Akdemii khudozhestv" (History of the religious painting workshop of the Academy of Arts). In G. N. Pavlov, ed., *Nasledie i sovremennost': Iskusstvo Rossii* (Heritage and contemporaneity: Russian art). St. Petersburg: Institut im. Repina, 1992.

Vostrishev, Mikhail. *Patriarkh Tikhon* (Patriarch Tikhon). Moscow: Molodaia Gvardiia, 1995.

Vrangel', Nikolai. "Iskusstvo i gosudar' Nikolai Pavlovich" (Art and His Majesty Nikolai Pavlovich). *Starye godi* (July–September, 1913): 53–64.

Vvedenskii, Aleksandr. *Tserkov' i revolutsiia: Ocherk vzaimootnoshenii, 1918–1922* (Church and revolution: Essay on interrelations, 1918–1922). Moscow, 1923.

Vybornov, Iurii. "Zhulik-ordenonostes" (Beetle-medal holder). *Rus' Pravoslavnaia,* May 1999.

Wortman, Richard. "Izobretenie traditsii v reprezentatsii rosiisskoi monarkhii" (The discovery of tradition in the representation of the Russian monarchy). *NLO,* 56 (April 2002).

———. "Rule by Sentiment: Alexander's Journeys through the Russian Empire." *American Historical Review* 95, no. 3 (June 1990): 745–771.

———. *Scenarios of Power: Myth and Ceremony in Russian Monarchy.* 2 vols. Princeton: Princeton University Press, 1995–2000.

Wright, Frank Lloyd. "Architecture and Life in the USSR." *Soviet Russia Today,* October 1937.

Zaionchkovsii, Petr. *Krizis samoderzhavia na rubezhe 1870–80–kh godov* (Crisis of autocracy on the verge of the 1870s–80s). Moscow: Izd-vo Moskovskogo universiteta, 1964.

Zakharova, Larisa. "Aleksandr II." In *Rossiiskie samoderzhtsy* (Russian autocrats). Ed. N. M. Maslova. Moscow: Mezhdunarodnye otnosheniia, 1993.

"Zalozhenie Khrama vo imia Khrista Spasitelia i vospominaniia ob izgnanii vraga iz Rossii" (Placing the cornerstone of the Cathedral of Christ the Savior and recollections of expelling the enemy from Russia). *Russkii vestnik* 19–20 (1817).

Zhikharev, Mikhail. "Petr Iakovlevich Chaadaev: Iz vospominanii sovremennika" (Chaadaev: Contemporary recollections). *Vestnik Evropy* 7 (1871): 203.

Zhivopisnyi Karamzin, ili Russkaia istoria v kartinkakh (Illustrated Karamzin, or Russian history in images). Moscow: Andrei Prevo, 1836.

Zhukovskii, Andrei. *O khudozhestvennykh arkhitekturnykh proizvedeniakh* (About artistic and architectural creations). St. Petersburg: Tip. N. Grecha, 1885.

Zhuravlev, Anatolii. *Dmitrii Chechulin.* Moscow: Stroizdat, 1985.

Zorin, Andrei. *Kormia dvuglavogo orla: Literatura i gosudarstvennaia ideologiia v Rossii v poslednei treti XVIII–pervoi treti XIX veka* (Feeding the doubleheaded eagle: Literature and state ideology in Russia in the last third of the eighteenth–first third of the nineteenth century). Moscow: Novoe literaturnoe obozrenie, 2001.

Zummer, Vsevolod. "Kniga Botkina kak material dlia biografii A. A. Ivanova" (Botkin's book as material for a biography of A. A. Ivanov). In *Mistetstvoznavstvo: Persha Kharkivska sektsia naukovo-doslidnychoi katedry mistetstvoznavstva* (Art history: The first Kharkiv section of the research department of art history). Kharkiv: Proletaryi, 1928.

Photo Credits

The illustrations in this volume are reproduced courtesy of the following sources.

Konstantin Akinsha Archive: 15, 50–52

Aleksei Kaluzhsky: 58

Konstantin Kokoshkin: 59

Galerie Alex Lachmann: 37, 38, 46–49, 53, 54

Museum of the Academy of Arts, St. Petersburg; courtesy Artem Zadikian: 17–19

Shchusev Museum of Architecture, Moscow; courtesy Artem Zadikian: 2, 3, 7, 8, 11, 12

N. K. Shilder, *Imperator Aleksandr Pervyi: Ego zhizn i tsarstvovanie* (St. Petersburg: A. S. Suvorin, 1897–98): 4

Slavic and Baltic Division, The New York Public Library, Astor, Lenox and Tilden Foundations: 16, 20–25

Artem Zadikian: 1, 5, 6, 9, 10, 13, 14, 26–36, 39–45, 55–57

Index